McGraw-Hill Education

500
GMAT Verbal
Questions

to know by test day

McGraw-Hill Education

500
GMAT Verbal
Questions

to know by test day

Kathy A. Zahler, MS

New York   Chicago   San Francisco   Athens   London   Madrid
Mexico City   Milan   New Delhi   Singapore   Sydney   Toronto

1 2 3 4 5 6 7 8 9 10   QFR/QFR   1 0 9 8 7 6 5 4

ISBN   978-0-07-181216-0
MHID   0-07-181216-4

e-ISBN   978-0-07-181217-7
e-MHID   0-07-181217-2

Library of Congress Control Number 2013948045

GMAT is a registered trademark of the Graduate Management Admission Council, which was not involved in the production of, and does not endorse, this product.

McGraw-Hill Education products are available at special quantity discounts to use as premiums and sales promotions or for use in corporate training programs. To contact a representative, please visit the Contact Us pages at www.mhprofessional.com.

This book is printed on acid-free paper.

CONTENTS

INTRODUCTION

Congratulations! You've taken a big step toward GMAT success by purchasing *McGraw-Hill Education: 500 GMAT Verbal Questions to Know by Test Day*. We are here to help you take the next step and score high on your GMAT exam so you can get into the business school of your choice!

This book gives you 500 GMAT-style multiple-choice questions that cover all the most essential course material on the verbal section as well as the analytical writing assessment. Each question is clearly explained in the answer key. The questions will give you valuable independent practice to supplement any earlier review you may have done.

This book and the others in the series were written by expert teachers who know the subject inside and out and can identify crucial information as well as the kinds of questions that are most likely to appear on the exam.

You might be the kind of student who needs extra study a few weeks before the exam for a final review. Or you might be the kind of student who puts off preparing until the last minute before the exam. No matter what your preparation style, you will benefit from reviewing these 500 questions, which closely parallel the content, format, and degree of difficulty of the questions on the actual GMAT exam. These questions and the explanations in the answer key are the ideal last-minute study tool for those final weeks before the test.

If you practice with all the questions and answers in this book, we are certain you will build the skills and confidence needed to excel on the GMAT. Good luck!

—The Editors of McGraw-Hill Education

PART **1**

Verbal

CHAPTER 1

Reading Comprehension

The questions in this group are based on the content of a passage. After reading the passage, choose the best answer to each question. Answer all questions following the passage on the basis of what is stated or implied in the passage.

Historians consider General Andrew Jackson's victory over the British at the Battle of New Orleans the greatest land victory of the War of 1812. The victory ensured America's sovereignty over the Louisiana Territory, which in turn led to a wave of new settlement in that area.

Today the battlefield is preserved as a tourist attraction. It features a monument whose cornerstone was laid in 1840 after Jackson visited the field on the 25th anniversary of the battle. Chalmette National Cemetery is also on the site. It houses the remains of only one veteran of the Battle of New Orleans; it is mainly for veterans of the Civil War (on the Union side), the Spanish-American War, World Wars I and II, and the Vietnam conflict.

Like all good historical restorations and most of our national historical parks, this one conjures up the history it celebrates. Visitors to the site may gain a panoramic view of the field of battle, with large reproductions of American cannons still fixed at several batteries and the front lines clearly visible. On the left, tourists may envision Colonel Robert Rennie's attack, which briefly overtook the American rampart. In the center, small-arms fire tore through the British Highlanders troops. On the right, the brigade run by General Samuel Gibbs came to grief under fire from General John Coffee's Tennessean troops.

1. Which of the following conclusions may be drawn directly from the first paragraph of the passage?
   (A) Had the battle been lost, America might have lost the Louisiana Territory.
   (B) Americans did not move into the Louisiana Territory before the battle.
   (C) Andrew Jackson was an early settler in the Louisiana Territory.
   (D) Most early inhabitants of the Louisiana Territory were British.
   (E) The battlefield is preserved in a way that makes visualization possible.

2. Based on the passage, which of the following is the most likely inference?
   - (A) The author believes that reconstructed historical sites serve no purpose.
   - (B) The author believes that American battlegrounds are especially haunting.
   - (C) The author believes that historical sites should help visitors imagine their history.
   - (D) The author believes that the Chalmette Cemetery should hold only War of 1812 veterans.
   - (E) The author considers Andrew Jackson an underrated figure in American history.

3. The first paragraph plays what role in the passage?
   - (A) It introduces the reader to characters who appear later in the passage.
   - (B) It provides a historical context for the information that follows.
   - (C) It sets the stage for the battle that will be described in detail.
   - (D) It lays out the author's theory about a specific moment in history.
   - (E) It provides a contrasting point of view to the author's own premise.

4. The site described in the passage would be most appropriate for
   - (A) historians and history buffs
   - (B) American and foreign tourists
   - (C) veterans of foreign wars
   - (D) both A and B
   - (E) A, B, and C

5. The author's attitude toward the battlefield today can best be described as one of
   - (A) appreciation
   - (B) disdain
   - (C) mystification
   - (D) reverence
   - (E) repudiation

For years, anecdotal evidence from around the world indicated that amphibians were under siege, especially in the Caribbean. Finally, proof of this hypothesis is available, thanks to the concerted, Internet-based effort of scientists involved with the Global Amphibian Assessment.

Amphibians have a unique vulnerability to environmental changes thanks to their permeable skin and their need of specific habitats to allow their metamorphosis from larva to adult. Studies indicate that they are at risk due to global climatic change, reduction in the ozone layer leading to an increased exposure to ultraviolet rays, interference with migratory pathways, drainage of wetlands, pollution by pesticides, erosion and sedimentation, and exposure to unknown pathogens thanks to the introduction of nonnative species. In other words, human progress is responsible for the losses this population is suffering.

Scientists have long considered amphibians a barometer of environmental health. In areas where amphibians are declining precipitously, environmental degradation is thought to be a major cause. Amphibians are not adaptable. They must have clean water in which to lay their eggs. They must have clean air to breathe after they grow to adulthood. Their "double life" as aquatic and land-dwelling animals means that they are at risk of a double dose of pollutants and other hazards.

The Global Amphibian Assessment concluded that nearly one-third of the world's amphibian species are under immediate threat of extinction. Nearly half of all species are declining in population. The largest numbers of threatened species are in Colombia, Mexico, and Ecuador, but the highest percentages of threatened species are in the Caribbean. In Haiti, for example, 9 out of 10 species of amphibians are threatened. In Jamaica, it's 8 out of 10, and in Puerto Rico, 7 out of 10.

Certainly, this is a disaster for amphibians, but scientists rush to point out that it may be equally a disaster for the rest of us on Earth. Even recent pandemics among amphibians may be caused by global changes. True, amphibians are ultra-sensitive to such changes, but can reptiles, fish, birds, and mammals be far behind?

6. Which of the following most accurately summarizes the main point of the passage?
   (A) The extinction of amphibians is due to global warming.
   (B) Amphibians really are a barometer of environmental health.
   (C) Only equatorial amphibians are currently under siege.
   (D) Amphibians' "double life" on land and in water may end up saving them.
   (E) Pandemics among amphibians are evident in South America.

7. The passage implies that the Global Amphibian Assessment has done science a favor by
   - (A) setting forth a hypothesis that connects the environment to species decline
   - (B) eliminating the need to study the connection between extinction and environment
   - (C) refuting a contention that had existed purely through anecdotal evidence
   - (D) collecting data to prove something that was previously just a hypothesis
   - (E) recovering and rehabilitating species that had previously faced extinction

8. The author's point in the first paragraph that amphibians are especially at risk in the Caribbean is best supported by evidence presented in which paragraph?
   - (A) 2
   - (B) 3
   - (C) 4
   - (D) 5
   - (E) none of the above

9. The author's purpose in the third paragraph is to
   - (A) provide background on the assessment study
   - (B) explain why amphibians are especially vulnerable
   - (C) list types of amphibians that are most at risk
   - (D) present examples of dangers from around the world
   - (E) suggest an action plan for scientists and nature lovers

A land bridge is land exposed when the sea recedes, connecting one expanse of land to another. One of the most famous land bridges was the Bering Land Bridge, often known as Beringia, which connected Alaska to Siberia across what is now the Bering Strait.

The Bering Land Bridge was not terribly long. If it still existed today, you could drive it in your car in about an hour. It appeared during the Ice Age, when enormous sheets of ice covered much of Europe and America. The ice sheets contained huge amounts of water north of the equator, and because of this, the sea level dropped precipitously, perhaps as much as 400 feet, revealing landmasses such as the Bering Land Bridge.

At this time, the ecology of the Northern Hemisphere was that of the mammoth steppe. It was a dry, frigid land filled with grasses, sedges, and tundra vegetation. It supported many large grazing animals including reindeer, bison, and musk oxen, as well as the lions that fed upon them. It also contained large camels, giant short-faced bears, and woolly mammoths. Many of the animals of the mammoth steppe used the bridge to cross from east to west and back again. Eventually, their human hunters tracked them from Asia to North America.

Ethnologists and geologists generally believe that humans used the Bering Land Bridge to populate the Americas, which up until about 24,000 years ago had no sign of human life. Ethnologists use evidence such as shared religions, similar houses and tools, and unique methods of cleaning and preserving food to show the link between the people of coastal Siberia and the people of coastal Alaska.

There are those among the Native American population who dispute the land bridge theory. For one thing, it contradicts most native teachings on the origins of the people. For another, it seems to undermine the notion that they are truly "native" to the North American continent.

10. According to this passage, the first people in North America lived
    (A) in what is now Central America
    (B) west of the Bering Strait
    (C) below sea level
    (D) in what is now Alaska
    (E) along the coast of Siberia

11. Based on information in the passage, about how long was the Bering Land Bridge?
    (A) Between 50 and 75 miles long
    (B) Between 90 and 120 miles long
    (C) Around 150 miles long
    (D) Around 200 miles long
    (E) Between 225 and 250 miles long

12. According to the passage, which of these would be considered a land bridge?

   (A) The Isthmus of Panama
   (B) The Chesapeake Bay
   (C) The Strait of Hormuz
   (D) The Khyber Pass
   (E) The island of Sicily

13. In the third paragraph, the author includes information about large mammals in order to

   (A) explain patterns of growth among animals of the mammoth steppe
   (B) indicate how tough animals needed to be to survive the Ice Age
   (C) contrast the climate of North America with the climate of Asia
   (D) suggest a reason for human migration from Asia to North America
   (E) contend that domesticating animals was one cause of human movement

14. The author's purpose in the fourth paragraph is to

   (A) introduce a theory and show some support for it
   (B) compare some processes used by geologists and ethnologists
   (C) list some possible reasons for the migrations of early humans
   (D) contradict a theory about an early use of the land bridge
   (E) show how ethnology has changed its focus over the years

15. The author suggests that some contemporary Native Americans object to the land bridge theory because it

   (A) equates them with Pleistocene man
   (B) challenges their history and status
   (C) relies on disputed science
   (D) belies the importance of southern tribes
   (E) fails to explain the connections among peoples

Aluminum is the most abundant metallic element in Earth's crust, but it is never found naturally as an element. Instead, it always appears naturally in its oxidized form as a hydroxide we call bauxite.

The extraction of aluminum from bauxite requires three stages. First, the ore is mined. Then it is refined to recover alumina. Finally, the alumina is smelted to produce aluminum. The mining is done via the open-cut method. Bulldozers remove the topsoil, and excavators or other types of power machinery are used to remove the underlying layer of bauxite. The bauxite may be washed to remove clay and other detritus.

Refining is done via the Bayer refining process, named after its inventor, Karl Bayer. Ground bauxite is fed into a digester, where it is mixed with a caustic soda. The aluminum oxide reacts with the soda to form a solution of sodium aluminate and a precipitate of sodium aluminums silicate. The solution is separated from the silicate through washing and pumping, and the alumina is precipitated from the solution, where it appears as crystals of alumina hydrate. The crystals are washed again to remove any remaining solution. Then they are heated to remove water, leaving the gritty alumina.

Smelting is done via the Hall-Heroult smelting process. An electric current is passed through a molten solution of alumina and cryolite, which is in a cell lined at the bottom and top with carbon. This forces the oxygen to combine with the carbon at the top of the cell, making carbon dioxide, while the molten metallic aluminum collects at the bottom of the cell, where it is siphoned off, cleaned up, and cast into bars, sheets, or whatever form is needed.

As with all mining of metals, bauxite mining presents certain hazards. Along with the usual mining issues of degraded soil and polluted runoff, chief among these hazards is the omnipresent bauxite dust, which clogs machinery and lungs, sometimes for miles around the mining site. Jamaica and Brazil have seen widespread protests recently against the major bauxite mining companies, which continue to insist that no link between bauxite dust and pervasive lung problems has been proved.

16. Based on the information in the second paragraph, you can conclude that bauxite is located
   (A) within the topsoil
   (B) wherever clay is found
   (C) below the topsoil
   (D) below Earth's crust
   (E) along riverbanks

17. According to the passage, all of these are produced by the Bayer process except
   (A) sodium aluminum silicate
   (B) sodium aluminate
   (C) aluminum manganese
   (D) alumina hydrate
   (E) alumina

18. The ideas in the second, third, and fourth paragraphs are related because they are
    (A) steps in a process
    (B) examples of a mineral
    (C) reasons for mining
    (D) comparisons among theories
    (E) suggested solutions

19. The process by which aluminum is extracted from bauxite is most similar to which of the following?
    (A) The building of steel bridges
    (B) The making of copper tubing
    (C) The manufacturing of glass
    (D) The mixing of cement
    (E) The growth of most grains

20. The author includes the discussion of protests primarily to show that
    (A) bauxite mining takes place in the Third World
    (B) workers are starting to fight back against the dangers of mining
    (C) mining companies have misled people for decades
    (D) the government of Brazil works with the mining companies
    (E) miners have a tradition of unionization

21. The tone of the passage suggests that the author would most likely believe which of the following?
    (A) Bauxite mining poses health problems.
    (B) The United States should use less aluminum.
    (C) Australian bauxite is the best quality.
    (D) Karl Bayer was something of a genius.
    (E) Mining is becoming cheaper and safer.

The discovery of electrons came about in a roundabout way. In the latter part of the 19th century, a popular demonstration by lecturers involved the cathode ray. They would evacuate air from the tube, pass high voltage through it, and show audiences the patterns of light that appeared. Were these really waves traveling through "ether"? Heinrich Hertz and Philipp Lenard conducted experiments that made this seem possible. On the other hand, English physicists had long posited that there must be a fundamental unit of electricity, a particle that connected matter and electricity. The Irish physicist George Johnstone Stoney had even gone so far as to calculate its size and to name it *electron*.

French physicist Jean Perrin determined that the cathode rays had negative charges. But it wasn't until English physicist J. J. Thomson designed an elegant set of experiments that the electron's existence was proved.

The first experiment determined that the negative charge of cathode rays could not be separated from the rays themselves using magnetism. The second found that the rays could bend when influenced by an electric field. The third measured the ratio of charge to mass of the rays by comparing the energy they carried and the amount of deflection possible when an electric field was introduced. Thomson discovered that the ratio was enormous, meaning that the rays were tiny or very highly charged or both.

His conclusions, published in 1897, were of the existence of a subatomic particle with a negative charge. It was not until Thomson's son George proved that electrons, although particles, had many of the properties of a wave that the mysteries of the cathode ray were truly solved.

George Thomson's concept of wave-particle duality, the notion that matter and light have properties of both waves and particles, was critical to the development of quantum mechanics. It was not a particularly new concept, having roots as far back as Isaac Newton's insistence that light was composed of particles, which he called *corpuscles*, the very word J. J. Thomson used to describe the particles of atoms he found in cathode rays.

22. Which of the following examples is presented as evidence that J. J. Thomson's theory about subatomic particles was not new?
    (A) The work of George Johnstone Stoney
    (B) The work of George Thomson
    (C) The work of Heinrich Hertz
    (D) The work of Philipp Lenard
    (E) A popular demonstration by lecturers

23. Thomson's first experiment indicated which of the following?
    (A) Unlike most rays, cathode rays were negatively charged.
    (B) Cathode rays could be diverted using electromagnetism.
    (C) The ray's negative charge was embedded within particles.
    (D) Most subatomic particles are tiny and highly charged.
    (E) Patterns of light form rays in the ether.

24. The discussion of corpuscles in the fifth paragraph shows primarily that

(A) people in the 1600s understood the parts of an atom
(B) Thomson borrowed a term from a much older theory
(C) atoms and blood cells are linked by similar structures
(D) Isaac Newton was trained as a medical doctor
(E) early investigators considered light a living being

25. The statement in the first paragraph that "the discovery of electrons came about in a roundabout way" indicates which belief on the part of the author?

(A) There is more to discover about electrons.
(B) Physicists had to use circular logic to come up with a theorem.
(C) Electrons could never have been discovered by a single scientist.
(D) Scientists ended up at the beginning when they searched for an answer.
(E) The discovery of electrons did not proceed step-by-step.

26. The tone of this passage suggests which about the author's attitude?

(A) She considers J. J. Thomson a splendid scientist.
(B) She prefers Isaac Newton to more recent scientists.
(C) She would like to know more about George Thomson.
(D) She believes that English scientists surpass the French.
(E) She finds the lengthy process of discovery disheartening.

27. Which of these inventions most relies on wave-particle duality in its everyday workings?

(A) A vacuum cleaner
(B) A high-voltage electric line
(C) An electron microscope
(D) A shortwave radio
(E) An inkjet printer

Elk were once found in the East, from Georgia north to New York and Connecticut. By the time of the Civil War, hunting and habitat destruction had caused their extinction in most eastern states. All of the eastern subspecies are now extinct. Elk County, Pennsylvania, was without elk for more than a century.

At the beginning of the 20th century, herds of elk in the Rocky Mountains faced death by starvation as encroaching farms depleted their winter feeding grounds, and finally the government decided to intercede. The elk were gathered up from Yellowstone National Park and 50 of them were shipped to Pennsylvania.

At that early date, 1913, there was little understanding of the kind of acclimatization required when moving large animals from one habitat to another. The elk were released from cattle cars and chased into the wild to fend for themselves. Two years later, 95 more elk were moved from Yellowstone to Pennsylvania.

The elk tended to move toward farming areas because that was where the food was. Although they were protected, their destruction of farmland caused farmers to poach them illegally. In a 1971 survey, researchers found about 65 animals. Intensive work by the Bureau of Forestry to improve elk habitat, especially through reclamation of old strip mines, brought those numbers up to 135 by the early 1980s. By the year 2000, there were more than 500 elk in Pennsylvania, including many in Elk County.

In 1984, hunters established the Rocky Mountain Elk Foundation, whose mission is to reintroduce elk in the states where they once roamed. At present, new herds are established in Arkansas, Kentucky, Michigan, and Wisconsin, in addition to Pennsylvania. There is talk of moving herds to Tennessee and to the Adirondack range in New York. It seems fairly clear that improving habitat for elk reintroduction improves conditions for other wildlife—wild turkey, whitetail deer, and black bear, among others.

Unlike in the 1910s, today reintroduction is vastly improved—far more closely monitored and controlled. Animals are checked for disease. Land trusts are used to preserve habitat and to keep the elk from moving too close to cropland.

28. According to this passage, a major early threat to elk populations was

    (A) wolves and cougars
    (B) vehicular traffic
    (C) disease
    (D) hunting
    (E) introduction of new species

29. Based on information in the passage, about how many elk were moved from Yellowstone to Pennsylvania in the mid-1910s?

    (A) 65
    (B) 95
    (C) 135
    (D) 145 -
    (E) 250

30. According to the passage, where might you see elk today?

    (A) The Tennessee Valley

    (B) Georgia

    (C) The Adirondacks

    (D) Arkansas

    (E) Ohio

31. According to the passage, what is true of the elk in Pennsylvania today?

    (A) They are the same as the elk who lived there 200 years ago.

    (B) They are a different subspecies from the old Pennsylvania elk.

    (C) They are a different subspecies from the elk found in the Rockies.

    (D) They are only distantly related to the elk found in Yellowstone.

    (E) They are closely related to northern European reindeer.

32. The passage claims that

    (A) reclamation of land is a bad idea

    (B) hunters have ulterior motives for reintroducing elk

    (C) species reintroduction has improved over time

    (D) elk reintroduction may be doomed to failure

    (E) moose should be the next species to be reintroduced

In 1593, a botanist brought back samples of tulips to Holland from Constantinople. He planted them with the intent of studying their medicinal value. His garden was ransacked, the bulbs were stolen, and that was the beginning of the tulip trade in Holland.

The rather pretty alterations caused by a mosaic virus made the plants even more desirable, and shortly thereafter, prices began to rise out of control. By the year 1635, buyers were purchasing promissory notes while the bulbs were still in the ground. The trade in tulip futures became frenzied.

Tulips have a built-in rarity, in that it takes years to grow one from seed, and most bulbs produce only one or two bulb clones annually. That scarcity kept the value up even when new varieties were introduced on the market.

The tulip craze soon found ordinary citizens selling everything they owned for a single bulb; quite literally, bulbs were worth their weight in gold. People traded oxen, silver, land, and houses for one tulip bulb. During the winter of 1636, when the craze was at its peak, a single bulb future might change hands half a dozen times in one day.

As wild as this market was, it was transacted entirely outside of the established Stock Exchange in Amsterdam. It was a people's exchange. Typically, sales took place at auctions, but often they were transacted at pubs or in town squares.

Like any craze in which potential profits seem too good to be true, tulipomania was doomed. In February 1637, at a bulb auction in Haarlem, the bottom fell out when no one agreed to pay the inflated prices. The ensuing panic took a matter of a few weeks; the government had to leap in to try to bail the country out, offering 10 cents on the dollar for bulb contracts until even that could not be sustained. Eventually, a panel of judges declared that all investment in tulips was gambling and not recoverable investment. Holland slowly fell into an economic depression that lasted for years and eventually overflowed its borders into the rest of Europe.

33. Which of the following statements most accurately captures the central thesis of the passage?

(A) Tulipomania was a localized craze with localized effects.
(B) Tulipomania shows the potential devastating effects of a craze.
(C) The Stock Exchange cannot prevent unregulated trading.
(D) The Stock Exchange developed as an answer to unregulated trading.
(E) Before the flower trade, speculation did not exist in Europe.

34. The passage suggests that the author would most likely believe that

(A) trading in futures may be ill-advised
(B) trading in commodities is safer than trading stock
(C) trading stocks is relatively risk-free
(D) trading at auctions is usually unwise
(E) flowering plants are a bad investment

35. Which of the following assertions does the author support with an example?

  I. Tulips have a built-in rarity.
 II. Sales were transacted in pubs and town squares.
III. Holland fell into a depression.

(A) I only
(B) III only
(C) I and II only
(D) I and III only
(E) I, II, and III

36. The author refers to the trade in tulips as a "people's exchange." This term is used to indicate

(A) fairness
(B) class warfare
(C) low prices
(D) efficiency
(E) informality

37. The 17th-century speculation on prospective tulip growth might be compared to today's

(A) fluctuation of oil and natural gas prices
– (B) exchange trading of options and futures
(C) hedge funds in the foreign exchange market
(D) issuance of risk-free municipal bonds
(E) bundling of low-rate mortgages

38. Auctions in the Netherlands continue to handle between 60 and 70 percent of the world's flower production and export. What question might this information reasonably suggest about tulipomania?

(A) Whether it resulted not only in a depression but also in the death of the auction system of commodity trading
(B) Whether it led the Dutch government to take over substantial debt for bulb dealers and their patrons
(C) Whether it changed the Dutch way of doing business to one that was more formal and controlled
(D) Whether it forced the Dutch to look into new, nonagricultural products for export and import
(E) Whether it stimulated the Dutch to explore more exotic sources of foreign commodities

The Red List is published annually by the World Conservation Union to indicate to the world which species are threatened, endangered, and extinct. The most recent list included nearly 16,000 endangered species, including, incredibly, nearly every ape on the planet.

The western lowland gorilla moved from "endangered" to "critically endangered" in 2007. "Critically endangered" indicates that its population and range are shrinking, and it is in imminent danger of extinction. The mountain gorilla, once studied by George Schaller and Dian Fossey in the 1960s, has also been endangered for years.

The gorilla has the misfortune to be native to an area that has been ravaged by war. Rwanda and the Congo are war-torn nations, and the resulting damage to habitat has affected gorillas as well as humans. Gorilla populations have also been ransacked by the Ebola virus, which has killed an estimated 90 percent of the gorilla population in each area of western and central Africa where it has been found.

Like humans, gorillas tend to have a single offspring at one time, with each one gestating for about nine months. Females do not mature until around age six, and nearly half of baby gorillas do not survive till breeding age.

The number-one threat to gorillas, however, is human greed. Humans are burning down the forests where the last remaining gorilla families live. They are doing this to harvest charcoal, which is used to fuel cooking fires throughout the region. In addition, they are poaching the last remaining gorillas for meat and for their hands or other parts, which are considered a delicacy in Africa and are used medicinally in parts of Asia.

Even the tourist industry, once thought to be a way to preserve the ape population, has proved deadly to the gorillas. Many have died from measles or respiratory infections caught from humans. Despite the best efforts of dedicated conservationists and African rangers, some give these vegetarian cousins of *Homo sapiens* no more than a decade before all wild specimens are eradicated.

39. The author's tone indicates that she feels the eradication of apes is
    (A) inevitable
    (B) shocking
    (C) intentional
    (D) impossible
    (E) accepted

40. Based on information in the passage, about how many gorillas have survived Ebola in regions where the virus is prevalent?
    (A) About 1 percent
    (B) About 1 in 10
    (C) About one-half
    (D) Only 9 in 10
    (E) About three-quarters

41. How are the ideas in the first two sentences of the second paragraph related?

    (A) Sentence 2 provides a contrast to sentence 1.
    (B) Sentence 2 is the next step after sentence 1.
    (C) Sentence 2 defines a term that appears in sentence 1.
    (D) Sentence 2 provides support for a theory in sentence 1.
    (E) Sentence 2 gives a reason for sentence 1.

42. Which of the following most accurately summarizes the main point of the passage?

    (A) Gorillas are not designed for survival.
    (B) Conservation is unrealistic.
    (C) Humans put gorillas at risk.
    (D) We all must protect our ape cousins.
    (E) We should build more parks and zoos.

43. The author's purpose in the fifth paragraph is to

    (A) introduce a hypothesis and support it with examples
    (B) compare some indignities perpetrated on apes
    (C) list some possible reasons for the extinction of species
    (D) contradict theories suggested in earlier paragraphs
    (E) provide examples of issues introduced in the fourth paragraph

44. By the end of the passage, the author concludes that

    (A) Africans care little about gorillas
    (B) the large apes should fight back
    (C) humans are largely evil
    (D) war is the main threat to gorillas
    (E) gorillas may not survive

The use of inhaled anesthetics can be traced back as far as the medieval Moors, who used narcotic-soaked sponges placed over the nostrils of patients. Some 300 years later, in 1275, Majorcan alchemist Raymundus Lullus is supposed to have discovered the chemical compound later called ether. The compound, which would have a brief but important run as the anesthetic of choice in Western medicine, was synthesized by German physician Valerius Cordus in 1540. Adding sulfuric acid, known at the time as "oil of vitriol," to ethyl alcohol resulted in the compound Cordus called "sweet vitriol."

During the next few centuries, ether was used by physicians for a variety of purposes. Its effectiveness as a hypnotic agent was well-known, and a favorite pastime of medical students in the early 19th century was the "ether frolic," an early version of the drunken frat party. Nevertheless, no record of ether's being used as an anesthetic in surgery appears until the 1840s.

Dr. Crawford Williamson Long of Jefferson, Georgia, removed neck tumors from a patient under ether anesthesia on March 30, 1842. However, he failed to publish the record of his experiment until 1848, by which time Dr. William T. G. Morton, a dentist in Hartford, Connecticut, had conducted a variety of experiments with ether on animals and himself, culminating in the painless extraction of a tooth from a patient under ether on September 30, 1846.

After reading about Morton's successful use of ether, doctors at Harvard invited him to demonstrate his technique. At Massachusetts General Hospital on October 16, 1846, Morton administered ether to a patient, and senior surgeon John Collins Warren removed a growth from the patient's neck as a crowd of doctors and dignitaries looked on. The operation is recorded in several paintings of the era, indicating its critical importance. Despite its volatility and side effects, ether continued to be used as an anesthetic until it was overtaken by less harmful potions. Morton, meanwhile, struggled unsuccessfully to be granted a patent for his "discovery" and then, when that failed, for his "technique." After years of litigation, he died penniless at age 49.

45. The statement in the first paragraph that ether would "have a brief but important run as the anesthetic of choice in Western medicine" implies that the author believes which of the following?

(A) Ether was not a particularly good anesthetic.
(B) Ether was not used long enough to judge its effectiveness.
(C) Ether was effective during the period when it was used.
(D) Ether was a noteworthy import from the East to the West.
(E) Ether had other, more critical uses during that time.

46. Which of these would be the best title for the passage?

(A) "Inhaled Anesthetics"
(B) "An Important Anesthetic"
(C) "How Anesthetics Have Changed"
(D) "Our Debt to Ancient Physicians"
(E) "The Dangers of Anesthesia"

47. Which of the following statements from the passage provides the least support for the author's claim that ether was an important discovery for physicians at the time?

   (A) "Dr. Crawford Williamson Long of Jefferson, Georgia, removed neck tumors from a patient under ether anesthesia on March 30, 1842."
   (B) "After reading about Morton's successful use of ether, doctors at Harvard invited him to demonstrate his technique."
   (C) "The operation is recorded in several paintings of the era, indicating its critical importance."
   (D) "Senior surgeon John Collins Warren removed a growth from the patient's neck as a crowd of doctors and dignitaries looked on."
   (E) "Nevertheless, no record of ether's being used as an anesthetic in surgery appears until the 1840s."

48. In the first paragraph, the author probably writes that Lullus "is supposed to have discovered" ether because

   (A) there is conflicting evidence about his discovery
   (B) Lullus did not really discover ether at all
   (C) although Lullus was meant to discover it, someone else did
   (D) no one can really "discover" a chemical compound
   (E) Lullus's training made him likely to make the discovery

49. How is the information in the fourth paragraph organized?

   (A) By reasons and examples
   (B) Using comparisons and contrasts
   (C) In time order
   (D) Using cause-and-effect relationships
   (E) In order of importance

50. The author probably includes information about Dr. Long in the third paragraph to show that

   (A) Morton was not the first to use ether in a surgical procedure
   (B) publishing results can mean the difference between fortune and penury
   (C) both dentists and doctors used ether to good effect
   (D) doctors in the Northeast often received more attention than doctors from the South
   (E) in contrast to earlier alchemists, doctors understood ether's dangers

At more than 195,000 square miles, Canada's Baffin Island is the fifth largest island in the world—more than twice the size of Great Britain. As large as it is, Baffin Island is home to only about 11,000 people, primarily due to its harsh climate. It is surrounded by sea ice and the Arctic Ocean, and the temperature rarely gets above 50 degrees Fahrenheit, even in July. In the center of the island, summer temperatures hover below 10 degrees Fahrenheit. In winter, temperatures throughout the island average well below zero.

Geologically speaking, Baffin Island represents a continuation of the Canadian Shield, an expanse of land scoured by glaciers that extends from the Arctic archipelago south into north-central United States and from the Northwest Territories all the way east to Labrador. It features rocky bluffs, a coastal strip of marshland, and a wide plain region that turns into a large plateau at the northern end of the island. Despite its inclement weather, it is a breeding ground for a remarkable variety of seabirds and the wintering place for narwhals, beluga whales, and walruses.

Things are changing on Baffin Island. Hunters are beginning to see melting of the sea ice. Trekkers are finding glaciers turned to slush in some places. Rock surfaces that have never seen the light of day are starting to emerge from the ice-covered tundra. The last decade has not warmed Baffin Island to the point where it is habitable for any but the hardiest souls—but it has definitely warmed it.

51. In the first line of paragraph 2 ("Geologically speaking . . . Labrador"), the author implies that

(A) Baffin Island is huge, but it is dwarfed by its surroundings
(B) at one time, Baffin Island was joined to the Canadian mainland
(C) glaciers separate Baffin Island from the mainland of Canada
(D) a single glacier helped to carve out Baffin and Labrador Islands
(E) Baffin Island is physically similar to some parts of northern Michigan

52. From the passage, it can be inferred that descriptions of changes on Baffin Island are mostly the product of

(A) scientific study
(B) satellite surveillance
(C) journalists' reports
(D) anecdotal observation
(E) pioneer narratives

53. The second paragraph plays what role in the passage?

(A) Descriptive
(B) Definitional
(C) Parenthetical
(D) Explanatory
(E) Rhetorical

The "most dangerous eight seconds in sports" is considered to be bull riding, in which a rider attempts to stay seated on a bucking bull for that length of time. Rules are strict: The rider must hold on with one hand and not touch the other hand to the bull for the length of the ride. The bull and rider begin the ride in a chute. In preparation for the ride, the rider rosins one hand, wraps a braided bullrope around the bull's neck, and then wraps the remainder of the rope around the rosined hand. When the rider signals readiness, the chute is opened, and the bull and rider fly out into the ring. The bull, selected for orneriness and speed, tries to buck the rider off before the allotted time is up. Two judges score both bull and rider on a scale of 0 to 50 points. Bulls are scored on agility and strength, and riders earn points for control and balance. Then the scores are added together. Scores above 90 are rare; rider scores of 0 (because of a fall) are common.

Certain bulls do well enough in competition to attain a measure of fame. One example is Little Yellow Jacket from North Dakota, who was voted best bucking bull two years in a row. Another is the enormous bull known as Outlaw, out of Calgary. It took 58 tries by 58 different riders before one rider was able to hang on to Outlaw for the required eight seconds. A third was Red Rock, from Texas, who apparently went his entire career without a successful ride, bucking off 309 riders between 1984 and 1987.

Of course, there are dozens of famous bull riders, new ones for every generation. There are a number of rodeo circuits, and riders may work their way up to the level of Professional Bull Riders. There they are guaranteed regular work and the possibility of many thousands in prize money. PBR bull riding is televised widely, with each event featuring the top 45 professional riders of the year.

54. The primary purpose of the passage is to

    (A) suggest reasons why bull riding should be outlawed
    (B) compare bull riders to athletes in other endeavors
    (C) describe and explain the rules of a popular sport
    (D) list a few beloved heroes of the sport of bull riding
    (E) review and elucidate the history of bull riding

55. Based on information in the passage, what could you assume if a rider scored a 20?

    (A) He fell off the bull before eight seconds was reached.
    (B) He showed unusual agility and strength on the bull.
    (C) His agility was less than average, but his balance was good.
    (D) He exhibited little control but did not fall off the bull.
    (E) His balance was not up to par, but he looked strong and agile.

56. In the second paragraph of the passage, the first sentence introduces the topic, and the other sentences provide

    (A) examples in support
    (B) examples in refutation
    (C) reasons for an opinion
    (D) causes and effects
    (E) comparisons and contrasts

Although Norway is today a Lutheran nation and thus not much associated with saints and miracles, the legend of Sunniva survives there as a testament to earlier values. On the island of Selja, there remain ruins of a great Christian center. Churches dating back to the 900s and a large monastery from somewhat later are part of the Selja ruins. On the island, too, is a large cave, where the legend is mostly set.

Sunniva was the Christian daughter of Irish King Otto. She was pursued by a heathen Viking, who wanted her hand in marriage. Seeking asylum, she set off in three ships with her followers, but her ships foundered without sails or oars, and she was castaway on the island of Selja. There she lived with her followers, pious men and women known as the *seljumun*, or "holy ones." The islanders suspected the strangers of eating their grazing animals, and they called on Earl Håkon to attack them and remove them from the island. Sunniva and her followers hid in a cave, but as their pursuers came near, the cave collapsed.

After that came a series of miracles. People reported seeing rays of light and smelling sweet odors emanating from the cave. Christian King Olav had the cave opened and found Sunniva's undisturbed body, which he placed in a crypt inside a church he built for her. The island became a site for pilgrimages and a major focus of Olav's Christianization of Norway. Sunniva is now the patron saint of Western Norway and particularly of Bergen.

57. It can be inferred that Sunniva rejected her would-be Viking lover because of her
    (A) faith
    (B) purity
    (C) royal blood
    (D) love for another
    (E) Irish heritage

58. Ancient Norwegians considered the fact that Sunniva's body was intact to be a miracle, but another logical explanation might be that
    (A) the rays of light came from flaming volcanic lava
    (B) King Olav kept her body interred in a crypt
    (C) the cave offered natural properties of preservation
    (D) Earl Håkon never managed to find Sunniva
    (E) Sunniva did not perish when the cave-in occurred

59. How might the organization of the passage be described?
    (A) Paragraph 1 introduces the topic; paragraph 2 tells the story; paragraph 3 presents the moral.
    (B) Paragraph 1 introduces the topic; paragraphs 2 and 3 narrate the legend.
    (C) Paragraphs 1 and 2 narrate the legend; paragraph 3 summarizes the story.
    (D) Paragraphs 1 and 2 introduce the topic; paragraph 3 extends the topic to the present day.
    (E) Paragraph 1 defines the terms; paragraph 2 tells the story; paragraph 3 offers an alternative.

The first Philippine Revolution occurred at the end of the 1800s, but it was fueled in part by a movement that had grown up earlier. Filipinos who had emigrated to Europe, either through exile or to study, began to come together to strive for equal rights for Filipino and Spanish citizens in the Philippines. They asked for representation on the Spanish parliament, freedoms of speech and assembly, and equal opportunities for Filipinos when it came to getting jobs in government.

La Solidaridad, a newspaper published in Spain by exiled Filipinos, was the main organ of this Propaganda Movement. La Solidaridad was the name of an organization as well as a newspaper, but it was the paper that mattered more. Between 1889 and 1895, the little paper, whose ambitions were modest and whose readership was small, lit a fire of nationalist pride under those few individuals who would go on to lead the Filipino people in their fight against Spanish exploitation.

Perhaps the most prominent member of the Propaganda Movement was José Rizal. A scientist by trade, he strove scientifically to refute Europeans' notions of Filipinos as an inferior people. His papers and orations were important, but his two novels, *Noli Me Tangere* (1886) and *El Filibusterismo* (1891), were even more influential. Their heavy-handed symbolism portrayed corruption and abuse in the Spanish-led government and clergy of the Philippines. Although Rizal mainly wanted equality and representation, his books led to a sense of Filipino self-respect that stimulated true revolution.

60. It can be inferred from the passage that in the Philippines around 1890,

    (A) *La Solidaridad* became the most important local newspaper
    (B) Filipino exiles returned to their impoverished nation
    (C) José Rizal produced experiments showing Filipino superiority
    (D) Spanish-born residents had more rights than the natives had
    (E) a revolution broke out with the goal of separation from Spain

61. The author suggests that the sense of cultural pride engendered by Rizal's books helped to goad Filipinos into revolution, but another possibility might be that

    (A) Rizal's scientific refutation of European biases angered the Spanish
    (B) Rizal's call for equality and representation was scorned by Filipinos
    (C) Rizal's descriptions of Spanish abuses aroused anger and bitterness
    (D) Rizal's books did more to convince Spaniards than to reassure Filipinos
    (E) Rizal's novels were thinly concealed biographies of real Filipinos

62. How might the organization of the passage be described?

    (A) Paragraph 1 introduces the topic; paragraphs 2 and 3 present examples in support.
    (B) Paragraph 1 introduces the topic; paragraphs 2 and 3 present reasons in support.
    (C) Paragraphs 1 and 2 present an argument; paragraph 3 summarizes the argument.
    (D) Paragraphs 1 and 2 introduce the topic; paragraph 3 offers alternatives.
    (E) Paragraph 1 introduces a cause; paragraphs 2 and 3 provide effects in order.

GreenBiz Group recently sent teams to interview executives at 15 major companies, from Cisco and Microsoft to Ford and General Electric. Their purpose was to determine where those companies stood when it comes to the convergence of energy, building, transportation, and information technologies.

The interviews were designed to look at the possibilities for a more connected future that offers both lower costs and lower carbon emissions while still expanding business. Among the questions they studied were: Which facilities might benefit from producing their own energy or managing their own water sources and use? How might logistics be altered to improve efficiency and complement the variables in each geographic region? How could offices be improved to limit waste and maximize communication?

According to their website, GreenBiz believes that "a revolution is taking place that is leading companies of all sizes and sectors to comprehensively address environmental issues as part of their strategy and operations—rethinking their policies, processes, and products, and their relationships with a variety of stakeholders and trading partners."

The owners of GreenBiz believe that corporations can be a force for good for the planet as well as for society, but that first corporate executives must see that green business is good business, and that the convergence of new technologies can result in new opportunities and growth. By providing a database on green business practices, GreenBiz hopes to guide corporations to make that philosophical leap.

63. Which of the following most accurately summarizes the main point of the passage?
   (A) GreenBiz thinks that companies have failed in their attempts to be a force for good.
   (B) With the help of GreenBiz, even large corporations can reduce their carbon footprint.
   (C) Without the help of GreenBiz, corporations will continue to put profits over environmentalism.
   (D) Recent changes in technology make it possible for corporations to increase profits while holding down costs.
   (E) GreenBiz works to educate executives on the transformations possible through greener technologies.

64. The database described in the passage would most likely be helpful for which of the following?

(A) A start-up medical supply company

(B) A professor of environmental science

(C) A school district's transportation director

(D) A freelance newspaper reporter

(E) An investor with stock in General Electric

65. The author mentions both Cisco and Ford in the first sentence for what purpose?

(A) To indicate that the study focused on manufacturing companies

(B) To demonstrate that both public and private corporations can benefit

(C) To establish that the study covered an international grid

(D) To show that new and old corporations were included in the study

(E) To prove that automobile companies were key to the interviewing process

The muckraking era between 1900 and World War I saw a new generation of reform-minded, watchdog journalists who wielded substantial influence with their investigations of corruption and dangerous working conditions. In an effort to counter this, corporations sought the help of a new industry, public relations.

Among the first and most influential of these agencies was Parker & Lee, founded in 1904 by George Parker and Ivy Ledbetter Lee. Lee had worked for a newspaper in New York and had run a publicity campaign for an unsuccessful presidential candidate. Parker, also a former reporter, had been the press agent for President Grover Cleveland. Together, they developed a number of tactics by which corporations might improve their public image.

During their brief partnership, Lee represented the head of the Pennsylvania Railroad. Following a tragic accident, Lee convinced the railroad to send out a frank press release detailing the incident before reporters could descend upon the scene. During a 1906 coal strike, Lee represented the coal companies and sent newspapers daily releases on the strike and negotiations. He did not believe in covering up but rather in controlling the release of the truth.

After his firm dissolved, Lee went out on his own. One of his most important jobs was as John D. Rockefeller's publicity counsel following the Ludlow massacre, the death of miners and families killed by local militia during a strike. Lee did much to soften the robber baron's image, urging him to be photographed handing out coins to indigent children. He worked behind the scenes, altering Rockefeller's business decisions and corporate policies to improve the company's overall relationship with the public.

Lee ran into trouble in the early 1930s because of associations with Germany's I. G. Farben Industries. In 1934 he was called to testify before Congress about providing propaganda for the Nazis through his work for Farben, a charge he denied. He may not have chosen his clients wisely, but there is no question that Lee established a prototype for public relations that is still widely used today from Silicon Valley to Washington, DC.

66. Which of the following statements most accurately captures the central idea of the passage?
   (A) Even the worst offenders in the corporate world can benefit from a sound public relations campaign.
   (B) Prior to 1900, corporations in America were losing the image battle to muckraking journalists.
   (C) Although he represented mostly American corporations, Ivy Ledbetter Lee was the first PR agent to work abroad as well.
   (D) Ivy Ledbetter Lee's innovations in the world of public relations included the press release and the personal photographer.
   (E) Ivy Ledbetter Lee developed modern PR while working for a wide spectrum of agencies and corporations.

67. The author most likely mentions the Ludlow massacre for what purpose?

    (A) To show what can ensue after a bout of bad publicity
    (B) To reveal one result of Lee's campaign for Rockefeller
    (C) To establish Rockefeller's need for a good publicity agent
    (D) To remind the reader of the need for muckraking journalism
    (E) To offer an example of the dangers of extraction industries

68. The PR benefit of Rockefeller's being photographed giving coins to poor children is most similar to that of photographs taken in which of these situations?

    (A) A beloved actor signing autographs for fans at Disney World
    (B) A candidate for mayor blowing up balloons at a street fair
    (C) A disgraced football player visiting a children's hospital
    (D) The Duchess of Cambridge throwing candy to schoolchildren
    (E) A computer mogul tossing out the first pitch at a ballgame

69. According to the passage, it can be inferred that Lee would have been least likely to do which of the following?

    (A) Lie about a politician's involvement with a scandal
    (B) Release photographs of a tycoon performing a service
    (C) Send out a press release about a client's hospitalization
    (D) Encourage a corporate client to improve working conditions
    (E) Talk to a reporter about a problem with a manufacturer's product

Monetarism, the economic theory associated with Milton Friedman (although it long preceded him), argues that major variations in the economy derive from changes in the supply of money, rather than, for example, fluctuations in stock prices. According to this theory, the way to maintain stability in the economic system is to ensure stability in the amount of money issued, increasing that amount only in relation to an increase in the gross domestic product (GDP).

Unlike Keynesians, monetarists believe that the role of government in economics should be minimal and that fiscal policy is often damaging to the overall economy. They tend to assume that markets work best when they are left to their own devices, preferring a laissez-faire course of inaction to governmental interference in the marketplace.

In the 1970s, this theory seemed to gibe with the inflation spikes that were occurring—although to some degree inflation was tagged to oil prices, there was also a clear rate of money growth that could be a secondary cause. Monetarists insisted that the Federal Reserve System should never manipulate the money supply in an attempt to stabilize the economy—that the economy was essentially stable as long as the money supply was stable, and no other discretionary policies were needed. However, inflation in the 1990s was unrelated to monetary policy, and in the 2000s, it became clear that pure monetary policy was unable to stimulate the economy in any lasting way.

Ultimately, monetarists seem to have succeeded in one thing only: Today's monetary authorities better understand the role of money in the stability of economies and recognize the need for caution in the manipulation of the money supply. Fiscal policy is no longer divorced from monetary policy, and the two work in tandem to inject stability into the system.

70. From the presentation of the information in the passage, it can reasonably be inferred that the author believes which of the following about monetarism?

(A) It is a failed theory with little bearing on today's economy.
(B) It is more relevant today than Keynesianism is.
(C) It should have focused less on the money supply and more on GDP.
(D) It took old laissez-faire theories and turned them upside down.
(E) Its main premise failed, but it still influences current policy.

71. Based on the passage, a true monetarist would most likely agree with which of the following statements?

(A) Changes in prices are not linked to expansion or contraction of the national money supply.
(B) An increase in money supply in one nation can easily destabilize the economy of a neighboring nation.
(C) To stabilize the economy, the government of an underdeveloped nation must invest in several industries simultaneously.
(D) The Great Depression represented a time of too little money infused throughout the system.
(E) Lowering taxes and decreasing regulation are required steps for any economic growth.

72. Which of the following titles would be most appropriate for this passage?

    (A) "Keynesian vs. Monetarist Thought"
    (B) "Nobelist Friedman and the Chicago School"
    (C) "A Brief Look at Monetarism"
    (D) "The Proper Role of Money"
    (E) "Failed Policies at the Fed"

73. The author implies which of the following about monetarist theory?

    (A) It was devised as a means to counter Keynesianism.
    (B) It was tied to politics and thus doomed to failure.
    (C) It weakened the role of the Federal Reserve System.
    (D) It failed to take globalization into account.
    (E) It fit patterns of the 1970s but not of the 1990s.

74. Based on the second paragraph, you might infer that the relationship of Keynesians to monetarists is most similar to the relationship between

    (A) monarchists and republicans
    (B) federalists and nationalists
    (C) globalists and regionalists
    (D) conservatives and neo-conservatives
    (E) statists and libertarians

Shared vocabulary is a critical component of any high-performing organization or institution. All organizations have a handful of terms and acronyms that are key to their functioning. A school district, for example, might regularly refer to RTI (response to intervention), differentiation, and benchmarking. If some teachers understand RTI in one way, and other teachers think the term means something else, chaos may ensue. District leadership needs to clarify the meaning of the acronym or term as they intend it to be used.

The same is true for any corporate entity. Does everyone in the office understand what you mean when you refer to scalable actions, competitive advantage, or core competencies? Are they all on the same page when they talk about success or excellence?

The meanings are not always in the individual terms, but rather in the organization's overall interpretation of those terms. If employees transfer in from a different company or even a different division, they may arrive with a different understanding of the meanings of some critical terminology regularly used in your office.

Some executives clarify terms at the beginning of staff meetings, just to ensure that everyone is speaking the same language from the onset of a project. Others publish key terms and definitions in an office handbook, which serves as a reference guide for everyone in the department. Successful teamwork and meaningful professional dialogue depend on an agreed-upon set of concepts and terms.

75. According to the passage, the author believes which of the following regarding acronyms?
    (A) They are an annoying but critical part of most organizations.
    (B) The words they stand for should be in parentheses after the abbreviation.
    (C) Employees should be in agreement on their meanings.
    (D) It is possible to confuse them if they use similar letters.
    (E) Leadership should avoid their use and use other terminology if possible.

76. As described in the passage, shared vocabulary in an organization is most similar to which of the following?
    (A) Teen slang used by parents
    (B) Sharing a meal with friends
    (C) Speaking in pig Latin
    (D) Learning a foreign language
    (E) Quarterback calls in a huddle

77. Why does the author mention *success* in the second paragraph?

    (A) To show that simple words have global connotations

    (B) As an example of a concept that most corporations share

    (C) To explain the goal of using shared corporate vocabulary

    (D) As an example of a term that needs a common definition

    (E) To stress the use of shared vocabulary in high-performing teams

78. Based on the final paragraph, which word describes the author's feeling about shared vocabulary?

    (A) Rare

    (B) Imperative

    (C) Overdone

    (D) Discretionary

    (E) Impractical

79. The author believes that shared vocabulary can help an organization to

    (A) distract the competition

    (B) create new terminology

    (C) reduce internal confusion

    (D) welcome new employees

    (E) resist unwanted change

AzPro Corporation in central New York State recently ran into trouble when nearby towns determined that their drinking water contained levels of arsenic exceeding the current standard of 10 ppb. Arsenic was detected at one well house at an average level of 15 ppb, and there is some indication that the levels may exceed 20 ppb at some private residences.

When people hear the word *arsenic*, they are often likely to conjure up Agatha Christie mysteries and to associate it with a gruesome, instant death. In fact, arsenic is a component in copper, lead, and other ores, and it is often naturally present in soil, groundwater, and surface water. However, it is its use in commercial pesticides such as those manufactured by AzPro that is the cause of concern here in central New York. The belief is that the use of testing areas surrounding the AzPro plant has enabled arsenic to enter the soil for decades, and that contaminated soil has leached components of pesticides into the groundwater surrounding the plant. AzPro has not used those testing areas since 1990; its recent practices are considered state-of-the-art when it comes to public health and safety.

If people are exposed to arsenic over a long period of time, they may develop skin problems, nerve or liver damage, or high blood pressure. There is evidence that arsenic, like lead, may contribute to learning deficiencies. High levels of arsenic may even increase the risk of certain cancers, notably bladder and skin cancers.

It is important to note that the safe level (maximum contaminant level, or MCL) for arsenic was recently lowered by the state from 50 ppb to 10 ppb. All of the current readings of arsenic surrounding AzPro are well below that earlier standard. Nevertheless, citizens who are concerned are encouraged to drink bottled water, and the towns will sample their well houses for contamination monthly. If it is determined that additional water treatment is required to lower the arsenic levels, AzPro has rightly agreed to pay for the installation of related equipment.

80. The author's attitude toward today's AzPro could best be characterized as

   (A) disgusted
   (B) disapproving
   (C) positive
   (D) baffled
   (E) fascinated

81. The third paragraph plays what role in the passage?

   (A) It explains why the presence of arsenic in water might be of concern.
   (B) It gives examples of heavy metals that can cause health problems.
   (C) It describes where arsenic may be found in nature.
   (D) It gives reasons for the use of arsenic in pesticides.
   (E) It presents a possible counterargument to the author's thesis.

82. The author of the passage would most likely agree with which of the following statements?

(A) The MCL for arsenic should have been lowered years ago.
(B) Even an MCL of 50 ppb does not pose a threat to human health.
(C) Current ppb levels of arsenic near AzPro should not cause great alarm.
(D) The testing of arsenic levels is all too often inaccurate and imprecise.
(E) Arsenic is not nearly the health threat that lead can be.

83. You might see MCLs applied to drinking water for all of these except

(A) microorganisms
(B) organic chemicals
(C) inorganic chemicals
(D) disinfectants
(E) effervescence

84. The author most likely mentions the old MCL for arsenic for what purpose?

(A) To show how standards change over time
(B) To indicate the arbitrariness of water testing
(C) To prove that AzPro violated no local standard
(D) To calm the nerves of citizens near the AzPro plant
(E) To scold the state for keeping old standards too long

Ground-source, or geothermal, cooling and heating is a green energy alternative with a variety of advantages. Geothermal heating works because a few feet below the surface of the Earth, the ground is warmer than the air above the surface of the Earth. By transporting that warmth to the surface, you may heat or cool a building.

The system uses two main components—the loop of underground pipes, which may be laid horizontally or vertically, and the heat pump inside the building to which those pipes connect. In cold weather, the ground loop circulates water or another liquid, which absorbs the heat from the Earth and transports it to the heat pump. That pump then extracts the heat from the liquid and distributes it as warm air throughout the building. With its heat removed, the water moves back through the pipes into the ground and circulates through again. In warm weather, the process is reversed—the heat pump removes heat from the hot air and transports it through the ground loop into the Earth, leaving cool air to be distributed through the house.

The system is energy efficient and environmentally clean. The cost comes with the installation of the system—it is difficult to retrofit but cost-effective when it is used for new construction. There are additional costs that cannot be overlooked. Running a heat pump takes energy in the form of electricity. Some people who retrofit an oil or gas system to geothermal find that their electric bills double or triple. Some get past that cost (and the decidedly un-green coal-powered electricity use) by installing solar panels and generating their own electricity. Others simply eat the cost, understanding that they are saving enormously on gas or oil costs and using a system with more than four times the efficiency of the most efficient gas heat.

Government loans and tax credits make even retrofitting to a geothermal system affordable. As gas and oil prices rise, geothermal heating looks like a better bet than ever. In addition, recent "super storms" have led people to recognize the power of geothermal heating as a weatherproof resource.

85. With which of the following generalizations about geothermal heating would the author of the passage most likely agree?

(A) Geothermal heating is an effective substitute for heating sources that use nonrenewable resources.

(B) Although it represents one form of green energy, geothermal heating is not universally appropriate.

(C) Because they use energy from the Earth, geothermal heating and cooling work best at low latitudes.

(D) A geothermal heating system with horizontal piping is far more efficient than one with vertical piping.

(E) State and federal governments should provide further incentives for switching to geothermal heat.

86. The passage is primarily concerned with
    (A) evaluating several forms of renewable energy
    (B) promoting residential use of geothermal heating
    (C) describing one green energy alternative
    (D) identifying recent discoveries about geothermal heat
    (E) explaining how geothermal heat benefits consumers

87. The author indicates that the purpose of the ground loop is to
    (A) remove water
    (B) extract heat
    (C) distribute air
    (D) convey heat
    (E) generate heat

88. The author mentions solar panels for what purpose?
    (A) To compare costs of geothermal and other alternative energy sources
    (B) To show that using one renewable source does not preclude using another
    (C) To contrast the relative efficiencies of two forms of power
    (D) To remind the reader that alternatives to coal exist
    (E) To suggest how the high electrical costs of a heat pump might be mitigated

89. From the presentation of information in the final paragraph, it can be reasonably inferred that the author believes which of the following about geothermal heating?
    (A) Its cost will continue to drop.
    (B) It is likely to grow in popularity.
    (C) It will be superseded by new forms of energy.
    (D) Its benefits will never outweigh its drawbacks.
    (E) It is the only answer to power losses due to super storms.

When Queen Beatrix of the Netherlands abdicated her throne in the spring of 2013, ceding the monarchy to her son Willem-Alexander, she ended more than a century of rule by women in her country.

William I was the first king of the Netherlands, self-promoted in March 1815 after the defeat of Napoleon and the departure of the French. He had six children by his wife, Wilhelmina. After her death, desiring to remarry a Belgian Catholic woman, William I abdicated in 1840 and was succeeded by his eldest son, now William II, who ruled for only nine years before succumbing to illness and dying at the age of 56. William II was followed by William III, who managed to outlive three of his four children, meaning that by the time of his death in 1890, only daughter Wilhelmina was left to succeed him. Her mother, William III's second wife Emma, was named regent, as Wilhelmina was then only 10 years old.

Wilhelmina was officially enthroned in 1898 and would go on to be the Nether-lands' longest ruling monarch. She abdicated in failing health after 57 years, ceding the throne to her only child (she had suffered a series of miscarriages and one stillbirth). That child, Juliana, herself went on to have four children, all of them girls, so it seemed clear that her successor would be the eldest of those girls, Beatrix. And in fact, Juliana abdicated in 1980, leaving the throne to Beatrix, the mother of three sons.

Beatrix was a popular monarch, despite her controversial marriage to a former member of the Hitler Youth. The marriage at the time was roundly despised by the Dutch, but they came around, apparently due to the sheer force of her husband's personality. Regardless of her popularity, Beatrix's abdication came as no surprise; abdication in favor of the younger generation has become something of a tradition for Dutch kings and queens, in contrast with the British monarchy, who tend to cling to their ceremonial roles for life.

90. Based on the passage, what made William II and William III different from William I and Queen Wilhelmina?

(A) They ceded the throne to daughters, not sons.
(B) They did not relinquish the throne to their offspring.
(C) They had good reasons for their abdications.
(D) They had children by more than one spouse.
(E) They served on the throne for far shorter periods.

91. The new king, Willem-Alexander, has three daughters. Based on this pas-sage, were Willem-Alexander to have a fourth child who was male, which of the following would be true?

(A) He would pass down the title to his son.
(B) He would pass down the title to his eldest daughter.
(C) He would pass down the title to whichever child he chose.
(D) He would be honor-bound to abdicate the throne at that time.
(E) The passage does not give enough information to make this determination.

92. The author's attitude toward the British monarchy could best be characterized as which of the following?

    (A) Tolerant
    (B) Sympathetic
    (C) Deferential
    (D) Critical
    (E) Outraged

93. The author most likely mentions the Hitler Youth for what purpose?

    (A) To show the tight bonds between the Dutch and the Germans
    (B) To remind the reader that today's Dutch rulers descend from the Germans
    (C) To reveal an obstacle that Queen Beatrix had to overcome
    (D) To point out historical prejudices that may still exist today
    (E) To poke fun at the Dutch monarchy for its lack of discretion

94. Which of the following situations is most similar to Beatrix's behavior in 2013?

    (A) Estée Lauder handing over the reins of her company to her son Leonard
    (B) Kiichiro Toyoda spinning off Toyota Motors from his father's company
    (C) CEO Danny Wegman naming his daughters president and vice president
    (D) Henry Ford taking back Ford Motor Company after son Edsel died
    (E) Son-in-law F. X. Rice taking over Utz Company on the death of William Utz

Clawback may be defined as monies that are distributed with the understanding that they may be taken back under certain circumstances. The term is used in a variety of contexts, but recently it most frequently appears in discussions of executive bonuses.

Scandals at Enron, Tyco, and WorldCom led to the Sarbanes-Oxley Act of 2002, which revised standards for the boards and management of public companies. Included in the act was a provision for clawback, requiring CEOs and CFOs of public companies to return bonuses, incentives, equity-based compensation, and profits on sales of company stock that they receive within the 12-month period following the public release of financial information that indicates willful noncompliance with financial reporting requirements under the federal securities laws.

The Dodd-Frank Act of 2010 went further, requiring clawback in the case of noncompliance whether it was or was not the fault of the executive. SEC Commissioner Troy Paredes declared that this sort of provision was "troubling," as it raised the possibility that an honest official might have his or her compensation revoked due to an accounting error.

Despite a rather large and well-publicized clawback in 2007, when the CEO and chairman of UnitedHealth was found guilty of misleading investors by backdating stock options and forced to repay $468 million, it is unclear how valuable clawback provisions have been to the regulation of corporations. In theory, financial managers and CEOs now have a personal incentive to publish correct and complete financial information. In practice, as John Cassidy suggested in a 2010 *New Yorker* article, the policy may be more of a public relations tool than a genuine reform with teeth.

95. The first paragraph plays what role in the passage?
    (A) Setting up a contrast
    (B) Laying out a theory
    (C) Establishing a premise
    (D) Offering a definition
    (E) Presenting evidence

96. Which of the following most accurately summarizes the main point of the passage?
    (A) Before the implementation of clawbacks, corporate finances were often dishonestly reported.
    (B) Clawbacks are newly required regulations meant to inspire CEOs and CFOs to provide accurate financial data.
    (C) Scandals at a few large corporations led to important changes for executives at those corporations.
    (D) The Sarbanes-Oxley Act offered regulatory provisions that were superseded by those in the Dodd-Frank Act.
    (E) To prevent honest executives from being falsely accused, the SEC is looking for changes to clawback provisions.

97. The author most likely mentions UnitedHealth for what purpose?

    (A) To show that clawbacks can prevent malfeasance

    (B) To give an example of an application of clawbacks

    (C) To remind the reader of one particular corporate scandal

    (D) To contrast corporations after Sarbanes-Oxley with corporations before

    (E) To support the assertion that clawbacks make little difference

98. John Cassidy's attitude toward the practice of clawbacks might be described as

    (A) hopeful

    (B) curious

    (C) dubious

    (D) confident

    (E) disapproving

99. Which of the following statements best expresses Commissioner Paredes's response to clawback provisions in Dodd-Frank as presented in the passage?

    (A) The provisions are impossible to implement equitably across the board.

    (B) The provisions penalize CEOs instead of the underlings who deserve punishment.

    (C) The provisions may be unfair to CEOs who have attempted to be scrupulous.

    (D) The provisions are an example of undue government regulation on industry.

    (E) The provisions allow certain executives to skirt regulations while others pay.

Ultrasonic devices are frequently used as a deterrent for cockroaches, mosquitoes, rats, mice, weasels, and even dogs and cats, but do they really work? The answer seems to be that the devices are effective only for a short period of time, and that animals rapidly habituate to the emitted output, eventually ignoring it as if it were simply ambient sound.

Ultrasonic repellents work by emitting high-frequency sounds—higher than humans can hear. People purchase ultrasound collars or outdoor bark detectors to keep dogs from barking. Gardeners use ultrasonic repellents to keep cats out of their flowers. Building superintendents install ultrasonic pest repellents in buildings infested with rodents or roaches. The devices are ubiquitous, yet there is a dearth of reliable data to prove their worth.

A survey of the literature in the mid-1990s indicated "only marginal repellency effects with six commercial ultrasonic devices." More important, research at the time discovered rapid habituation on the part of the pests, such that within three days to a week, all effects were negated, and the pests returned.

There are other negatives involved. Ultrasound cannot travel through walls, meaning that the devices work only in open spaces. The sounds are weak and cannot be effective more than a few feet from the source.

Recently, the Federal Trade Commission (FTC) has begun to crack down on manufacturers of ultrasonic pest repellents, requiring that efficacy claims be supported by scientific evidence. It is clear that advertiser claims are unsubstantiated by research. Nevertheless, people's desire to rid themselves of unwanted pests or unpleasant pet behavior causes them to ignore warnings and purchase these devices by the carload. Some even swear that they work, either because they see immediate results and do not look for more long-term success, or because the results they see are due to any number of other, unrelated factors.

100. Which of the following is an assumption underlying the last sentence in the passage?
   (A) Ultrasonic repellents are tested in controlled conditions.
   (B) Ultrasonic devices permanently eradicate certain kinds of pests.
   (C) Manufacturers of ultrasonic repellents fool buyers.
   (D) Users of ultrasonic devices do not understand science.
   (E) Ultrasonic devices do not work in the long term.

101. The author of the passage would most likely agree with which of the following statements?
   (A) Consumers are risking their health by purchasing ultrasonic repellents.
   (B) Consumers may be disappointed by the results of their ultrasonic purchases.
   (C) Consumers may rely on manufacturers' labeling when purchasing pest repellents.
   (D) Consumers should spend their money on professional pest control services.
   (E) Consumers are repeatedly duped into purchasing unreliable products.

102. Which of the following statements best expresses the FTC's response to ultrasonic repellents as presented in the passage?

    (A) The FTC insists that manufacturers prove any advertising claims.

    (B) The FTC has banned ultrasonic devices for most purposes.

    (C) The FTC has issued a warning for consumers of ultrasonic devices.

    (D) The FTC will allow certain manufacturers to continue making repellents.

    (E) The FTC is regulating the manufacture and purchase of ultrasonic devices.

103. The passage can best be described as which of the following?

    (A) A review of the literature on ultrasonic devices

    (B) A reflection on the popularity of a certain kind of repellent

    (C) An investigation of cause and effect in ultrasonic repellents

    (D) An opinion piece on a particular manufactured item

    (E) A call to action for consumers of a fraudulent device

104. Based on the author's presentation, the ultrasonic devices described in the passage would most likely be useful in which of the following situations?

    (A) Permanently ridding a basement of rats

    (B) Training a German shepherd

    (C) Keeping bugs away from a short outdoor event

    (D) Preventing rabbits from destroying a vegetable garden

    (E) Killing weasels in a chicken coop

According to Professor Philip Sicker of Fordham University, without some form of impediment, a classic love story could not exist, or at best would be short and trite. One prototype for the love story might be the medieval legend "Tristan and Iseult," in which the two lovers are kept apart by a variety of barriers. Iseult is promised to another man, which prevents Tristan and Iseult from marrying. They carry on an illicit affair until they are found out and separated, and eventually in death have a reuniting of souls. Sicker sees this as the template for all interesting love narratives in Western literature; only the barrier changes to match the times.

In the 19th century, says Sicker, the barrier was usually the forbidden nature of adulterous love, with desire intensified by the proscription against love outside marriage. Examples of this in literature include *Anna Karenina* and *Madame Bovary*.

In the 20th century, on the other hand, love and its boundaries became greatly psychologized, as in the novels of Marcel Proust or Thomas Mann. No longer was marriage enough of an impediment; lovers are torn apart by age, class, race, sexual orientation, mental illness, and so on.

"A love story doesn't go very far," says Sicker, "if people feel exactly the same way—if there are no obstacles to [that love]." For passionate, romantic love to generate the kind of plot that is compelling for the reader, an impediment to that love must exist to ratchet up the desire and the conflict.

There are examples of characters for whom romantic love is self-destructive, who do not generate the sort of hopeful rooting for success that most readers bring to a love story. Emma Bovary, in her self-deluded, narcissistic longing for love, is not a heroine that readers admire. Humbert Humbert, the much older lover of the prepubescent girl in *Lolita*, tries hard to gain the sympathy of the reader while at the same time referring to his behavior and desires as maniacal. Such narratives construct yet another impediment—a barrier between character and reader, as the reader is conflicted about the love story itself.

105. Which of the following most accurately captures the central idea of the passage?
   (A) Romantic love may be smooth, but it is more often destructive.
   (B) To enjoy a love story, readers must root for the main characters.
   (C) Classic love stories feature a struggle to attain the love object.
   (D) Adultery is no longer an impediment to true romantic love.
   (E) Readers prefer a love story in which lovers are finally united.

106. Which of the following novels has an impediment similar to those described in the last paragraph?

(A) *Lorna Doone*, in which Lorna is promised to another but is abducted by John, whose father was killed by Lorna's relatives

(B) *Villette*, in which teacher Lucy falls in love with a difficult professor who is loved by the proprietress of the school

(C) *My Ántonia*, in which Jim looks back sadly on his unconsummated teenage crush on a wild Bohemian girl

(D) *The Good Soldier*, in which philanderer Edward falls for his own ward but is foiled by his wife's revelation of his sins

(E) *The Snow Goose*, in which the girl Fritha bonds with disabled artist Philip over a wounded goose and only after his death realizes her love for him

107. According to the passage, barriers play what crucial role in love stories?

(A) They heighten conflict and desire.

(B) They cause conflict in the reader.

(C) They prevent happy endings.

(D) They reveal hidden longings.

(E) They elongate the narrative.

108. The quote in the fourth paragraph is most likely included to

(A) clarify the professor's theory

(B) offer a contrasting view

(C) provide a cogent example

(D) introduce the speaker to the reader

(E) reveal an illuminating detail

109. The professor appears to believe that "Tristan and Iseult" is

(A) archaic

(B) unorthodox

(C) cautionary

(D) archetypal

(E) heartbreaking

In the U.S. Census Bureau's 2013 study of the geographic locations of concentrated wealth, the top 5 percent of households are determined to be those earning at least $191,469 annually. As in the general population, most of those high-income households are clustered in high-population areas, especially along the East and West Coasts.

Unsurprisingly, the Census Bureau found that the highest concentration of wealth in the years 2007 to 2011 was around the New York City area, especially in the suburbs, with Bridgeport-Stamford-Norwalk, Connecticut, at the top of the heap, with nearly 18 percent of households in that top 5 percent of earners nationwide. The area we know as Silicon Valley, comprising San Jose-Sunnyvale-Santa Clara, California, came in second, with nearly 16 percent of households among the top 5 percent. Following those two regions were the suburbs around Washington, DC; the suburbs around San Francisco, CA; the New Jersey suburbs of New York City; and the Long Island suburbs of New York City.

Some statistics were unexpected, at least to this writer: Boulder, Colorado, is richer than posh Santa Barbara, California. Hartford, Connecticut, is richer than Honolulu, Hawaii. Of the 366 metropolitan statistical areas studied, the two with the lowest concentration of wealth (1.1 percent) are Danville, Illinois, and Danville, Virginia—a statistic the Census Bureau calls out and notes as a "coincidence."

The study does not consider cost of living, which in expensive areas such as San Francisco can limit the buying power of a high income.

110. Which of the following most accurately summarizes the main point of the passage?
    (A) Wealth in the United States tends to be concentrated in the suburbs of large cities.
    (B) The disparity between rich and poor in the United States continues to grow.
    (C) High-income earners have left the central cities for surrounding towns.
    (D) The Census Bureau has given us a new definition of *wealthy*.
    (E) If you make more than $200,000 annually, you probably live near New York City.

111. The author most likely mentions Santa Barbara for what purpose?

    (A) To show that Silicon Valley cities have a high concentration of wealth

    (B) To contrast a wealthy city with an impoverished city

    (C) As a reminder that some cities lost wealth in the recent recession

    (D) To suggest that not all wealthy cities are concentrated on coastlines

    (E) As an example of a city that is reputed to be very wealthy

112. Based on the final sentence, which of the following could be inferred about the author's beliefs about the Census Bureau's study?

    (A) The Census Bureau should have taken other data into account.

    (B) Wealth is relative to an area's cost of living.

    (C) The U.S. census does not count everyone.

    (D) Income is irrelevant when it comes to measuring wealth.

    (E) Certain cities should have been omitted from the study.

As assembly lines and machinery reduced the need in American factories for skilled workers, employers discovered that they could cut their labor costs dramatically by hiring women and children to do the low-skill tasks on the modern factory floor. The numbers of women in the workforce increased 330 percent over the 20 years between 1880 and 1900. As women began to work in offices and factories, many ceased their labors in domestic service. Their new positions paid not much more than those menial jobs they had once taken in laundries or kitchens, but the work, although dangerous and repetitive, was often far easier on their health.

Office work became a goal for working women, because it offered conditions that were clean and pleasant in most cases. Whereas in 1880, only 4 percent of office workers were women, by 1920, equal numbers of women and men performed clerical tasks.

This is not to suggest that women and men were equal in the workforce, of course; women made far less in hourly wages than men did, and they were rarely given supervisory tasks or allowed in most cases to handle money. One man might supervise a pool of several dozen low-paid women.

As for children, they had always worked in large numbers, particularly on family farms. The need for children to aid with planting and harvesting is the reason our antiquated school calendars still include a summer vacation. However, with the mechanization of factories, thousands of children went to work, often under grueling conditions and for incredibly low wages. In 1890 nearly 20 percent of all children between the ages of 10 and 15 were employed in some capacity. Even after factory work began to be regulated, parents often lied about their children's ages just to preserve the tiny income their offspring contributed to the family welfare. Following compulsory education laws and Progressive era reforms, the number of children in the workforce began to decline, but it was still not uncommon after 1900 to see children peddling newspapers, delivering messages, and shining shoes in large cities during the school day.

113. According to the passage, the author believes which of the following regarding women in office jobs?

(A) Women preferred these jobs to factory or domestic work.
(B) Women enabled men to take on more managerial tasks.
(C) Office jobs paid better wages than any other form of women's work.
(D) Office jobs had restricted hours, enabling women to care for their children.
(E) Mechanization allowed one woman to do the work of several men.

114. The third paragraph plays what role in the passage?

    (A) It refutes an earlier allegation about women in the workforce.

    (B) It contrasts two different roles of women in the workforce.

    (C) It clarifies the status of women in the workforce.

    (D) It offers an explanation for the increase of women in the workforce.

    (E) It classifies several strata of women in the workforce.

115. From the presentation of information in the final paragraph, it can be inferred that the author believes which of the following about the current school calendar?

    (A) It is essential for working families.

    (B) It helps farm families involve their children.

    (C) It changed with Progressive era reforms.

    (D) It is traditional but outmoded.

    (E) Compulsory education made it obsolete.

People speak of an "Ivy League Education" as though it is a standardized experience—as though students at Brown and Cornell receive the same input and achieve the same outcomes. The fact of the matter is that each of the eight Ivies has its own personality, its own focus, and its own philosophy of education, and not all Ivies are right for all students.

Take two undergraduate programs of similar size, the one at Princeton and the one at Columbia. When you apply to Princeton, you apply to the university itself, not to a department or program or college. When you apply to Columbia, you apply either to Columbia College for a liberal arts degree or to Columbia Engineering for a degree in science.

Freshman and sophomore years at Princeton are spent exploring courses across disciplines while determining a major course of study. Distribution requirements include one course apiece in epistemology and cognition, ethical thought and moral values, historical analysis, and quantitative reasoning, and two courses each in literature and the arts, science and technology, and social analysis.

Columbia freshmen and sophomores spend their time immersed in the Core Curriculum, an approach to education that Columbia has used since 1919. Students work in small seminars studying seminal works in history, music, art, literature, philosophy, and science. Students in Columbia Engineering take half of this humanities Core and supplement it with technical courses in physics, chemistry, mathematics, engineering, and computer science.

Once Princeton sophomores select a major, which may result in an AB degree or in a BSE degree depending on whether it focuses on humanities or sciences, they may choose to supplement this major with a certificate program in any of 47 areas from Jazz Studies to Biophysics. Many students choose a certificate program that complements their majors, but just as many choose one that is completely unrelated and simply allows them to explore a passion or interest.

Columbia undergraduates have an opportunity to choose among several tracks. They may pursue a preprofessional degree such as Pre-Law; they may work toward a BA from Columbia College followed by a BS from Columbia Engineering in a five-year program; they may explore music in depth through the Columbia-Julliard Exchange; or they may opt for an accelerated program that enables them to receive both a BA and JD degree in just six years.

The other six Ivies are just as different from one another as Columbia is from Princeton. It behooves high school applicants to think long and hard about the kind of education they want before selecting an institution to provide it.

116. Compared to freshman and sophomore years at Columbia, the first two years of undergraduate academics at Princeton might be considered more

    (A) interdisciplinary
    (B) reactionary
    (C) classical
    (D) technical
    (E) seminar-based

117. Based on the information given in the passage, it can be inferred that Princeton might be a better choice for which kind of entering high school student?

(A) One with an interest in international studies

(B) One whose ambition is to work in civil rights law

(C) One with a love for both creative writing and science

(D) One who hopes to earn a bachelor's degree in two disciplines

(E) One who expects to read all the Great Books with great professors

118. Which of the following most accurately describes the structure of the passage?

(A) Order of importance

(B) Cause and effect

(C) Chronological order

(D) Reasons and examples

(E) Comparison and contrast

119. The first paragraph plays what role in the passage?

(A) It sets the scene for the upcoming revelations that will be listed in order of occurrence.

(B) It defines the terms that will be used in the passage to follow and explains their importance.

(C) It lays forth a personal bias of the author's that will then be upheld by a relating of personal experiences.

(D) It offers a refutation of a commonly held belief that will then be explored with examples.

(E) It broadly introduces a topic of concern that will be dissected in the paragraphs to follow.

120. The author of the passage would most likely agree with which of the following statements?

(A) High school students would be wise to apply to more than one Ivy League school.

(B) High school students should never apply both to Columbia and to Princeton.

(C) High school students should choose the Ivy that best fits their natures and needs.

(D) High school students improve their odds if they apply to all eight Ivies.

(E) High school students should have a career in mind before applying to Princeton or Columbia.

At one time, hundreds of thousands of *Panthera tigris*, tigers, wandered the Asian land-scape. Today a handful of collaborative conservation programs are all that protect tigers from disappearing entirely. One of those programs, "Tigers Forever," seeks not only to keep tigers from being eradicated but also to increase their numbers by half over the next decade.

The threats to tigers are many. Owners of livestock shoot tigers with impunity to save their sheep, goats, and other animals. Hunters track and trap tigers for the illegal wild animal market, where a live tiger might fetch $20,000, a skin up to $1,500, and a kilo of tiger bones for traditional medicine perhaps $100. In places where the average income might be $3,500, tigers provide windfall profits to those brave enough to hunt them.

Added to this trouble for tigers is the loss of habitat that threatens all Asian large mammals. Tigers depend on a large range to satisfy their hunting needs. The encroachment of human development, logging, and agriculture on tiger habitats reduces tigers' territories to tiny patches of land, and the human overhunting of the deer and wild pigs that the tigers feed upon lessens their chances for survival.

Tigers Forever builds upon work done by the Wildlife Conservation Society (WCS) in India, Thailand, and Siberia. In partnership with the WCS, a group called Panthera is working in five countries—Indonesia, Malaysia, Myanmar, India, and Lao PDR (Laos)—to eliminate the direct hunting and killing of wild tigers. Tigers Forever focuses on law enforcement and the training of local officials with the goal of enforc-ing protection, apprehending hunters, and acting proactively to root out networks of poachers. Working in partnership with localities has proved a far better method than imposing regulations from outside, and the best results thus far seem to be occurring in nations with strong and active governments. The conservation of tigers in India is by all accounts a rousing success; tigers in Lao PDR, on the other hand, where illegal deforestation is a rampant national disgrace, remain on the decline.

121. Which of the following most accurately summarizes the main point of the passage?

   (A) Tigers are limited in Asia to a few small areas of protection.
   (B) Organizations are working in tandem to save Asian tigers.
   (C) Tigers Forever has had good luck improving tiger survival rates.
   (D) Five countries have succeeded in saving their own tiger populations.
   (E) India is one of the few places where tigers are thriving.

122. The average income of $3,500 is mentioned in the second paragraph for what purpose?

   (A) To focus the reader's attention on a basic inequity
   (B) To explain why nonprofit organizations such as WCS are needed
   (C) To contrast exorbitant food prices with real family incomes
   (D) To indicate an incentive for illegal poaching of wild animals
   (E) To show that these countries are too poor to initiate conservation efforts

123. By contrasting India and Lao PDR in the final paragraph, the author seems to be saying that

(A) tiger eradication can be reversed only through collective effort
(B) successful conservation requires a strong regulatory environment
(C) cultural differences may hinder the achievement of conservation goals
(D) conservation of the environment should supersede conservation of animals
(E) assuming that one plan would work across Asia was probably ill-advised

124. Based on the statements in the last paragraph, which of the following describes the author's attitude toward Lao PDR?

(A) Approval
(B) Indifference
(C) Skepticism
(D) Contempt
(E) Perplexity

125. The description of the work being done by Tigers Forever is closest to which of these overseas U.S. endeavors?

(A) Training Afghan soldiers to fight the Taliban
(B) Working on offshore hospital ships in western Africa
(C) Collecting data on whale populations in the Bering Sea
(D) Taking satellite photos of deforestation in South America
(E) Sending first responders to assist after the Haitian earthquake

The attractive moniker "walled garden" is given to those Internet environments that control user access to applications and services. Although at times, gardens are walled to protect the user, as when children's sites are protected from inappropriate outside content, for the most part, walls are built to enable vendors to control and charge for access.

An original purveyor of the walled garden model was AOL, which for a long time was many users' only access to the Internet. AOL was a closed platform, with content that was custom designed and movement restricted by the "walls" surrounding the platform itself. Often, AOL customers did not know what they were missing; the territory beyond the wall was simply invisible to them.

Today, Amazon's Kindle follows a similar closed platform model. Once users are inside, they are directed to apps sold solely through the Kindle store. Apple's iPad is similarly restrictive, as are many of the new smartphones. As soon as the maker of a device starts limiting consumer access to the entirety of the Internet, the walled garden model is clearly in use. Hackers are now getting into the game: As subscribers become frustrated, new open source software springs up, enabling them to bypass the wall and convert content into more accessible modes.

Even Facebook, often considered to be the future of social media, is a walled garden of sorts. Outsiders cannot access private content inside Facebook, and a standard search engine cannot locate much of what exists there.

So the question for the consumer becomes: Do you want an easily navigable format that is restricted, or do you want complete access at all times to everything, however daunting that might be? The answer depends on the kind of consumer you are, on how much you value Internet as opposed to Intranet content, and perhaps on how comfortable you are with chaos.

126. According to the passage, what effect are hackers having on walled gardens?
    (A) They are establishing their own closed platform models.
    (B) They are inventing software that improves accessibility.
    (C) They are enabling access to once-private content.
    (D) They are improving the navigability of closed platforms.
    (E) They are allowing consumers to avoid paying for content.

127. Based on information in the passage, *walled garden* seems like an apt nickname for this sort of platform because it connotes
    (A) a prison-like, punitive atmosphere
    (B) a region that is overgrown and untidy
    (C) the formality of a nobleman's parkland
    (D) an environment that is pleasant but circumscribed
    (E) an area of safety and comfort in a dangerous world

128. The author of the passage would most likely agree with which of the following statements?

   (A) Walled gardens should only be used to protect children.
   (B) Walled gardens are simply a way for providers to make money.
   (C) Walled gardens are for consumers who care little about the Internet.
   (D) Walled gardens may make the Internet easier to navigate.
   (E) Walled gardens have no place in today's social media.

129. How would you describe the structure of the passage?

   (A) Definition and examples
   (B) Cause and effect
   (C) Spatial organization
   (D) Problem and solution
   (E) Theory and reasons

130. The author's use of the word *chaos* in the final sentence indicates that her attitude toward consumers who are drawn to walled gardens is one of

   (A) discouragement
   (B) amusement
   (C) antipathy
   (D) confusion
   (E) understanding

There are those who champion *Moby Dick*, and those who favor *The Adventures of Huckleberry Finn*, but there can be little doubt that the novel that had the greatest impact on American history was 1852's *Uncle Tom's Cabin*. While it is rarely read for fun today, in its day it was the bestseller of all bestsellers, and its influence was felt for years.

Author Harriet Beecher Stowe was born into a family of ministers, teachers, and thinkers and received a classical education rarely available to girls at the time. While living in Cincinnati, Ohio, an important stop on the Underground Railroad, she became involved in the antislavery movement. She married an active participant in that movement, and for a time the two of them offered their home as a way station for runaway slaves.

Stowe and her husband moved to Maine, an actively antislavery state, and she decided to write about what she had seen along the Ohio River in her time in Cincinnati. She fueled her writing with borrowings from slave narratives of the time, which were beginning to be popular among abolitionist readers. *Uncle Tom's Cabin*, which at one time bore the subtitle "The Man That Was a Thing," was published first as a 40-part serial and then as a book. It sold hundreds of thousands of copies in its first year in print, both in the United States and abroad, and introduced many Northerners to the realities of slavery while enraging Southerners with its critique of their way of life. Southern criticism of the novel even led Stowe to publish a "Key to Uncle Tom's Cabin," in which she dissected characters and events and offered real-life equivalents for each.

The melodrama of the novel, which has been widely panned since its publication, was the style of the times, especially for an audience of women, and it was that audience that built the novel's reputation and spread its message. People who could not be bothered to read political tracts treated the novel as gospel and began to flock to the abolitionist cause. It is important to recognize that even in states that disapproved of slavery, Northerners had little sympathy for blacks, whom they often reviled as inferior. Stowe attributed familiar emotions and powerful beliefs to the slaves in her novel, bringing them to life in a way that changed attitudes across the Northern states. Especially significant was the message of familial love; scenes in which families were split apart were affecting and disturbing to Stowe's readers, who often had never before considered this contemptible aspect of slavery.

Within a decade of its publication, Stowe's novel had exacerbated the divide between proslavery and antislavery readers to the degree that Lincoln's election seemed preordained and war inevitable. At no time before or since has a work of American fiction so inspired the course of American history.

131. Of the following titles, which would be most appropriate for the contents of this passage?
    (A) "The Man That Was a Thing"
    (B) "The Life and Works of Harriet Beecher Stowe"
    (C) "One Novel's Cultural and Historical Impact"
    (D) "A Northerner's Look at Southern Customs"
    (E) "From Antislavery to Abolitionist"

132. The author appears to believe that Stowe was

  (A) misguided
  (B) misunderstood
  (C) well educated
  (D) insensitive
  (E) droll

133. From information in the fourth paragraph, it can reasonably be inferred that the most immediately influential readers of Stowe's work were

  (A) Southern women
  (B) Southern landowners
  (C) Northern women
  (D) young people
  (E) politicians

134. Based on the fourth paragraph, which of the following could be inferred about the author's attitude toward Stowe's readers?

  (A) They were woefully ignorant but easily swayed.
  (B) They were perceptive and eager to learn.
  (C) They remained unsympathetic and callous.
  (D) They found change abhorrent and difficult.
  (E) They had little tolerance for realistic fiction.

135. Which of the following modern events is most similar in effect to the publication of *Uncle Tom's Cabin* as described in the passage?

  (A) Spielberg's film *Lincoln* leads to a reappraising of the 16th president.
  (B) *The Plague of Doves*, a novel exploring racial discord, is a Pulitzer finalist.
  (C) *Times* reporter Marie Colvin is killed while covering the Syrian civil war.
  (D) *The Help*, a novel about black maids in the 1960s, becomes a best-seller in 2009.
  (E) Egyptian bloggers and videographers stimulate Arab Spring uprisings.

We tend to view termites only in terms of their destructive potential, but perhaps it is time to think of their potential for good. Yes, they are agricultural pests and cause millions of dollars in damage to wood structures, but perhaps they have some useful properties as well.

It may come as a shock to you to learn that in certain cultures, termites are part of the human diet. In parts of Africa and southern Asia, people eat winged termites roasted or fried (after first removing their wings). They are said to have a nutty taste and to be rich in protein.

Termites are important in other ways. They create habitats for other species, whether by hollowing trees or by building large termite mounds. They clear away flammable materials on the savanna, lessening the possibility of grass fires. In addition, termites are notoriously efficient energy producers. They break down wood products quickly, releasing hydrogen as they do so. Scientists are studying their biochemical processes in hopes of reproducing them on a large scale as a source of renewable energy.

Of course, these positive qualities do nothing to assuage the fears of homeowners. The subterranean consumers thrive on dark, damp places in your home, tunneling and foraging as they go. Without your ever recognizing their existence, they may thoroughly undermine the wood throughout your dwelling, leaving only the external grain. To prevent such infestations, store firewood well away from your home, keep any mulch at least six inches from your foundation, and check old furniture for telltale tunnels and ridges before moving it into your living space.

136. Which of the following conclusions may be drawn directly from the second paragraph of the passage?

(A) The author has actually tasted roasted or fried termites.

(B) The author has heard about the consumption of termites.

(C) The author does not believe that people ever eat termites.

(D) The author is disgusted by the notion of eating termites.

(E) The author is surprised about human consumption of termites.

137. The author's list of termites' uses in the third paragraph is reflective of which of the following types of text structure?

(A) Opinion and examples

(B) Problem-solution

(C) Comparison-contrast

(D) Space order

(E) Cause and effect

138. Which of the following statements best describes the author's bias?
- (A) She is biased against termites.
- (B) She thinks termites are both good and bad.
- (C) She approves of everything termites do.
- (D) She is biased in favor of termites.
- (E) She holds no opinion of termites.

139. According to the passage, termites play what role in energy production?
- (A) Their digestive processes release hydrogen.
- (B) Their respiration converts water to oxygen.
- (C) They convert cellulose to flammable fuel.
- (D) They produce renewable energy via transpiration.
- (E) They manufacture hydrogen in their spiracles.

140. Unlike the previous paragraphs, the final paragraph plays what role in the passage?
- (A) It focuses on the habits and powers of the termite.
- (B) It illustrates termites' role in ecology.
- (C) It stresses termites' negative qualities.
- (D) It develops a theory about termite behavior.
- (E) It presents scientific facts about termites.

The Arecibo Observatory, near the north shore of Puerto Rico, is a key component of Cornell University's National Astronomy and Ionosphere Center (NAIC). In a joint venture with the National Science Foundation, the observatory exists to provide observation time and support for scientists worldwide. A panel of judges determines the "most promising" research proposals among the hundreds that are presented to the observatory each year. Those scientists are invited to Puerto Rico for viewing time on Arecibo's giant telescope.

Scientists who visit the observatory are typically involved in one of three studies: radio astronomy, which is the study of natural radio energy produced by faraway galaxies and stars; atmospheric science, which is the study of the Earth's upper atmosphere, including its temperature, density, and composition; and radar astronomy, which is the study of planets and their moons, asteroids, and comets. The enormous telescope assists with all three studies.

The Arecibo telescope does not resemble what most of us think of when we hear the word *telescope*. Its reflective surface covers a remarkable 20 acres. Dangling above it are towers and cables, subreflectors and antennas, all of which can be positioned using 26 motors to transmit radio waves and receive echoes with astonishing precision.

Arecibo has been the site of hundreds of fascinating discoveries. Among these are the rate of rotation of the planet Mercury, determined two years after the telescope launched in 1963; two new classes of pulsars; and the first planets ever spotted outside of our solar system. Today, one of the most important goals of the observatory is to document and quantify global climate change by monitoring changes in temperature, hydrogen composition, and wind fields in the ionosphere.

Although at one time, scientists had to travel to Puerto Rico to share viewing time on the giant telescope, today there are new protocols that enable remote viewing. At the University of Texas at Brownsville, students are helping to design a remote-control command center that will control the positioning of the telescope from 2,000 miles away. Students and professors will use the command center to study radio pulsars, rotating neutron stars that release radiation in regular pulses.

141. Based on the information in the third paragraph, you can conclude that most telescopes

(A) do not have reflective surfaces
(B) contain radio antennas
(C) are not as large as Arecibo's
(D) cannot be repositioned
(E) contain a variety of antennae

142. All of these are typical studies at Arecibo except

    (A) the nature of the ionosphere
    (B) production of remote-controlled devices
    (C) radio waves produced by galaxies
    (D) investigations of distant asteroids
    (E) cloud formation and density

143. The main point of the fourth paragraph is to

    (A) provide the history of the observatory
    (B) describe Arecibo in some detail
    (C) compare and contrast astronomical studies
    (D) list some of Arecibo's successes
    (E) explain the nature of climate change

144. The remote-control command center will most likely

    (A) result in remarkable research findings
    (B) save scientists the cost of traveling
    (C) fail to achieve its goal of assisting students
    (D) be used primarily for atmospheric studies
    (E) allow Arecibo to expand over time

145. The tone of the passage suggests that the author finds Arecibo

    (A) expensive to maintain
    (B) scientifically intriguing
    (C) old-fashioned in its approach
    (D) too involved in popular science
    (E) remote and inaccessible

Ballast waifs are seeds that arrive on one shore from another in the soil placed in a ship's hold as ballast. One remarkably lovely and dreadfully damaging ballast waif is *Lythrum salicaria*, the bright purple, spiky flower known commonly as purple loosestrife. Purple loosestrife is not a newcomer to U.S. shores; it arrived from Eurasia, almost certainly via ship, some 200 years ago.

For all its beauty, purple loosestrife is a menace. The same long growing season that makes it so beloved by gardeners makes it a seed-making machine. A mature plant may produce two or three million seeds a year. It also propagates underground, sending out shoots and stems in all directions.

Scientists took little notice of purple loosestrife until sometime in the 1930s, when a particular strain began colonizing along the St. Lawrence River, an area rife with the sort of wetlands purple loosestrife likes best. Purple loosestrife does not just propagate wildly; it also adapts easily to changes in environment. As it starts up in a new area, it quickly outcompetes native grasses, sedges, and other flowering plants, forming dense stands of purple loosestrife where once heterogeneous wetland meadows existed. This not only eradicates the native plants, but it also removes food sources for migratory birds and other animals.

In recent years, purple loosestrife has had a devastating impact on native cattails and wild rice. It has invaded and destroyed spawning areas for fish. In rural areas, it is beginning to move away from wetlands and adapt to drier areas, encroaching on agricultural lands. In urban areas, it is blocking pipes and drainage canals. It has moved steadily westward and is now found in all states but Florida.

Attempts to control purple loosestrife have been only partially successful. It has proved resistant to many herbicides, and it is impervious to burning, as its rootstock lies beneath the surface and can reproduce from there. It can be mowed down and plowed under, and then replaced with a less invasive plant. This is very labor intensive in marshy areas that are substantially overgrown, but it may be the only way of eliminating the pest.

146. According to the passage, all of these are true except
   (A) Purple loosestrife propagates through an underground system.
   (B) Purple loosestrife is found in urban and rural settings.
   (C) Purple loosestrife is best eradicated through controlled burning.
   (D) Purple loosestrife is not native to North or South America.
   (E) Purple loosestrife is easily able to eradicate competition.

147. Which of these would be the best title for the passage?
   (A) "A Floral Invasion"
   (B) "A Gardener's Worst Nightmare"
   (C) "Migrating Plants"
   (D) "Controlling Pesky Plants"
   (E) "Developing New Herbicides"

148. The author's mention of the St. Lawrence River shows primarily that

    (A) ballast waifs prefer to travel on freshwater conveyances

    (B) purple loosestrife does well in marshy areas along rivers

    (C) most ballast waifs survive best in northern regions

    (D) purple loosestrife can be replaced by less damaging plants

    (E) cleaning up a river may help to eliminate pests

149. Which fact about purple loosestrife adds to its power of endurance?

    (A) Easy adaptability

    (B) Spiky stems and flowers

    (C) Introduction as a ballast waif

    (D) Preference for wetlands

    (E) Range of purple coloration

150. The author suggests that people enjoy growing purple loosestrife because it

    (A) keeps out other weeds

    (B) makes millions of seeds

    (C) has a long growing season

    (D) reduces weevils and insects

    (E) grows well in sandy soil

151. According to the passage, where would purple loosestrife least easily thrive?

    (A) Among swampy areas of northern New Jersey

    (B) In the wetland meadows of eastern Michigan

    (C) Along the inland waterways of North Carolina

    (D) Above the tree line in the mountains of Utah

    (E) In the moist grasslands of western Illinois

Yahoo CEO Marissa Mayer made waves once more when she banned her employees from telecommuting and gave them an ultimatum: Work at the office or quit. From one of the few women in a leadership position in an industry where flexibility in the workplace has been common if not required, this was a radical move.

Protesters flocked to point out that Mayer, herself a new mother, had installed at her own expense a nursery next door to her office, something no other working parent could possibly afford to do. Surely this made her new rule for her workers all the more unfair.

On the flip side of the argument were those who pointed out that Mayer was hired to turn around a floundering company, and that company metrics indicated that one cause of that floundering might be the numbers of people who were not logging on to the Yahoo system as often as they should, were not producing as they once had, and were often found to be working on projects outside the Yahoo purview. Shouldn't Mayer have the right to demand a certain level of commitment from her employees, even if that meant she had to keep an eye on them, physically, within the confines of the Yahoo office complex?

There are a variety of conflicting assumptions contributing to this situation. Mayer, being a young woman, is expected by many to represent the New Woman in industry and thus to embrace the freedoms that her foremothers fought to achieve, one of which is the flexibility to work from home. On the other hand, Mayer's youth is thought by some to dictate her pulling away from the conventions of the women's movement and moving back toward a tradition of teamwork and synchronous communication. Meanwhile, those who look at the bottom line and who know Yahoo intimately insist that Mayer had no choice in the matter—that one of the reasons for Yahoo's demise was its far-flung workforce and lack of cohesion. Perhaps only time will tell whether Mayer's decision was the right one for Yahoo; we might all check back in a year's time to see where things stand.

152. In the first paragraph, why does the author refer to Mayer's decision as "radical"?

   (A) It represented something that had never been tried before.
   (B) It defied the traditions of that particular industry.
   (C) It was almost militant in its adoption of feminist theory.
   (D) It showed a fanatical commitment to company turnaround.
   (E) It was extreme in its "all-or-nothing" approach.

153. According to the passage, people who supported Mayer's decision did so because of which of the following?

   (A) It has been proved that telecommuting leads to a lack of productivity.
   (B) Yahoo worked better back when everyone worked in the same office space.
   (C) Compared to previous data, Yahoo workers seemed to be slacking off.
   (D) She herself was able to balance work and family life without difficulty.
   (E) Synchronicity is critical, especially for companies involved in high tech.

154. The author of the passage would most likely agree with which of the following statements?

    (A) Mayer has made a grave error in pulling her employees back into the office.

    (B) Working from home has been shown to increase, not decrease productivity.

    (C) Yahoo's history indicates that Mayer's controlling attitude may backfire.

    (D) Mayer is far too young to be held to the standards of the women's movement.

    (E) Mayer's plan for Yahoo deserves to move forward and be judged later on.

155. How could the author's attitude toward Mayer be characterized?

    (A) Detached

    (B) Derisive

    (C) Deferential

    (D) Derogatory

    (E) Doting

156. The author of the passage is primarily concerned with

    (A) explaining the motivation for a decision

    (B) showing the negative effects of a decision

    (C) revealing the politics behind a decision

    (D) presenting the attitudes toward a decision

    (E) exploring the possible results of a decision

January 2013 marked the nation's largest income drop in 20 years, with personal income declining by 3.6 percent compared to the month before. The Commerce Department announced that the decline was the greatest since the same month in 1993. Surprisingly, the same month brought a sudden increase in consumer spending, specifically on services rather than goods. (In January, especially a cold and snowy January, it is common to see increased spending on utilities.) In fact, January's drop in spending on durable goods such as large appliances and consumer electronics is troublesome, because consumers tend to cut back on big-ticket items when they feel economic stress.

A decline in income was expected, given the expiration of the payroll tax cut and higher tax rates for wealthy Americans, but it looked especially dramatic because many companies, anticipating that change, paid special dividends and bonuses prior to the start of the new year in January. In other words, income in December was unusually high, causing post-payroll-tax-cut income to appear even more dismal.

The drop in income and increase in spending led naturally to a sharp decrease in the rate of savings, to the lowest level recorded since 2007. On average, consumers saved about 2.4 percent of their disposable income in January, compared to 6.4 percent in December.

It is important not to conflate this unusual one-month dip with the very real and steady decline of median middle-class income. A 2012 Pew Research report declared that only half of American households now rank as middle income, down from 62 percent in the 1970s. Households in the wealthiest 1 percent of U.S. citizens have 288 times the wealth of the average middle-class family. This ongoing decline in income leads to less disposable income, higher levels of debt, decreased savings, and increased dependence on government assistance.

157. Which of the following expresses the author's attitude toward the drop in consumer spending on goods as opposed to services?

(A) Unsurprised
(B) Perturbed
(C) Indifferent
(D) Irate
(E) Baffled

158. According to the passage, dividends played what role in the income decline?

(A) They covered up the decrease in salaries in December.
(B) They led to an unexpected increase in spending.
(C) They failed to cause the predicted improvement in savings.
(D) They caused December's income to look unnaturally high.
(E) They prevented companies from absorbing tax cuts.

159. Based on the information presented in the passage, what prediction might you make about personal income in February?

(A) It will rebound to December's levels.

(B) It will drop more than it did in January.

(C) It may drop, but not as much as in January.

(D) It will parallel trends in consumer spending.

(E) It will increase for the top 1 percent of Americans.

160. The final paragraph plays what role in the passage?

(A) It contrasts an unnatural decline with an enduring and authentic decline.

(B) It indicates how sudden decreases can play a role in middle-income decline.

(C) It compares a decline in income for wealthy Americans to that of the middle class.

(D) It suggests a correlation between one kind of income decline and another.

(E) It shows what happens to income decline when tax cuts are figured in.

The Janissaries were an elite corps of Turkish soldiers whose music was particularly suited to a military corps. Janissary music used kettledrums, cymbals, triangles, tambourines, and unusual forms of percussion such as the "Jingling Johnny," a tall, decorated pole hung with bells. By 1720, the sound had made its way to Europe by way of a gift from the Turkish sultan to the Polish army of Augustus II. Within a few years, Janissary percussion had been added to military bands in Russia, Austria, and Prussia. So-called "Turkish music" became wildly popular, and it did not take long for the lively military style to find its way into classical composition. This sudden craze presaged the Orientalism that would flavor European art in the next century.

Here in America, when we think of martial music, we think of John Philip Sousa and beloved marches on the order of "The Stars and Stripes Forever." However, 100 years earlier, Joseph Haydn used a Janissary style in his *Military Symphony No. 100 in G Major*, and Ludwig van Beethoven included a "Turkish March" in his *The Ruins of Athens*. Wolfgang Amadeus Mozart based his opera *The Abduction from the Seraglio* on Janissary percussion. As the 19th century began, it became popular to add a "Janissary stop" to pianos and harpsichords, to provide a percussive accompaniment similar to that produced by the kettledrums of the Janissary corps.

As quickly as it had come, Janissary music passed out of favor, and by the middle of the 19th century, European and American bands had become formal, trained accessories to regiments, consisting typically of flute and piccolo, clarinets, oboe, saxophones, bassoons, horns, cornets, trombones, and percussion. In this country, the importance of martial music may have reached its peak during the Civil War, when every unit and regiment had its own small band. However, even today, according to *Mother Jones*, the Pentagon is the largest employer of musicians anywhere in the world, spending nearly $200 million of taxpayers' money annually on bands from Guam to Washington, DC—approximately 10 times what the federal government spends on K–12 music education. No longer do these bands follow men into battle, however; their purpose today is largely ceremonial, and you are more likely to hear them at a state funeral than at the rear of a forced march.

161. The discussion of Haydn and Mozart best illustrates the author's point that

(A) not all martial music is Janissary in flavor
(B) Janissary music was European in origin
(C) martial music influenced classical composers
(D) Orientalism affected painting as well as music
(E) martial music was not merely percussive

162. Which of the following assertions does the author support with an example?

    I. Janissary music used unusual forms of percussion.

    II. You might hear martial music at a state funeral.

    III. John Philip Sousa wrote beloved marches.

(A) I only

(B) II only

(C) I and III only

(D) II and III only

(E) I, II, and III

163. In the 18th century, enlisting in the army became known as "following the drum." If the author included this information in the passage, it would probably be used to

(A) support the notion that martial music was a critical part of military culture

(B) provide an example of idiomatic expressions based on music and art

(C) add details to the segment on the influence of martial music in the Civil War

(D) illustrate the change that followed the introduction of Janissary music

(E) explain why drums are often used in the music of Haydn

164. The author's mention of the level of funding provided for music education is most likely meant as a

(A) fascinating comparison

(B) critical comment

(C) humorous aside

(D) predictive claim

(E) assertion of proof

165. Which of the following statements most accurately captures the central idea of the passage?

(A) Music from Turkey continues to influence martial music even today.

(B) Most of our current martial instrumentation derives from an Orientalist tradition.

(C) In the time before brass instruments, martial music relied on percussion.

(D) Janissary percussion was popular for a time with European armies and composers.

(E) Whereas military bands once worked the battlefields, today they are ceremonial.

CHAPTER 2

Critical Reasoning

For the following questions, select the best of the answer choices given.

166. Attempts to control purple loosestrife (*Lythrum salicaria*) have been only partially successful. It has proved resistant to many herbicides, and it is impervious to burning, as its rootstock lies beneath the surface and can reproduce from there. It can be mowed down and plowed under, and then replaced with a less invasive plant. This is very labor intensive in marshy areas that are substantially overgrown, but it may be the only way of eliminating the pest.

Which of the following information, if true, would provide the least support for the author's argument?

(A) *Lythrum salicaria* has been removed from some gardens through the careful use of an Australian slug.

(B) Replanted meadows where purple loosestrife once grew are slowly being taken over by a new, hardier strain of *Lythrum salicaria*.

(C) Cattails are coming back to some New York swampland once devastated by the incursion of *Lythrum salicaria*.

(D) Chopping up the rootstock of *Lythrum salicaria* with a plow adds an unexpected bonus in the form of nitrogen-rich fertilizer.

(E) Mowing and replanting *Lythrum salicaria* cost small communities along the Missouri River nearly $1 million last year.

167. A land bridge is land exposed when the sea recedes, connecting one expanse of land to another. One of the most famous land bridges was the Bering Land Bridge, often known as Beringia, which connected Alaska to Siberia across what is now the Bering Strait. Ethnologists and geologists generally believe that humans used the Bering Land Bridge to populate the Americas, which up until about 24,000 years ago had no sign of human life.

Which of the following findings best supports the author's contention that Siberia was once connected to North America?

(A) Native American legends from the American Northwest feature enormous whales and large fish.

(B) People of coastal Siberia have features that distinguish them from people in the rest of Russia.

(C) Hunters in both Siberia and coastal Alaska continue to hunt seals, walrus, and sea lions.

(D) Large animal fossils found in both places prove that identical species once populated both regions.

(E) As a waterway, the Bering Strait connects the Arctic and Pacific Oceans over the polar ice cap.

168. The clearest sign that we are not ready to abandon our metanarratives comes in the current and ongoing clash between those who accept evolutionary theory and those who accept the Bible as the written word of God. The latter grant the Earth 6,000 years of life, the former give it several million more, and never the twain shall meet. Each of these viewpoints is a metanarrative, a big story that governs people's understanding of the world. Like many metanarratives, each of these completely negates the other.

Which of the following can be correctly inferred from the preceding statements?

(A) Metanarratives are neither wholly true nor entirely false.

(B) In the modern world, no two metanarratives are alike.

(C) People tend to decipher their world through metanarratives.

(D) Biblical scholars do not accept evolutionary theory.

(E) Evolutionary theory negates most of what is written in the Bible.

169. Ether had a brief but important run as the anesthetic of choice in Western medicine, beginning when Dr. Crawford Williamson Long of Jefferson, Georgia, removed neck tumors from a patient under ether anesthesia on March 30, 1842. However, Dr. Long failed to publish the record of his experiment until 1848, by which time Dr. William T. G. Morton, a dentist in Hartford, Connecticut, had conducted a variety of experiments with ether on animals and himself, culminating in the painless extraction of a tooth from a patient under ether on September 30, 1846.

What evidence could the author have included that would best support the contention that ether was important to the history of medicine?

(A) The chemical makeup of diethyl ether—CH_3-CH_2-O-CH_2-CH_3

(B) Names and occupations of the patients on whom Dr. Long and Dr. Morton worked

(C) A comparison of chloroform to nitrous oxide when used as anesthesia

(D) Examples of how ether was used in battlefield medicine during the Civil War

(E) Lists of the compounds used as anesthesia in modern operating rooms

170. Gorilla populations have been ransacked by the Ebola virus, which has killed an estimated 90 percent of the gorilla population in each area of western and central Africa where it has been found. Like humans, gorillas tend to have a single offspring at one time, with each one gestating for about nine months. Females do not mature until around age six, and nearly half of baby gorillas do not survive till breeding age. The number-one threat to gorillas, however, is human greed. Humans are burning down the forests where the last remaining gorilla families live. They are doing this to harvest charcoal, which is used to fuel cooking fires throughout the region. In addition, they are poaching the last remaining gorillas for meat and for their hands or other parts, which are considered a delicacy in Africa and are used medicinally in parts of Asia. Despite the best efforts of dedicated conservationists and African rangers, some give these vegetarian cousins of *Homo sapiens* no more than a decade before all wild specimens are eradicated.

Which new information, if true, would most challenge the claim that gorillas have only a decade before extinction in the wild?

(A) A new transboundary law outlawing any human incursion into gorilla habitat

(B) The discovery of a vaccine against Ebola in humans

(C) Successful breeding of Mountain with Lowland gorillas in a zoo setting

(D) Observations of several twin babies in existing gorilla families

(E) Signs warning tourists to stay away from gorilla breeding grounds

171. As the world celebrates International Woman's Day, the United States remains one of the few nations not to have ratified the United Nations' Convention to Eliminate All Forms of Discrimination Against Women. The Senate has held hearings on the treaty several times over the past two decades, but conservatives have stopped its movement, thus allowing even the countries that have ratified the agreement to soften their commitment to women's rights.

The preceding argument relies on which of the following assumptions?

(A) The United States is able to influence the behavior of other nations.
(B) The United Nations is regarded as inferior by the U.S. Senate.
(C) International Woman's Day is not celebrated in the United States.
(D) There are more conservatives than liberals in the U.S. Congress.
(E) The United States lags behind most other nations in fighting discrimination.

172. Westco Corporation developed a new lawn tractor and tested it in a variety of situations. Following two weeks of intense testing, 1 out of 5 of the tractors were found to have minor operating problems, while 1 out of 20 tractors needed significant repairs. Given these results, the company moved production of the lawn tractor forward.

Which of the following, if true, most strongly supports Westco's decision to begin production of this lawn tractor?

(A) Previous Westco tractors, tested over two weeks in 2005 and 2009, had far worse results and had to be remodeled.
(B) The intensity of the testing conditions means that a tractor with $\frac{19}{20}$ of its machines functioning after two weeks is suitably durable for the market.
(C) Consumers expect that their lawns will never offer the difficult conditions encountered in the two-week test.
(D) Most models of lawn tractors at Westco engage in testing of anywhere from two to four weeks.
(E) The significant repairs required by 1 out of 20 of the tractors were primarily due to engine overheating.

173. Thomas Bowdler was, from all the evidence, an unlikely editor. He was born in 1754 near Bath, England, to a wealthy family. He studied medicine but never really practiced, preferring to exercise philanthropy and to play chess, at which he was a master. In his retirement, he decided to try his hand at editorial work. Shakespeare's dramas were his first project. He added nothing to the texts, but by cutting and paraphrasing strove to remove anything that "could give just offense to the religious and virtuous mind."

The preceding statements, if true, best support which of the following assertions?

(A) Bowdler, though untrained, proved to be a clever editor.
(B) Bowdler was less an editor than a critic and censor.
(C) Bowdler's work breathed new life into Shakespeare's dramas.
(D) Bowdler failed to make Shakespeare accessible to his peers.
(E) Bowdler was a better doctor than he was a man of letters.

174. An unusual strain of bird flu has once again hit China, causing several cities to suspend their live poultry trade. Authorities have killed several thousand chickens, ducks, and pigeons over a wide zone. Since H7N9 is rarely or never transmitted from person to person, the 16 cases of human H7N9 reported so far appear to be _____.

Which of the following best completes the passage?

(A) unrelated to other strains of influenza
(B) causing pneumonia and breathing difficulties
(C) linked to direct contact with infected birds
(D) evidence of a mutated virus
(E) predictors of a possible worldwide pandemic

175. It has come to my attention that our county's planning commission is wedded to the concept of nodal development in our rural towns. This concept is problematic for several reasons. First, to succeed, nodes must have a critical mass of inhabitants. Studies suggest that 2,500 is the smallest possible group required to support retail businesses within a node. **Our rural nodes would have far fewer residents—at most, 1,500.**

In the preceding argument, the portion in boldface plays which of the following roles?

(A) It is a conclusion that must be proven in order for the argument to be valid.
(B) It is an assumption that provides little support for the argument's conclusion.
(C) It is a premise that has little validity in the context of the argument.
(D) It provides specific evidence to support the writer's premise.
(E) It provides specific evidence to counter the writer's conclusion.

176. John received an A (4.0) in his writing course and Bs (3.0) in biology, German, and government. His grade point average for the semester came to a 3.0.

Which of the following, if true, would best explain the paradox described?

(A) His writing course was worth double the credit of his other courses.
(B) He changed his German course to pass/fail and did not get a grade.
(C) Biology is given as a two-semester course.
(D) John also received a C in comparative literature.
(E) The government course required a final exam.

177. After five years of declining market share, the board of Arrow Chicken Feed called for some changes. The marketing budget was doubled, and for the first time, ads were placed on radio both in-state and in the surrounding states. Within six months, Arrow was beating its nearest two competitors in sales of most products.

To evaluate whether the board's decision to double the marketing budget led to the increase in market share, which of the following would be most useful to know?

(A) How many farms are in the home state where Arrow Chicken Feed is located?
(B) Did Arrow's nearest competitors make changes to their marketing plans?
(C) How do Arrow's customers typically learn about new products?
(D) Was anything cut back to make room for the increase in marketing costs?
(E) Does Arrow Chicken Feed plan to expand into other farm products?

178. Either Jason's Deli or Sunburst Café sells coffee-flavored frozen yogurt. I recently purchased coffee-flavored frozen yogurt at Sunburst Café. It appears that Jason's Deli does not sell frozen yogurt in that flavor.

The reasoning in the preceding argument most closely parallels which of the following?

(A) If carnivores are mammals, then carnivores are animals. Since wolves are carnivores, it follows that wolves are animals.
(B) Unless we get rid of charter schools, public schools will go down in flames for lack of resources. It seems evident that charter schools are here to stay, so we may as well say goodbye to public schools.
(C) We may choose to re-elect the congressman or to elect his rival. If we elect the congressman, things will go on as usual. If we elect his rival, nothing will change. Thus, it matters little what we do.
(D) Columbia Contracting has succeeded despite refusing to send its manufacturing overseas. Therefore, at least one company is thriving without outsourcing.
(E) This week, Dr. Pendergrass is either in Paris or Berlin. If she is in Paris, she is attending a conference. If she is in Berlin, she is visiting friends. Dr. Pendergrass is thus either attending a conference or visiting friends.

179. The recently injured athlete's monthly drug test was positive for marijuana. Although the athlete insisted that he had not used the drug, he did admit to spending some time at a party where others were smoking. The doctor, however, insisted that contact of that sort could not result in a positive indicator.

Which of the following, if true, would contribute most to an explanation of the results of the drug test?

(A) Taking large amounts of ibuprofen can result in false positives for marijuana.

(B) Secondhand smoke exposes innocent bystanders to a variety of toxic chemicals.

(C) Excessive exercise has been found to mask certain effects of marijuana use.

(D) The athlete had tested positive for amphetamines three years earlier.

(E) The team doctor sends all test samples out to an independent laboratory.

180. For years, mercury was used in thermometers because it is a bright silvery metal that is liquid at room temperature and has a high coefficient of expansion. However, mercury has the disadvantage of being extremely toxic. Although the amount in an oral thermometer is minuscule, the chance of ingesting or inhaling it is enough that **the EPA recommends using alternatives in the home**.

In the preceding argument, the portion in boldface plays which of the following roles?

(A) It is a conclusion, which is supported by other pieces of the argument.

(B) It is a premise that weakens the author's main argument.

(C) It is a premise that supports the author's main argument.

(D) It is an assumption that undermines the conclusion.

(E) It is evidence that supports another premise of the argument.

181. Microcalcifications show up on mammograms as tiny, salt-like white specks. They are not of particular concern unless they display certain patterns throughout the breast, in which case they may indicate a precancerous condition or even an early stage of breast cancer. In such a case, a doctor may call for a needle biopsy or stereotactic biopsy, and if those results indicate the presence of a low-grade tumor, a surgical biopsy may follow.

Based on this passage, when would a doctor call for a needle biopsy?

(A) When microcalcifications first appear

(B) When microcalcifications display certain patterns

(C) When microcalcifications form a low-grade tumor

(D) When a stereotactic biopsy indicates microcalcifications

(E) Whenever white specs appear on mammograms

182. Once again, Google tops the Forbes list of the best companies to work for. Its 30,000-plus employees benefit from the subsidized massage, wellness centers, and seven-acre sports complex on its sprawling Mountain View site. Google workers rave that they are never more than a short walk away from a well-stocked kitchen.

     The preceding argument relies on which of the following presuppositions?

     (A) Google workers are spoiled.
     (B) Forbes looked primarily at tech companies.
     (C) A healthy worker is a happy worker.
     (D) Google spends more on perks than on salaries.
     (E) Perks keep workers contentedly employed.

183. A poll of village residents indicated that nearly 60 percent were not satisfied with the communication they received from the village government prior to the budget vote and throughout the year. The village proceeded to begin posting meeting minutes on the village website, to mail occasional one-page newsletters, and to send e-mail alerts to villagers about topics of general interest.

     Which of the following, if true, provides the strongest reason to expect that the villagers will give a "satisfactory" rank to the communication skills of the village government on next year's survey?

     (A) A majority of villagers protested the latest bond proposal of $9 million for a new water project.
     (B) Three villagers stood up at the last board meeting before the survey to complain about the lack of communication.
     (C) Other villages in the area post their minutes and offer regular newsletters.
     (D) Villagers suggested that their favorite modes of communication would be mail, e-mail, and website.
     (E) Villagers remarked on this year's poll that they wanted to be able to attend more board meetings.

184. As a candidate for president, Al Smith had several strikes against him. He was the Catholic son of Irish and Italian-German immigrants, making him anathema to nativists, the xenophobes who underwent a resurgence in the 1920s. He was from New York City, viewed even in the early 20th century as disconnected from the national character. He was a progressive, which made conservatives of all stripes nervous. And he favored the repeal of Prohibition, a position that lost him the backing of many party leaders.

     Which of the following can be correctly inferred from the preceding statements?

     (A) Al Smith may have been too far out of the mainstream to win an election.
     (B) Al Smith came from a city, but most Americans lived in rural areas.
     (C) There were more conservatives than progressives in the 1920s.
     (D) Al Smith worked hard to appeal to a variety of constituencies.
     (E) Prohibition had been put into place through the work of party leaders.

185. If Kai gets into Penn State, he will enroll in its business program. Assuming that he does enroll in its business program, he will complete his degree in three years. Therefore, if Kai gets into Penn State this year, he will graduate in three years.

The pattern of reasoning in the preceding argument most closely matches which of the following?

(A) If you take up a bad habit such as gambling, it is foolish to argue that such a habit is harmful. If you truly believe that gambling is harmful, you will not gamble.

(B) If you choose your college wisely, you are likely to have a pleasant experience. Suzanne, sadly, chose her college based on nothing more than a hunch. As you might expect, her experience was less than optimal.

(C) It is hardly worth the effort to get upset because bad weather prevents you from participating in a favorite event. The odds of bad weather in this region are about one in four, so you must plan as though any event might be cancelled or moved indoors.

(D) Should it start to rain, Doward will turn off the sprinkler system. Once he turns off the system, it will not automatically reset for 24 hours. In other words, if it rains this morning, the sprinkler system won't reset before tomorrow morning.

(E) Once Jon joins the union, he will not be allowed to train anyone who might potentially replace him. Right now, Jon is not a member of the union, so he is not covered by that protection.

186. When voters turned down the school budget in a May vote, the administration scrambled to prepare a second budget. The president of the school board insisted that the new budget contain fewer administrative positions, as she posited that people had voted "no" due to dislike of a top-heavy administration.

Which of these investigations would be most useful in evaluating the board president's claim?

(A) Comparing the number of administrators to the number in other districts

(B) Adding up the salaries and benefits for all district administrators

(C) Graphing five years of correlation between numbers of students and administrators

(D) Surveying neighborhood districts to determine which budgets passed

(E) Exit-polling voters to determine the reasons for their votes

187. Marla used the same ingredients—sugar, salt, flour, molasses, butter, ginger, salt, baking soda, and an egg—to make four batches of gingerbread. She baked each batch in a pan in the oven for 30 minutes. When she had finished, she discovered that three batches were fine, but one was completely inedible.

    Which of the following, if true, would best explain the paradox described?

    (A) The oven was preheated to 350 degrees.
    (B) Marla mixed up the salt and the sugar on the last batch.
    (C) The recipe calls for ½ cup of light molasses.
    (D) Marla used four pans, all the same size.
    (E) Marla moved quickly once the first batch was done.

188. Whenever Mr. Rollins flies Jet Blue to New York, he flies business class because he has a deal through his company. Today Mr. Rollins is flying to New York in coach. Apparently he is not flying Jet Blue.

    The pattern of reasoning in the preceding argument most closely matches which of the following?

    (A) If Will does well in his database management class, he will be in line for a promotion. Will scored a 100 on his final exam. He will soon receive a new title and salary increase.
    (B) Greta will take either the train or the bus home from school. If she takes the train, she will leave at midnight. If she takes the bus, she will leave at noon. She must plan for a departure in the middle of the night or midday.
    (C) If Lionel is in the theater, you will always find him in a center orchestra seat. Tonight, Lionel is not in a center orchestra seat. He must not be attending this performance at the theater.
    (D) Male lions look fierce, but in fact, it is the females who do most of the hunting and guard the young cubs. In other words, you are safer in a cage with a male lion than with a female.
    (E) The lecturer today will be either Dr. Lorenz or his assistant, Dr. Crenshaw. Dr. Crenshaw is currently out of town. Therefore, we can expect to hear from Dr. Lorenz.

189. A spate of accidents at the corner of Settlement and Vine Streets warrants the county's immediate attention. **One of our neighbors recently punctured a tire on the ragged edge of the torn-up road surface.** The resident at the corner reported that a driver skidded on gravel the other morning, plowed through her fence, backed up, and drove off without a word.

In the preceding argument, the portion in boldface plays which of the following roles?

(A) It is a conclusion that must be proven in order for the argument to be valid.
(B) It is an assumption that provides some support for the author's argument.
(C) It is a premise that has questionable validity in the context of the argument.
(D) It provides evidence to support the author's conclusion.
(E) It provides evidence to refute the author's conclusion.

190. The village of Teeburg has received grant money to study whether it should retain or dissolve its village police department. The department, which currently represents 30 percent of the annual budget of the village, has two full-time and several part-time employees. Since the village is also within the purview of the county sheriff and the state police, who are housed just five miles away, the village department may be considered a luxury.

The argument's conclusion logically depends on which of the following?

(A) There is not a significant amount of crime in Teeburg.
(B) State police or sheriff's deputies could easily patrol Teeburg.
(C) Villages and small towns have little need for police departments.
(D) The grant will show that Teeburg can cut positions and save money.
(E) Teeburg could maintain the same amount of safety with fewer employees.

191. A trial of a new diabetes medicine combined with a stringent diet resulted in positive results for 75 percent of the trial subjects, all of whom were able to control blood sugar levels without resorting to insulin shots. However, nearly 100 of the 400 test subjects saw spikes in their blood sugar over the course of the trial, leading the manufacturer to head back to the drawing board.

Which of the following, if true, would most weaken the manufacturer's conclusion as described?

(A) Establishing that several of the 400 test subjects suffered from other, unrelated conditions
(B) Noting that insulin shots with diet and exercise are traditionally the best way to control diabetes
(C) Determining that a stringent diet with no medicine at all resulted in a positive result for 30 percent of subjects
(D) Recognizing that a variety of medicines with 75 percent positive results achieved market readiness
(E) Finding that many test subjects with negative results had made false claims on their dietary reports

192. Parental involvement in children's education tends to peak in the mid-elementary years and decline rapidly in middle school and high school. Many school districts don't bother to continue PTOs or PTAs in middle school and high school because they cannot attract the critical mass needed to keep those organizations going. It's a shame, really, because middle school tends to be the time when children most require their parents' attention and oversight.

Which of the following, if true, would most strengthen the author's conclusion in the passage's final sentence?

(A) Middle school parents tend not to volunteer in the classroom but prefer to serve as advisers or coaches.

(B) Typically, children in middle school are breaking away from parents and searching for some autonomy.

(C) The burdens of puberty cause middle schoolers to be needier in some ways than their younger siblings are.

(D) Middle schools may emphasize grades and correct responses more than they emphasize love of learning.

(E) Students in middle school and high school may be distracted from academia by social interactions.

193. A recent poll of 6,000 small businesses found that the five cities friendliest to business were Oklahoma City, Dallas–Fort Worth, San Antonio, Austin, and Atlanta. The study looked at cost of living, hiring, licensing, regulation, zoning, taxes, workforce availability, and support systems for entrepreneurs, among other measures. It is not surprising that three of the top five cities are in Texas; the Lone Star State has long been known for _____.

Which of the following best completes the preceding passage?

(A) oil and gas exploration

(B) its enormous size and bigger-than-life attitude

(C) cultural pride and a diverse population

(D) low taxes and minimal bureaucratic controls

(E) a unique blend of history and innovation

194. **Removing another foreign language from the curriculum at Middleview High will have dire results.** Today's global economy dictates a need for multilingual workers, so the more languages our students are exposed to, the better for their future careers. A recent study found that students with multiple fluencies got into top colleges compared to students with only one foreign language and no AP courses in that language.

In the preceding argument, the portion in boldface plays which of the following roles?

(A) It is a conclusion that must be proven in order for the argument to be valid.

(B) It is an assumption that provides some support for the author's argument.

(C) It is a premise that has validity in the context of the argument.

(D) It provides evidence to support the author's conclusion.

(E) It provides evidence to refute the author's conclusion.

195. The controversy surrounding Rigoberta Menchú's Nobel Peace Prize is all about her memoir. It started when anthropologist David Stoll began independent research on the same era about which Rigoberta wrote and discovered discrepancies in her recall of events. Massacres she described were not remembered by the locals, one of her brothers died by shooting rather than by fire, dates were incorrect, and so on. Stoll's discoveries were enough to roil up conservative historians and columnists, who declared Rigoberta's book the grossest propaganda and her career, therefore, unworthy of the Nobel Peace Prize.

If the previous statements are true, which of the following must be true?

(A) Rigoberta Menchú's Nobel Peace Prize will soon be rescinded.

(B) Many conservatives believed David Stoll's accounts of events.

(C) Memoirs are habitually biased by inaccurate memories.

(D) The Nobel Prize will no longer be based on personal narratives.

(E) Historically, most Nobel Prizes were awarded without controversy.

196. One small-town newspaper recently determined that it was making significantly more on website advertising than on circulation subscriptions. In reaction to this news, the publisher decided to produce only the online version for most of the week, but to continue with a print version on Wednesdays and Saturdays.

Which of the following, if true, best supports the conclusion reached?

(A) Subscription prices have not increased over the past five years.

(B) At other papers that have gone this route, readership has declined.

(C) Even some major magazines have moved to online-only publication.

(D) Online advertising is expected to plateau over the next few years.

(E) Readership is always highest on Wednesday and Saturday coupon days.

197. In 1984, hunters established the Rocky Mountain Elk Foundation, whose mission is to reintroduce elk in the states where they once roamed. At present, new herds are established in Arkansas, Kentucky, Michigan, and Wisconsin in addition to Pennsylvania. There is talk of moving herds to Tennessee and to the Adirondack range in New York. It seems fairly clear that improving habitat for elk reintroduction improves conditions for other wildlife—wild turkey, whitetail deer, and black bear, among others. This reintroduction is being closely monitored and controlled. Animals are checked for disease. Land trusts are used to preserve habitat and to keep the elk from moving too close to cropland.

Which of the following findings best supports the author's contention that elk repopulation is carefully monitored?

(A) Farming to raise deer, elk, and reindeer is increasingly popular.
(B) Before 1997 there had not been a wild elk in Kentucky in 150 years.
(C) Rocky Mountain elk were among the original animals at the Hearst Zoo.
(D) Jackson County is testing potential elk herds for chronic wasting disease.
(E) Adirondack conditions are similar to those found in the elks' western habitat.

198. Although all its 15 employees started at minimum wage, Jake's Grocery paid several longer term employees $8.50 an hour, somewhat above the minimum wage at the time. However, when the state raised the minimum wage to $9.00 an hour, all employees found that they were once again starting at minimum wage. Jake justified this by pointing out that the forced increase in wages was significant enough that if he kept longer term employees at a proportionally higher wage, it would mean that one or more employees would have to be laid off.

Which additional piece of evidence would most weaken this conclusion?

(A) Data indicating that Jake hired three new workers in the past year
(B) Data showing that Jake's profits increased twofold over five years
(C) Data illustrating increased layoffs in the small grocery industry
(D) Data showing that minimum wage workers contribute to the economy
(E) Data proving that a living wage in the area required a salary of $12.15 an hour

199. The value of farmland has gone up enormously in the past five years, according to the assessment office. This is primarily due to the fact that large tracts of land are hard to come by, as most in the county were developed over the past three decades. We can expect the cost per acre of farmland to continue to grow through 2020.

Which of the following is an assumption made in drawing this conclusion?

(A) Fewer and fewer large tracts of land will be available in the years to come.
(B) Development will slow as the price of land becomes exorbitant.
(C) As farmers lose their farms, developers will move in quickly.
(D) The cost per acre of farmland rarely decreases, even in a recession.
(E) After three decades of development, large purchases have nearly ceased.

200. According to United Nations statistics, by the year 2030, more than 60 percent of the world population will be urban, up from 30 percent in 1950. Unlike the population growth in developed nations, the birth rate in less developed nations is high, meaning that the cities will continue to grow even as migration slows from the rural areas. Megacities such as New York, on the other hand, have populations that have leveled off over time.

Which new information, if true, might challenge the author's contention that certain cities will continue to grow despite a slowing of migration from the countryside?

(A) Scientists are creating new strains of rice and wheat that require far less in the way of hands-on care.
(B) The number of people living below the poverty level will climb in less developed and developed nations.
(C) Inflationary trends in heating oil and gasoline prices will limit most people's discretionary spending.
(D) New methods of birth control will limit the population explosion in the developing world.
(E) Demographers foresee ecological overload, homelessness, and infrastructure strained to the breaking point.

201. Herbal remedies fall under the auspices of the FDA, but they are not regulated the way medicines or foods might be. Instead, they fall under the category of dietary supplements, meaning that they must meet certain quality standards, but manufacturers do not need to seek FDA approval before placing products on the market. It is fairly clear that such oversight is insufficient and that many herbal remedies should be treated by the FDA as medicines.

Which of the following, if true, provides the strongest support for the previous argument?

(A) Herbs often contain antioxidants and essential oils that provide anti-inflammatory relief.

(B) Burdock apparently has a certain diuretic property that helps the body to expel toxins.

(C) Up to 80 percent of some Asian and African cultures rely on herbal remedies in part for healthcare.

(D) Certain herbal remedies increase heart rate, which can be lethal for cardiac patients.

(E) A variety of industrial plants are grown expressly to be used in modern prescription medicines.

202. How does the doctor respond to the patient in the following scenario?

PATIENT: I have followed your advice about diet and exercise, and I have seen no results. It is clear to me that improving my health depends upon finding the right combination of medications.

DOCTOR: Your conclusion is flawed. Although medication might address some of your health problems, you need to give the diet and exercise plan time to work. My estimate was that you would see positive results in six months, but you have only given the plan three months in all.

(A) By pointing out a flaw in the patient's original premise

(B) By indicating a paradox in the patient's assumptions

(C) By demonstrating a presupposition that better reflects reality

(D) By showing the patient how to strengthen his own argument

(E) By drawing a conclusion about the patient's power of reasoning

203. Sixty-eight children at Merrydale School came down with an intestinal illness after lunch. After testing the food in the cafeteria, health department workers determined that there were no disease-inducing bacteria in the chicken casserole served that day. Nevertheless, of the children who were ill, half were out of school for at least 24 hours.

Which of the following, if true, would best explain the paradox described?

(A) Half of the children recovered quickly from their illnesses.
(B) The children who became ill ate hot dogs as their entrée.
(C) Many young children are allergic to peanuts or wheat.
(D) The director of the health department was newly appointed.
(E) Merrydale School had suffered outbreaks of illness before.

204. Dozens of practitioners in small clinics in rural America are closing up shop and moving to southern Australia to practice medicine in a friendly environment where doctors are critically needed. Critics of American healthcare blame this outflow on the shrinking of Medicare reimbursements that started in the 1990s, making it increasingly difficult for rural doctors to meet expenses.

Which of the following must be studied in order to evaluate the validity of the critics' argument?

(A) The percentage of rural patients who rely upon Medicare
(B) Comparative licensing in Australia and America
(C) Lack of medical technology in rural America
(D) Relative respect for primary care physicians in Australia and America
(E) Medicare reimbursements at large urban hospitals

205. Equality and community appealed to the people from other cultures who joined the Shakers in the late 1700s. Unlike most sects, the Shakers were firmly inclusive. The Shakers attracted Native Americans, free blacks, and non-Christians, and _____.

Which of the following best completes the preceding passage?

(A) white men were relegated to minor posts
(B) the group became ever more isolated
(C) only true Quakers were turned away
(D) most would leave after a year or two
(E) all were welcomed into the commune

206. Because of the outflow from the sewage treatment plant, a stream to the lake has been contaminated, resulting in the closing of the Boy Scout Camp to swimming this summer. The town has called for the complete closure of the treatment plant while the cleanup takes place.

Opponents of the town's plan might cite which of the following as their strongest criticism of the proposal?

(A) The Boy Scout Camp has suffered from declining enrollment for five years.
(B) Test results show contamination of the stream but not of the lake.
(C) The plant is the only source of sewage treatment on that side of the lake.
(D) Houses along the lakeshore have septic tanks and do not use the sewer system.
(E) Workers at the treatment plant will be moved to a plant across the lake.

207. In investigating my ancestry, I have determined that the U.S. branch of my mother's family arrived in Canada in the 1910s, with my great-grandfather traveling to Saskatoon and working in logging camps and my great-grandmother running a rooming house not far from there with her family. Although it is not clear where they first disembarked from their Norwegian ships, there is no record of them at Ellis Island, so I am sure they did not arrive in the States until they had been in Canada for several years.

The author's conclusion would be most strengthened by which piece of evidence?

(A) Photographs of the great-grandparents in Chicago in the 1930s
(B) A ledger from the great-grandmother's family's rooming house
(C) Ships' records showing both great-grandparents arriving in Quebec in 1912
(D) Newspaper reports on the numbers of Norwegian emigrants to Canada
(E) A certificate of the great-grandparents' marriage in Saskatoon

208. In 2010 the voter turnout in New York State ranked dead last in the nation. Yes, it was an off-year, midterm election, but pundits noted that the turnout was significantly less than in other, similar years. Those same pundits remarked that the negativity of New York's campaigns, which featured a variety of chillingly nasty ads, kept the electorate home.

Which of the following is an assumption made in drawing this conclusion?

(A) Negative advertising repels and discourages voters.
(B) Voters refuse to watch negative advertising.
(C) Fewer voters turn out for midterm elections.
(D) New York has always ranked near the bottom in voter turnout.
(E) Positive ads get political messages across better.

209. Although some cities have seen immigration expand their borders, for most megacities, it is migration from within the country that has caused the city to grow. An example is China, where some 150 million rural inhabitants have migrated to cities in just the past 10 years. In many cases, the cities house the only possibilities of employment in this global economy.

The preceding statements most strongly support which of the following conclusions?

(A) Megacities are a product of economic realities.
(B) China has the most megacities in the world.
(C) Only farming jobs exist in rural China.
(D) Immigration is rarely a cause for urban growth.
(E) A high percentage of Beijing's population is non-Chinese.

210. Although they are renowned for their disposition and brains, chocolate labs are also prone to allergies and hip dysplasia, possibly because of over-breeding in the 1960s and 1970s. Since that time, breeders have become more cautious, and it should be quite easy now to find a chocolate lab pup that is healthy and allergy-free.

The author's conclusion would be most strengthened if it were found that

(A) most dogs do not develop allergies before the age of three
(B) overbreeding is found to cause health problems in horses
(C) studies indicate a decline in chocolate lab allergies from 1970 to 2010
(D) DNA results on certain chocolate labs show evidence of cross-breeding
(E) veterinarians have developed new treatments for hip dysplasia in large dogs

211. Before the House vote on drone policy, Congressman Arnold's staff conducted a poll to determine which way the congressman should vote. The congressman vowed to vote based on the wishes of the majority of his constituents.

The answer to which of the following questions would be most useful in evaluating the value of Congressman Arnold's poll?

(A) Do Arnold's constituents have particular expertise in military matters?
(B) Did the staff poll a representative sample of voters throughout the district?
(C) Was the poll conducted in more than one format (e.g., phone plus e-mail)?
(D) Did the results of the poll match Arnold's own thinking on the topic?
(E) Were the pollsters honest about the reasons for conducting the poll?

212. The PC market declined in 2013, and many insisted that this was based on dislike of the new Windows operating system. Even with the well-publicized option for an app that enables users to bypass the new system and work with one similar to the more popular former version, sales continue to decline.

Which of the following would help to explain the discrepancy described?

(A) The former operating system is no more admired than the new one.
(B) The new Windows operating system is difficult to navigate.
(C) Demand for PCs is up in foreign countries but down in the United States.
(D) Users are spending their money on tablets rather than PCs.
(E) More people are purchasing hardware and software on the Internet.

213. How does the employer respond to the employee in the following situation?

EMPLOYEE: I have worked in the office for nine months, during which time two other employees on my team have received promotions. I am concerned that you are overlooking the great work I am doing and wonder if you are being unfair.

EMPLOYER: Your work has been first-rate, but your contract clearly states that you are not eligible for promotion during your first year's probationary period. In a few months, we can review where we are and reconsider your position.

(A) By attacking the employee's argument as deceptive
(B) By indicating that the employee's definition of fairness does not match her own
(C) By questioning the employee's premise that others have received promotions
(D) By showing the employee that one of his premises is immaterial
(E) By offering a counterargument to the employee's argument

214. Wendy hopes to open a cake shop in her little village. Assuming she gets the paperwork done in time to establish herself as a local business, she will open this year. If she is able to open her cake shop this year, she will hire her daughter-in-law Amy as her assistant. So if the paperwork gets done, Amy will start to work for Wendy this year.

The pattern of reasoning in the previous argument most closely matches which of the following?

(A) Wilkommen Energy Services will only drill for gas in areas where there are no bans. There are bans on gas drilling throughout Tucker County, so do not expect Wilkommen to start drilling there anytime soon.

(B) If Danielle's landlord lets her have a pet, she plans to get a rescue dog from the SPCA. She will only adopt a female dog because she finds them easier to train. Thus, Danielle will adopt a female dog if her landlord comes through with the approval for a pet.

(C) The service at Gerry's Coffee Shop is always slow, but it is slowest on Saturdays. Today is Sunday, so you can expect fairly speedy service.

(D) Either Maurice or his cousin Bernard will drive the bus when the third-graders visit the zoo. Since Bernard is busy on the date of the field trip, Maurice will serve as the children's driver for the day.

(E) If I do not eat lunch with my aunts, I will have dinner with them instead. I am currently lunching with my aunts, so I certainly won't join them for dinner.

215. When polled about their favorite teachers, nearly 40 percent of the students at Boylston High chose one of their math teachers. This was true whether the students were freshmen or seniors and whether they had done well or poorly in math class. Clearly, at Boylston High, success in a class is not an indication of affection for a teacher.

The preceding argument relies on which of the following suppositions?

(A) Fewer than 40 percent of Boylston High students chose English teachers.

(B) Most students at Boylston High did exceptionally well in math class.

(C) Students chose their science teachers only if they had done well in science class.

(D) The pattern for those who chose other teachers was similar to that for math.

(E) Only a small percentage of Boylston students participated in the poll.

216. As a traffic calming measure, the hamlet of Eller's Hollow has invested several thousand dollars in painting the shoulders of the main road green. "The green color," said one alderperson, "fools drivers into feeling that the shoulder is grassy, and that the two-lane road, which is 28 feet across with its 2-foot shoulders, is narrower than it is. This in turn protects bicyclists who are riding along that shoulder and prevents drivers from speeding, as they would on a wider road."

Which of the following study results, if true, would most seriously weaken the alderperson's conclusion?

(A) As lane width decreases, volume of traffic tends to decrease.
(B) Driver speed only increases when lane width increases to 15 feet.
(C) Painted lane markings have a clear effect on driver safety.
(D) Cities in the United States have doubled their bike lanes since 2005.
(E) Most speeding in Eller's Hollow happens during commuting time.

217. United States wine exports continue to rise, with California wines still dominating the market. The fastest-growing wine export states are not at all what you might expect. Would you believe Florida? New Jersey? Washington State? The fact is that without the overseas market, wines from New Jersey would probably not find a buyer, because, after all, who in the States is likely to purchase a Paterson Pinot or a Camden Cabernet? It's most likely to be indiscriminate Asian consumers who are eagerly snapping up any wine from any state in the United States.

Which of the following, if true, provides the strongest support for the preceding argument?

(A) Exports of wine from Washington State rose by $9 million over five years.
(B) Wines from Napa Valley still outsell wines from any other state.
(C) New Jersey wineries have been producing since colonial times.
(D) California wine sales alone are up 30 percent in China and 18 percent in Vietnam.
(E) Wine consumption continues to grow despite a sluggish economy.

218. The Beats were of their time, and they transcended their time. The highway system that crisscrossed the United States in the 1950s gave them the power to move. Suburbia and the man in the gray flannel suit gave them something to despise. The cold war gave them angst and disillusionment. Jazz and the drug culture gave them a way out. Without the Beats to pave the way, Sixties culture would have looked quite different.

The previous statements, if true, best support which of the following assertions?

   (A) Jazz and travel inspired the Beats, who in turn inspired Sixties culture.
   (B) The Beats inspired the man in the gray flannel suit and Sixties culture.
   (C) Sixties culture inspired the Beats, who found a haven in drugs and jazz.
   (D) If not for the Beats, jazz and the drug culture would have died out by 1960.
   (E) The Beats' hatred for their own culture led them to embrace Sixties culture.

219. Despite the increase in the cost of beef, the price of a hamburger at Barney's Big Meal has not increased in five years. Nevertheless, Barney's continues to report sales and profits similar to those it has reported for the past decade.

Which of the following, if true, would best explain the paradox described?

   (A) Barney's is using beef obtained from outside the United States.
   (B) More people are buying hamburgers than ever before.
   (C) Hamburgers come with sides of pickles and chips.
   (D) Barney's Big Meal no longer sells hamburgers.
   (E) Barney's has reduced its serving sizes.

220. For years, scientists have reported on the placebo effect, in which a hopeful outlook is all it takes to improve health. Researchers have determined that a change in mindset can alter the neurochemistry of the brain. In addition, hope for the future can promote healthy actions around diet and exercise and the avoidance of unhealthy habits.

The preceding argument is structured to lead to what conclusion?

   (A) Researchers continue to explore the mind-body connection.
   (B) A change in mindset can counter healthful habits.
   (C) The placebo effect has been replaced by neurochemistry.
   (D) Unhealthy habits get in the way of a hopeful attitude.
   (E) Hope may exert a strong influence on healing and health.

221. Before deciding which of two local job offers to accept, Sara phoned six of her closest friends to receive their advice and counsel. She determined that she would go with whichever position the majority of her friends recommended.

The answer to which of the following questions would be most useful in evaluating the value of Sara's informal poll of her friends?

(A) Do any of Sara's friends live and work outside her city?
(B) Did Sara apply for any positions that were not local?
(C) Do all six of Sara's friends work in the same field as Sara?
(D) Are the six friends equally divided by gender?
(E) Do both positions offer similar salaries and benefits?

222. In the sparsely populated, rural sections of the state, superintendents' salaries are capped at $160,000. School districts in those regions have found that their pool of applicants has declined dramatically since the cap was introduced. The cap has ensured that small, rural schools have less chance of attracting competent leadership.

Which of the following is an assumption made in drawing this conclusion?

(A) Fewer people overall are vying for superintendent positions.
(B) Rural schools offer an undesirable environment for dynamic superintendents.
(C) Superintendent candidates worry more about salary than about location.
(D) Competence is inversely proportional to salary expectations.
(E) Richer districts regularly attract a large pool of superintendent applicants.

223. The town removed the beaver dam along Rickford Road in 2012. In the time since then, there have been no incidents of flooding along that road, **but the site has also seen overgrowth of young trees that the beavers had previously kept trimmed**. In addition, local fishermen complain about the loss of the best fishing pond in the area. It appears that the beavers were an asset to the community.

In the previous argument, the portion in boldface plays which of the following roles?

(A) It is a conclusion that must be proven in order for the argument to be valid.
(B) It is an assumption that provides some support for the author's argument.
(C) It is a premise that has questionable validity in the context of the argument.
(D) It provides evidence to support the author's conclusion.
(E) It provides evidence to refute the author's conclusion.

224. According to the National Association of Social Workers, some 80 percent of prison inmates spent part of their childhood in the foster care system. And although that particular statistic might reveal more about the circumstances that led children to foster care than about the system itself, the National Center on Child Abuse and Neglect did find that children were 11 times more likely to be abused in state care than in their own homes.

If the preceding statements are true, which of the following must be true?

(A) Foster care leads inevitably to physical abuse and jail time.
(B) Foster care is preferable to childhood in a dysfunctional home.
(C) Foster care is sometimes the more damaging of two alternatives.
(D) Without foster care, prisons would be less overcrowded.
(E) Without foster care, children might enter the prison system earlier.

225. Women have spent decades arguing for family-friendly workplace policies such as parental leave, quality child care, and flexible hours. It is time, says Kathleen McCartney, that we viewed such policies as supporting parental employment, not simply as tools that enable women to "have it all." Sadly, we continue to view women as the biologically driven caretakers of children, a view that limits the possibility of parity in the workplace.

Which of the following, if true, provides the strongest support for the preceding argument?

(A) Until the Industrial Revolution, women and men often worked side by side in and around the home.
(B) In most places, paid parental leave is tied to the amount of time an employee has worked for the company.
(C) Yahoo's decision to limit telecommuting was framed by the media as specifically harmful to women.
(D) Kathleen McCartney recently left Harvard to become the president of Smith College, a college for women.
(E) Some flextime workers may opt to work four 10-hour days instead of five 8-hour days.

226. Kalinda planned to drive from her office in Winchester to the plant in Cumberland. She had a choice of roads. Taking Route 51 was slightly more direct and would take just under an hour and a half for a distance of 63 miles. Taking 522N took her out of her way but on a much faster highway for a distance of 80 miles in about the same time. Kalinda's odometer measured 11,645 miles at the start of her trip and 11,708 at the end. She clearly took the more direct route.

Which of the following is most like the preceding argument in its logical structure?

(A) No matter who is elected as county judge, D. A. Wilkinson will remain in office. It looks as though the people will elect either Kelly O'Hara or Donnell Willis to the bench. So one of them will serve with D. A. Wilkinson.

(B) The northern two-thirds of Assateague Island is in Maryland, while the southern third is in Virginia. Chincoteague National Wildlife Refuge is not in the northern two-thirds of the island. Therefore, it must be located in Virginia.

(C) Although people call them ladybugs, the little insects are not really bugs at all. True bugs are insects of the order Hemiptera. Cicadas and leafhoppers are two examples of true bugs.

(D) Lynette plans to bake either brownies or a cake. Her brownie recipe calls for an oven temperature of 350. The cake requires a temperature of 325. Lynette preheats the oven for 350. She must be planning to bake the brownies.

(E) When you refer to Aargau, you may mean either a canton in northern Switzerland or a fictional planet in *Star Wars*. The city of Aarau is the capital of Aargau, and it is not fictional. Thus, Aarau must be a city in Switzerland.

227. A developer who has been unable to sell four-bedroom townhouses in the village is contemplating subdividing the units into smaller, two-bedroom apartments. He believes that the expense will be worth it because he will more easily rent such apartments.

The answer to which of the following questions would be least relevant to the developer's decision whether or not to subdivide?

(A) What is the renting population of the village?
(B) How many two-bedroom units currently exist in the village?
(C) What would the cost of subdividing be?
(D) How many of the apartments will face the road?
(E) How much rent could be charged for a two-bedroom unit?

228. Closing the two primary schools in town and moving all children to the larger elementary school would be a grave mistake. Studies show that students do best academically in small, easy-to-navigate schools. Our little schools, with 95 students apiece, are right on track to provide the quality education our students deserve.

Which of the following, if true, would most weaken this conclusion?

(A) Studies of small schools define "small" as housing 250–500 students.
(B) Primary schools serve only children from ages 4 or 5 to 7 or 8.
(C) The town's larger school uses the same textbooks as the small schools do.
(D) The population of the town has declined over the past decade.
(E) Renovating the primary school buildings will cost more than $2 million.

229. Marcus and his twin are nearly identical; only their parents can tell them apart from a distance. Nevertheless, they are differentiated by their interests: Marcus is a hands-on engineer, whereas his brother has always been more artistic and less academically inclined. Sending both of them to MIT, as their parents are planning, is clearly a mistake.

The argument's conclusion logically depends on which of the following presuppositions?

(A) Twins should be separated to allow for social growth.
(B) College is wasted on those who are artistically inclined.
(C) Identical twins often have identical interests.
(D) Sending two children to MIT is an impractical expense.
(E) MIT is best for those with a predilection for science.

230. How does the environmentalist respond to the logger in the following exchange?

LOGGER: Clearing this forest, which we do judiciously, enables new growth to establish itself. We plant 10 new trees for each tree we cut down. In many ways, our labor is contributing to the health of the forest.

ENVIRONMENTALIST: Although you plant saplings, their roots cannot do the work of old-growth forests in holding together the soil and preventing erosion. As habitats change, your work has contributed to the reduction of biodiversity in the region. Your labor is in fact contributing to the death of the forest.

(A) By offering additional premises that lead to a different conclusion
(B) By indicating an oversight in the logger's assumptions
(C) By reducing the logger's argument to a single, unsupported premise
(D) By showing the logger how to strengthen his own argument
(E) By inferring the motivation behind the logger's argument

231. Stuart had scheduled oral surgery for late July with the expectation that insurance would cover 85 percent of the cost, but he lost his job and thus his health insurance at the end of June. Stuart called the oral surgeon just before his appointment, got the procedure pushed to August, and managed to pay just 20 percent of the cost of the August surgery.

   Which of the following would help to explain the apparent paradox described?

   (A) Stuart's original employer negotiated a new plan with Stuart's union.
   (B) The oral surgeon rescheduled Stuart for a time of year with few surgeries.
   (C) In July, Stuart was hired by an employer with an 80/20 health insurance policy.
   (D) Stuart decided to have just two wisdom teeth pulled instead of all four.
   (E) The cost of health care in Stuart's city declined by a small amount in July.

232. Donnelly School District is contemplating joining a central business office consortium, or CBO. They may use such a consortium for payroll, purchasing, and even human resources. The head of the consortium insists that the savings in personnel more than make up for the cost of joining, and the service is just as good as an in-house business office would be.

   Which of the following would be least relevant in evaluating the argument presented?

   (A) How many personnel does Donnelly currently pay to conduct the services performed by the consortium?
   (B) Would Donnelly need to retain any business office personnel to oversee the work of the consortium?
   (C) Is the staff at the CBO as well trained and competent as Donnelly's current staff is?
   (D) How many other school districts have joined the consortium over the last several years?
   (E) Since joining, have the members of the consortium been satisfied with the level of service provided?

Anyone who completes the training session before noon will be allowed to take the rest of the day off. Helene completed the training by 11:30, so she will be taking the rest of the day off.

The reasoning in the preceding argument most closely parallels which of the following?

(A) Solutions with a pH less than 7 are considered acidic. Human skin has a pH of around 5.5. Therefore, human skin is acidic.

(B) The Hadda beetle is in the class Insecta. All members of that class are part of the phylum Arthropoda. Arachnids are also members of Arthropoda. Therefore, the Hadda beetle is an arachnid.

(C) The fee to access Sulphur Creek Reservoir for boating is $3 on weekdays and $5 on weekends. Today is not Saturday or Sunday, so the fee will be $3.

(D) The lyricist of "Many Sorrows" is the brother of the man who composed the tune. The composers of "Recently" are not brothers. The men who wrote "Many Sorrows" must have had nothing to do with the writing of "Recently."

(E) Passerine birds of the crow family include the carrion crow and the fan-tailed raven, which is similar in size but has very large wings. The members of the scout troop noticed two members of the crow family with large wings. They assumed that those were fan-tailed ravens.

234. Harvard has partnered with MIT to design a new form of grading software for students who are enrolled in massive open online courses (MOOCs). The software offers students immediate feedback, but it limits the teaching connection that takes place as a professor red-pencils a student's argument. Software can pull out obvious errors such as misplaced modifiers or passive voice, but it cannot tell students why misplaced modifiers result in misleading communication or how to make their voice more active.

The previous argument is structured to lead to what conclusion?

(A) We can expect more large courses to use this software in the future.

(B) Software is no replacement for direct discourse with a professor.

(C) No one learned to write by designing grading software.

(D) Grading software needs to grow in sophistication and complexity.

(E) Professors should use grading software only to supplement their lectures.

235. Facebook appears to be losing popularity with teenagers, just as its popularity grows with adults. That may not be coincidence: Some teens point out that they are annoyed when their older relatives comment on their posts, and that they do not wish to read the long posts and links that adults tend to include. Teens are rapidly turning to Instagram and Twitter, quick, snappy apps that better appeal to their short attention spans.

This conclusion relies on which of the following presuppositions?

(A) Facebook is slower and stodgier than Instagram and Twitter.
(B) Teenagers are never loyal to social networking sites.
(C) Adults will soon leave Facebook for Twitter and Instagram, too.
(D) Facebook was once far more popular with adults than with teens.
(E) Social networking may be too complex for today's teenagers.

236. Health care in the United States is often viewed as managing disease, not managing health. As a nation, we spend 75 percent of healthcare dollars on healthcare costs due to chronic illnesses such as diabetes or coronary heart disease. If we focused on supporting lifestyle changes that might prevent those diseases, we would save billions.

Which of the following, if true, would most bolster the preceding argument?

(A) Angioplasties and stents cost $60 billion a year but do not prevent heart attacks or prolong life in most patients.
(B) One insurance company saved $30,000 per patient in the first year on those who participated in a lifestyle-altering program.
(C) Prediabetes and type 2 diabetes are estimated to affect millions of Americans over the next decade.
(D) Lifestyle choices may include what we eat, how much stress we endure, and whether or not we smoke.
(E) New high-tech diagnostic tools enable doctors to predict who will suffer from heart disease in the future.

237. The British divided up Cetshwayo's kingdom into 13 mini-chiefdoms, granting 11 to Zulus, 1 to a pro-British Basuto chief, and 1 to a white African mercenary. This plan led to many years of civil war, and in 1882 the British restored Cetshwayo to his throne, leaving his son in charge of a nearby territory. In 1883 that son joined with a band of Boer mercenaries and invaded his father's kraal, forcing his father into exile, where he soon died under mysterious circumstances.

If the previous statements are true, which of the following must be true?

(A) Boer mercenaries took advantage of civil war to gain power.
(B) More than 10 times more Zulus than Basutos lived in Cetshwayo's kingdom.
(C) Had the British not restored Cetshwayo, war would have continued.
(D) One effect of British imperialist policies on Africa was civil war.
(E) Pro-British rulers often came to bad ends in 1880s Africa.

238. Expanding the Marbury Mall would be the wrong decision. **Although the present mall has a small footprint compared to other local malls, its size is adequate for the population.** Expecting that large numbers of people will travel across the lake and over the mountains to visit a mall when their malls are just as good is foolish.

In the preceding argument, the portion in boldface plays which of the following roles?

(A) The first clause offers a valid premise, and the second concludes the argument.

(B) The first clause anticipates a counterargument, and the second responds to that counterargument.

(C) The first clause presents the author's conclusion, and the second supplies evidence in support.

(D) The first clause presents evidence in support of the conclusion, and the second presents evidence in opposition.

(E) The first clause offers a premise in support of the conclusion, and the second presents an assumption.

239. The cruise ship docked in Florida a day early following an outbreak of gastrointestinal illness among passengers and crew. At least 110 passengers out of 1,900 reported symptoms, and 3 out of 750 crew members fell ill as the ship sailed through the Gulf of Mexico after spending two days in Havana. This latest outbreak led cruise line shares to sink 5 percent as tourists everywhere cancelled planned cruises, citing health hazards.

The conclusion tourists drew relies on which of these presuppositions?

(A) An illness rate of less than 10 percent is insignificant.

(B) Sailing through the Gulf of Mexico carries a risk.

(C) Crew members are responsible for illness on cruise ships.

(D) Caribbean cruises pose higher risks than European cruises.

(E) The gastrointestinal illness was contracted on board ship.

240. A local school district is considering outsourcing its IT work to an outside agency. The agency promised the school board that it could save the district $100,000 a year in salaries and benefits, and that it would continue to receive the same 24/7 service currently available from its two district employees.

Which of the following most undermines the preceding argument?

(A) The current district employees earn a total of $150,000 in salaries alone.

(B) One district employee recently spent a weekend repairing a damaged server.

(C) The agency has access to workers with a wide range of IT specialties.

(D) Unlike the district, the agency uses hourly workers who are eligible for overtime.

(E) The agency has offered to hire one of the laid-off district employees.

241. At the airport, animal carriers are the last to be loaded onto planes so that they may be the first to be unloaded. Unfortunately, this means that animals are often left on the tarmac in very hot or cold weather for long periods of time. Passengers should think twice about taking their animals with them on plane trips; the animals will be more comfortable staying with a house sitter or spending time in a nice kennel.

Which additional piece of evidence would best support this conclusion?

(A) The process of vaccinating and microchipping pets for international travel may take months.

(B) Certain breeds of dog, especially those with short nasal passages, travel less well than others.

(C) More than two million pets and other live animals are transported by air every year.

(D) Like the cabin where human passengers fly, the cargo hold is pressurized.

(E) The recent death by hypothermia of a hairless kitten on a commercial flight made headlines.

242. The Dryden Rotary has adopted a stretch of highway and conducts cleanups twice a year. Participants have noticed that the spring cleanup is easy, with little trash in the ditches and along the road. The fall cleanup, on the other hand, often takes several hours and involves dozens of trash bags.

Which of the following, if true, would best explain the discrepancy described?

(A) Fewer Rotarians are available to help in the early spring cleanup; more attend the fall cleanup.

(B) The stretch of highway has peak traffic between the hours of 7 a.m. and 9 a.m. and again just after 5 p.m.

(C) Having spent the long winter indoors for the most part, the Rotarians enjoy cleaning up in springtime.

(D) Spring is a time of renewal, whereas fall is the time when nature seems to die back.

(E) People are more likely to throw trash out of an open car window in summer than in winter.

243. Following a survey of all employees, Rebar Associates built a small gym in the basement to accommodate workers' wishes. The CEO expressed his strong belief that such an addition would create a more productive workplace.

The answer to which of the following questions would be most useful in evaluating the value of the gym to productivity?

(A) Is there an upswing in output in the hour following workers' workouts?
(B) Does every worker take advantage of the gym at least weekly?
(C) Do more workers use the gym at lunchtime or after work hours?
(D) How have other firms incorporated healthful activities for their workers?
(E) Are workers losing weight and eating healthier foods?

244. George Thomson's concept of wave-particle duality, the notion that matter and light have properties of both waves and particles, was critical to the development of quantum mechanics. It was not a particularly new concept, having roots as far back as Isaac Newton's insistence that light is composed of particles.

The author's claim that George Thomson's work was critical to quantum mechanics could best be supported by the inclusion of

(A) the theories of light proposed by Isaac Newton and Christiaan Huygens
(B) experiments showing the results of gravity on light and sound waves
(C) de Broglie's equation relating wavelength to momentum
(D) a definition of quantum mechanics that mentions wave-particle duality
(E) excerpts from Thomson's Nobel Prize acceptance speech

245. How does the school board member respond to the developer in the following?

DEVELOPER: Building this complex across from the high school will help the school district. It will bring in needed taxes by increasing the population in the village. Children in the complex will be able to walk to school with ease, and we will pay to add a crosswalk and a light.

SCHOOL BOARD MEMBER: Although we appreciate the crosswalk and light and understand that you have the freedom to build whatever you want on your property, it is incorrect to suggest that this complex will increase the tax base by increasing the population. Although you will pay property tax on the development, your clients will be renters and will pay no taxes at all.

(A) By offering a counterexample to the developer's suggestion
(B) By revealing an assumption that bolsters the developer's argument
(C) By demonstrating a fatal flaw in the developer's premise
(D) By showing a disconnection between the developer's key points
(E) By drawing a conclusion about the developer's motivation

246. After one of her German shepherds developed a skin allergy, Rhonda changed the dog's food on advice from the vet. Although the dog's coat turned shiny and sleek over the next several weeks, the dog continued to scratch its neck and lick its paws.

Which of the following, if true, would help to explain the discrepancy described?

(A) The sleekness of the dog's coat was caused by oils in the new food.
(B) Rhonda fed the dog somewhat more than the vet had suggested.
(C) German shepherds are susceptible to a variety of allergens.
(D) Rhonda's vet received money from the dog food company.
(E) The dog's allergen was airborne rather than food based.

247. In the Chicano neighborhoods of the southwestern United States, political muralism still explodes onto bare walls in the form of graffiti. Edward Seymour's 1949 invention of canned spray paint provided would-be artists with an easy mode of expression, and the graffiti mural took off as an art form in the 1960s and 1970s. It began as "outlaw art," but it rapidly _____.

Which of the following best completes the passage?

(A) left the prisons and moved into the world of suburbia
(B) drew critics for its lack of formalism and petty politics
(C) lost its artistic quality and became almost mundane
(D) devolved into the messy ravings of teenage hoodlums
(E) acquired a kind of cachet as an exciting form of public art

248. It is rapidly becoming possible to execute cyber-scams without having the victim download anything at all. New threat reports show that criminals are targeting smartphones because they are filled with personal information and are often wide open. Your computer at work, protected by firewalls and malware detection software, is likely to be far safer than your mobile device.

Which of the following is an assumption made in drawing this conclusion?

(A) Mobile devices are unprotected by firewalls.
(B) Computers are unaffected by cyber-scams.
(C) People store personal information on mobile devices only.
(D) It is not necessary to download anything to a mobile phone.
(E) People use their smartphones in unprotected areas.

249. Lawn signs for candidates are nothing but annoying eyesores. Every October, they litter the landscape, but surely no one's vote is captured by a simple blue-on-white or white-on-red sign. It would be better by far if candidates spent a few days before the election meeting with as many constituents as possible. This would likely garner more votes than any irritating signs might do.

Which of the following, if true, would most weaken this conclusion?

(A) Despite the increased cost, many politicians are moving toward more visible four-color signage.
(B) Successful candidates spend hours going door-to-door and meeting their constituents.
(C) Consumers and voters need to see a brand or name seven times before they retain it.
(D) Certain neighborhoods and villages have rules or laws about size and placement of signs.
(E) White lettering on a blue background is more visible from the roadway than other color combinations.

250. Once the bones found under a parking lot in Leicester were definitively proven to be those of King Richard III, a custody battle began. Officials in Leicester determined that the bones should be reinterred in a local cathedral, while citizens of the city of York immediately began a petition drive calling for the king to return to that city. Richard had no connection to Leicester, other than having been killed nearby. It seems obvious that York is the better of the two options.

The author's conclusion would be most strengthened if it were found that

(A) Richard had in fact spent his teenage years near Leicester
(B) Richard wrote of his desire to be buried in York's cathedral
(C) there is a Richard III Museum in the city of York
(D) Leicester, like York, has mounted a petition campaign
(E) Shakespeare called Richard's brother "this son of York"

251. The Olympic Committee intends to drop wrestling from the 2020 Games. This is not the wrestling that is more like acting and involves costumes and masks; it is the wrestling that was part of the first Olympics in 708 BC and continues to be a respected sport today in most places in the world. Wrestling is not confined to athletic powerhouses such as Russia and the United States; many of the Olympic winners have come from smaller countries where wrestling is held in high esteem. So when the committee suggests that wrestling might lack "relevance" in today's world of sports, whom are they addressing?

The preceding argument is structured to lead to what conclusion?

(A) After all, badminton is still on the roster, and it was certainly not around in Greece in 708 BC.

(B) Perhaps if Olympians start wearing costumes and masks, they can convince the committee to keep their sport.

(C) Other sports that are often won by athletes from small countries include fencing and weightlifting.

(D) The committee should remember that it represents all Olympians, not just a select few, and they should retain wrestling as a sport in the Summer Games.

(E) The Olympic Committee should be disbanded and replaced by a nonpartisan group of former athletes.

252. The Cockneys, traditionally, were those working-class citizens born within earshot of the bells of St. Mary-le-Bow, Cheapside. The word itself was a slap at the ignorant townsfolk by country gentry, who likened their urban brothers and sisters to deformed eggs, known as "cokeney" or "cock's eggs."

The previous statements most strongly support which of the following conclusions?

(A) Cockneys no longer exist in the traditional sense.

(B) Since a cock cannot lay eggs, *cockney* means "unworkable."

(C) Certain country dwellers were once worldlier than town dwellers.

(D) Cheapside lies very near the rural outskirts of London.

(E) Being compared to farm creatures was once a great insult.

253. Since the 1985 NCAA "March Madness" tournament, only once have all four number 1 seeds made it to the Final Four. In fact, three times, none of the top four number 1 seeds competed in the Final Four. The lowest seed to make it to the Final Four was ranked number 11 in its conference. Based on this, it's fair to predict that this year's Final Four will contain no more than two number 1 teams.

The prediction is based on which of the following assumptions?

(A) Past performance is an indication of future outcomes.
(B) Upsets rarely happen in the March Madness tournament.
(C) Teams ranked number 1 are invariably the best teams out there.
(D) The way teams are ranked has little to do with ability.
(E) Most years, two number 1 teams have competed against each other.

254. Before enrolling their daughter in preschool, Dawn and her husband called five of the families whose children had attended the preschool in the previous year.

The answer to which of the following questions would be most useful in evaluating the value of Dawn's calls to the families?

(A) Did any of the families have more than one child who had attended the preschool?
(B) Were the families given as references by the preschool, or were they randomly chosen?
(C) Were all five of the former preschool attendees still living in the area?
(D) Has Dawn's daughter had any previous experience in a home daycare setting?
(E) Was this the only preschool that Dawn and her husband were considering for their child?

255. A mosquito infestation in 2010 was blamed on high temperatures and unusually damp weather, which combined to create the warm puddles in which the insects breed. In 2011 the mosquito population was down significantly. The weather was probably less tropical that year, providing fewer opportunities for breeding.

Which of the following, if true, provides the strongest support for the preceding argument?

(A) Mosquitoes breed prolifically in semitropical climates.
(B) Drought conditions in the summer of 2011 harmed several crops.
(C) Mosquitoes were carriers of West Nile virus in several areas.
(D) Spraying of mosquitoes was widespread across the region.
(E) Mosquitoes need no more than a few inches of water in which to lay eggs.

256. Students in a nutrition lab ran an atomic absorption spectrophotometer, checking for amounts of zinc in the digestive products of astronauts. The students found trace amounts of zinc in each of the samples they tested. They concluded that some characteristic of space travel yet to be determined caused zinc to be poorly absorbed.

Which of the following most undermines this conclusion?

(A) The amount of zinc in astronaut by-products was equivalent to that in tests performed on other humans of similar ages and weights.

(B) The atomic absorption spectrophotometer was also used to test for concentrations of sodium, potassium, and magnesium.

(C) Zinc plays a critical role in protein synthesis, cell division, immune function, and other aspects of cellular metabolism.

(D) Zinc deficiency is rare but may appear in alcoholics, certain vegetarians, and people with sickle-cell disease.

(E) Because gravity does not exist above our atmosphere, space toilets use suction to draw waste into a holding container.

257. The admissions department at Cranmore College revealed that although test scores and transcripts are certainly important, Cranmore's foremost interest is in building an entering class that is diverse in all ways—racially, culturally, economically, geographically, and so on. Thus, in the unlikely but possible event that they are comparing two application packets from would-be freshmen from Paducah, both with stunning scores and A averages from their neighboring high schools, admissions officers may reject one of the applicants _____.

Which of the following best completes the passage?

(A) simply due to his proximity to the other

(B) because her scores are a few points lower

(C) as being unready for Cranmore's rigor

(D) without even examining extracurriculars

(E) if the concentration he desires is overpopulated

258. Coloration in Labrador retrievers is complicated. The main alleles are sometimes described this way:

B = black
b = chocolate
E = able to express dark coat color
e = unable to express dark coat color

Yellow labs, then, always have a genotype that ends in ee; it could be BBee, Bbee, or bbee. Black labs must have a dominant B and a dominant E; they may be BBEe, BbEe, BBEE, or BbEE. Chocolates have recessive b and dominant E; they may be bbEe or bbEE.

Two black labs were bred, and all of the puppies were yellow. What explains this apparent discrepancy?

(A) Both parents had genotypes BBee.
(B) Both parents had genotypes BbEe.
(C) Both parents had genotypes BBEE.
(D) Both parents had genotypes BbEE.
(E) Both parents had genotypes bbEe.

259. How does the editorial director respond to the marketing manager in the following exchange?

MARKETING MANAGER: With the public's new awareness of the Common Core State Standards, it is logical to assume that parents will soon exhibit concern about their children's ability to perform well on 21st-century assessments. Because of this concern, and the current void in the market, we strongly suggest that we develop a series of related test prep books for home use.

EDITORIAL DIRECTOR: It is worth recalling that such a preemptive move was a great moneymaker when we first entered the state testing market. Parents snapped up our titles in most of the 50 states in an effort to prepare their children for that high-stakes testing. Can we afford to miss this opportunity?

(A) By presenting a counterargument that suggests a change in direction
(B) By pointing out a minor flaw in the marketing manager's assumptions
(C) By demonstrating a reason for holding back on the marketing manager's proposal
(D) By asking a question that challenges one of the marketing manager's premises
(E) By offering an example that bolsters the marketing manager's argument

260. The average wage for recent community college graduates in Tennessee this year is $38,948, more than $1,300 higher than the average salaries for graduates of the state's four-year colleges and universities. In Virginia, recent community college graduates make an average of $40,000 at what are considered "middle-skills" jobs. That's almost $2,500 more than recent bachelor's degree recipients. Since an associate's degree from a community college costs significantly less than a four-year degree, it's time to consider community college a great investment for any and all high school graduates.

Which of the following is an assumption made in drawing this conclusion?

(A) Costs of degrees will remain similar for the next decade or two.
(B) All high school graduates aim for careers in "middle-skill" jobs.
(C) Graduates of four-year colleges are less skilled than community college students.
(D) $2,500 a year is not worth the stigma of an associate's degree.
(E) The number of applicants to community colleges is rapidly increasing.

261. At great expense, the people of Freeburg banded together to replace the old wooden playground with a brand-new play structure made from recycled plastics. The mayor cut the ribbon, claiming that parents' safety concerns about arsenic and splinters could now be laid to rest. Nevertheless, within the first week of operation, two children ended up in the clinic with wooden splinters embedded in their hands.

Which of the following, if true, would help to explain the discrepancy described?

(A) Recycled plastic can crack at points of severe pressure.
(B) Arsenic is a by-product of the preservative once used to pressure treat lumber.
(C) Some of the old materials were left piled behind the new playground.
(D) People may get splinters from glass, metal, or fragments of plastic.
(E) Splinters typically lodge in the subcutaneous layer of the skin.

262. The company began turning a profit after five years, realizing most of its income each year from the sale of medical supplies, with a consistent 5 percent coming from consulting for pharmaceutical companies.

Which of the following statements can be inferred from the preceding statement?

(A) The company is seeing steady growth in its sale of medical supplies.
(B) Consulting should play a larger role if the company is to grow.
(C) Income from consulting has not grown in five years.
(D) Total dollar sales have remained relatively constant over five years.
(E) Consulting consistently earns less than sales of medical supplies.

263. Sam is known in his neighborhood for his two large Great Danes, which he walks to and from the park with regularity. Occasionally, he drives around in his SUV with one or another of the dogs in the passenger seat. One of Sam's neighbors was recently surprised to see Sam at the vet with a pet carrier too small to hold a beagle, much less a Great Dane. He asked Sam later whether Sam had been taking care of someone else's pet, but Sam said no.

Which of the following, if true, would best explain the discrepancy described?

(A) Great Danes grow two or three inches a month in their first year of life.
(B) Sam arrived at the vet's with an empty pet carrier and left with one of his dogs.
(C) Sam's dogs were staying at the vet overnight after receiving their shots.
(D) The animal in the pet carrier belonged to Sam's neighbor.
(E) Sam owns several domestic rabbits in addition to his Great Danes.

264. Most developing nations are wrestling with the problem of how to care for an aging population. According to a new study, European nations are generally providing better for their older citizens, based on indicators of life expectancy, healthcare spending, physician accessibility, and out-of-pocket spending ability. Instead of looking at retirement communities in the United States, which ranked 19th below the Slovak Republic, U.S. retirees should consider moving to Luxembourg, Switzerland, or Norway.

Which of the following is an assumption made in drawing this conclusion?

(A) Physician accessibility is less critical than overall healthcare spending.
(B) Life expectancy is higher in the Slovak Republic than in Norway.
(C) Immigrants from the United States would receive the same benefits as Europeans.
(D) Moving to Luxembourg is easier than buying into a retirement community.
(E) A retirement community anywhere is no guarantee of a healthy lifestyle.

265. Two members of the Constitutional Accountability Center think tank recently posted an opinion about cameras in the Supreme Court. At present, the Court does not allow cameras, due to the justices' belief that their questions and comments might be taken out of context and the seriousness of the proceedings impinged upon. The writers point out that this "sound biting" of opinions and arguments is already taking place, since reporters may write about the proceedings, and those writings may lead to phrases taken out of context and even lampooned in editorials or on late-night television. They argue that what they call the "majesty" of the hearings is an impressive and educational experience that can only be felt by watching the debates live.

The writers' argument is structured to lead to what conclusion?

(A) Sound bites should be forbidden, and only full coverage allowed.
(B) Reporters should not be allowed to take quotes out of context.
(C) Camera coverage of the hearings would be a service to the public.
(D) Lampooning the justice system is inappropriate and disrespectful.
(E) The justices are correct when they suggest that their words may be misconstrued.

266. Results from a recent study indicated that adults who eat a healthy diet including yogurt with live cultures suffer less frequently from gastric diseases of varying types. Therefore, adults with a history of gastric diseases should start eating yogurt.

The reasoning in the preceding argument most closely parallels which of the following?

(A) A clothing shop recently determined that it would do better marketing to a younger audience. With that in mind, it began advertising in places where students would see its ads.
(B) It is clear from the census that a preponderance of wealthy citizens live in the suburbs of eastern cities. Apparently, people who want to make money should move east.
(C) Every Friday, the Dairy Bar gives away free samples of frozen yogurt. It is now Friday, so we can probably visit the Dairy Bar for some free samples.
(D) Kris was sure that her score on the exam was higher than that of her peers. After talking with some friends, she discovered that several had higher scores than she did. Now she believes that her score is lower than that of her peers.
(E) Driving students who watched the video tended to pass their test on the first try, but so did students who simply practiced driving on a simulator. To get a 100 percent passing rate, the driving school should insist that all students both watch the video and use the simulator.

267. Citing her strong belief that municipalities needed to curb property taxes and would only do so if forced, the governor called for a 2 percent cap on the property tax levy, to be implemented immediately. The cap may only be overridden by a two-thirds vote of a county's legislators.

Which of the following must be studied in order to evaluate the argument presented?

(A) Do any counties currently have a property tax levy under 2 percent?
(B) Do one-third of the county legislators support the idea of a tax cap?
(C) Have taxes risen significantly in the past 5 to 10 years?
(D) In other states with a cap, has the overall property tax rate declined substantially?
(E) Is it possible to curb spending and thus to slow down the growth of taxes?

268. The karat rating of gold is based on this equation: $x = 24 \ (M_g/M_m)$, where x is the karat rating, M_g is the mass of gold in the material, and M_m is the total mass of the material. Thus, 18-karat gold is 75 percent gold—18 parts gold and 6 parts copper or some other metal. However, 24-karat gold jewelry is typically only about 99.9 percent gold.

Which of the following, if true, would best explain the paradox described?

(A) When gold is pounded or twisted, bits of it may flake off.
(B) The value of M_m is less for jewelry than for a gold bar.
(C) Gold is too soft to be used in pure form in jewelry.
(D) Gold jewelry has less value than other gold objects.
(E) Alloys of gold may contain silver, copper, platinum, or zinc.

269. In order to win the Triple Crown, a horse must win the Kentucky Derby, the Preakness, and the Belmont Stakes. The Derby comes first, on the first Saturday in May, and attendance is always far higher there than at either the Preakness or the Belmont. This is almost certainly because Triple Crown winners are so rare that racing fans lose interest quickly after the Derby is over.

Which of the following undermines the preceding argument?

(A) The Derby is a 1¼-mile course, the Preakness is 1³⁄₁₆ miles, and the Belmont is longest at 1½ miles.
(B) All three races are for three-year-old thoroughbred colts or fillies only.
(C) Although the Belmont Stakes is the oldest of the Triple Crown races, the Derby is more steeped in tradition and pageantry.
(D) Since 1930, the Belmont has been run five weeks after the Derby and three weeks after the Preakness.
(E) In the history of the Triple Crown, only 11 horses have won all three races.

270. Marcos planned to attend either Harvard or Wharton. No matter which one he attended, he knew that he would spend his first three years after school in an internship with his family's business before moving into a management position. Marcos was accepted into Wharton. Therefore, he expects to start his internship after graduation.

Which of the following is most like the previous argument in its logical structure?

(A) If Stu got into Cornell, he planned to study Industrial and Labor Relations. If he studied Industrial and Labor Relations, he would look for a job in management after college. Stu got into Cornell, so he will look for a job in management when he graduates.

(B) A certain singer was offered contracts by two record companies. The first record company promised her a full tour schedule and a two-record deal. The second company promised her three records and an abbreviated U.S. tour. The singer is now touring Asia. She must have accepted the first company's deal.

(C) The cost of a park pass will go up on July 1, so many people are purchasing passes today. Today must be a date in June.

(D) The point of this survey is to reach as many nonvoters as possible. Because of that, we have not used voter rolls to find our participants but are instead sending out mailers based on motor vehicles records.

(E) Villagers could vote for or against Proposition A in November's election. In either case, the water project would go ahead as planned. Most villagers voted against the proposition. Nevertheless, the water project is expected to begin on schedule.

271. A soft drink company performed a blind taste test in which it asked a random sample of participants to try small cups of the company's current diet cola and a test cola made with a brand-new, all-natural, noncaloric sweetener. Of the participants, 9 out of 10 preferred the new test cola. The company decided to use the new sweetener in all of its products.

Which additional piece of evidence would best support this conclusion?

(A) The cost of the new sweetener is slightly higher than the one currently used.

(B) The company's sales of diet sodas have always exceeded those of sugared sodas.

(C) The soft drink company has improved its market share over the last two quarters.

(D) Another test done with orange sodas instead of colas produced similar results.

(E) There is currently no universal standard or definition for "all-natural" claims.

272. The Parks Department has an opportunity to hire 10 adolescent workers from the local juvenile facility to perform a variety of needed summer tasks for minimum wage. To hire adult workers to do the same tasks would mean paying $2/hour more per worker-hour, and the department budget is already under strain.

    The answer to which of the following questions would be least relevant to the department's decision on whether to hire the juvenile workers?

    (A) Will the department need to pay for adult supervision for the juvenile workers?

    (B) Do the juveniles have the strength to perform the required manual labor?

    (C) Are 10 juvenile workers equivalent to 10 adult workers, or could fewer adults be hired?

    (D) Do most of the tasks for the park department's summer workers take place outdoors or indoors?

    (E) Will the required hours of work meet state rules for hiring adolescent workers?

273. Lester would have received the office award for the first time if he had been able to achieve the monthly "pie in the sky" goal in sales. Once again, Lester's office mate won the award. Lester must not have met the sales goal.

    The reasoning in the preceding argument most closely parallels which of the following?

    (A) African elephants are classified as vulnerable, whereas Asian elephants are considered endangered. The elephants in our local zoo are labeled "endangered," so they must be Asian elephants.

    (B) Horses that enter to run on western tracks such as Santa Anita are scratched, usually for health reasons, a little more than 10 percent of the time. On eastern tracks such as Aqueduct, Belmont, or Saratoga, horses are scratched far more often, with about one out of five entries scratched. If you favor a particular horse, you are more likely to see it run if it is racing in Southern California than in New York.

    (C) If Bridget had signed up for a CAD class last semester, she would be eligible for the engineering seminar this semester. The seminar professor says that Bridget is not yet eligible for her class, so Bridget must not have taken the CAD prerequisite.

    (D) Newfoundland and Labrador, which make up the easternmost province of Canada, have a combined area of around 405,000 square kilometers. Although Labrador is significantly larger, more than 90 percent of the province's population lives on the Island of Newfoundland and its surrounding smaller islands, meaning that Labrador is sparsely populated.

    (E) Scottish Gaelic is not the same as Scots. Unlike Scots, which is Germanic in origin, Scottish Gaelic is a Celtic language. Although it is similar to Irish Gaelic, it is recognized as a separate language.

274. Quagmire, Inc. has experienced a high turnover of IT directors, with four recent hires lasting less than two years apiece. To rectify the situation, the CEO has decided to increase the pay for the next director by 15 percent, thus providing a more attractive and competitive package for recruits.

Which of the following must be studied in order to evaluate the validity of the CEO's plan?

(A) Do workers at Quagmire have flexible hours?
(B) Does Quagmire need to update its technology plan?
(C) Are the computers at Quagmire in good condition?
(D) How many people does the IT director supervise?
(E) Are the IT directors leaving for more lucrative positions?

275. Frédéric Chopin, the brilliant Polish composer and pianist, from childhood withstood a series of lung infections that sapped his strength and rendered him weak and listless. His death at a young age (39) was assumed for many years to have been from consumption, or tuberculosis. However, in 2008, a new theory was proposed—that Chopin had in fact suffered from cystic fibrosis.

Which of the following, if true, would most weaken the new theory about Chopin's illness?

(A) An 1829 portrait of Chopin shows him with the pale skin typical of consumptives.
(B) As late as 1959, the median survival rate of patients with cystic fibrosis was six months.
(C) The gene mutation that causes cystic fibrosis is most prevalent in people of European descent.
(D) The first accurate description of cystic fibrosis was made by American doctor Dorothy Hansine Andersen.
(E) Lung diseases include infections such as pneumonia and influenza and disorders such as asthma and COPD.

276. The director of technology is working out a deal for the new overseas initiative. Either Dell will provide PCs or Apple will provide iPads for the four schools to be built in the Northern Territories. Apple cannot provide the iPads. Therefore, the schools will receive PCs from Dell.

Which of the following is most like the preceding argument in its logical structure?

(A) Our new swimsuit line was to be manufactured either from the traditional spandex material or potentially from a new elastic fabric from India. Because the fabric from India will not be available in time, we will continue to work with spandex.

(B) Supplies of grain to Somalia went by ship until piracy became a serious issue along that country's coastline. Today, grain is often airlifted in, or it is brought with some difficulty overland.

(C) A burro is a small donkey, whereas a mule is a cross between a male donkey and a female horse. Because horse-donkey crosses are nearly always sterile, mules cannot reproduce.

(D) Software applications for most PCs include word processing, databases, spreadsheets, and so on. In the early days of personal computing, owners often had to write their own programs. Today the owner who knows even the basics about his or her applications is rare.

(E) If Desmond and Maria get married in June, then her relatives from Colombia will make the trip north. If Maria's relatives travel north, the couple will postpone their honeymoon to spend time with the family. So if the wedding takes place in June, the honeymoon will happen at a later date.

277. A worker at Durwood Industries recently proposed to an OSHA inspector that Durwood be required to retrain workers annually in safety techniques. Although Durwood has an initial safety workshop for new recruits, it does not require longtime workers to retrain, and older workers tend to be the ones who end up on disability.

Which of the following questions would be most useful in evaluating the worker's claim?

(A) How much is Durwood currently paying out in disability benefits?
(B) Has Durwood recently updated any equipment or techniques?
(C) Who currently provides the safety instruction for new hires?
(D) What is the average age of a new recruit at Durwood Industries?
(E) Are older workers receiving injuries due to negligence or just to age?

278. Stocks tumbled on April 5 following a disappointing jobs report that showed the lowest monthly gain in nearly a year. Typically, when the labor force participation rate sinks, investors defect from stocks and rush to safer havens. As expected, _____.

Which of the following best completes the passage?

(A) nearly 500,000 people dropped entirely out of the labor market
(B) gold and U.S. Treasuries gained a good deal of ground overnight
(C) the Labor Department's monthly report showed gains below expectations
(D) economists had predicted a gain of close to 190,000 jobs
(E) a couple of health-related stocks were up in early trading

279. Lake Zakher is a man-made lake in the United Arab Emirates and a favorite spot for birdwatchers. It is the unexpected by-product of a system of desalination in the desert. Despite its beauty, the lake is something of an ecological nightmare, according to many biologists, who fear that its unnatural addition to the landscape will damage a fragile ecosystem.

Which additional piece of evidence, if true, would best support this conclusion?

(A) The process of desalination releases salt water into the ocean.
(B) UAE authorities hope to encourage water conservation and recycling.
(C) Herons and teal now nest along the shores of the new lake.
(D) The UAE uses more energy per capita than any nation in the world.
(E) Humidity from evaporation has adversely affected desert insects near the lake.

280. The Pritzker Architecture Prize, considered the Nobel Prize of architecture, has been awarded annually since 1971 to a living architect whose body of built work embodies "talent, vision, and commitment." There have been only two female recipients of the award, one in 2004 and one in 2010. In future years, we can expect the numbers of male and female winners to equalize, since graduates of architecture schools are now nearly 40 percent female.

Which of the following, if true, would most seriously weaken the author's conclusion?

(A) The Pritzker Award is sponsored by the Hyatt Foundation.
(B) The two female recipients were born in Iraq and in Japan.
(C) Only 12 percent of practicing architects are women.
(D) The most recent winner was a male architect from Japan.
(E) Public buildings and corporate structures earn the most accolades.

281. Italy's credit rating received another downgrade recently, which came as no surprise either to Italians or to those who watch the markets. The recession in Italy is one of the worst in Europe. What really caused the downgrade, however, was almost certainly Italy's continued political instability.

The conclusion drawn in the final sentence logically depends on which of the following?

(A) Other nations in Europe have greater political stability.
(B) Political stability is important for economic growth.
(C) Credit downgrades are based on economics, not politics.
(D) Italy's credit rating is still investment-grade.
(E) A new government may be formed over the next few weeks.

282. As more and more taxpayers file their returns electronically, the IRS is reporting fewer errors. Prior to this, the most common error was the miscalculation of tax owed. Exemptions and earned income tax credits were frequently reported incorrectly. While some errors still occur, plugging in numbers from a W-2 form and having a computer do the calculations greatly reduces the chance of math mistakes.

The previous statements most strongly support which of the following conclusions?

(A) Filing electronically leads to a likelihood of quicker, more accurate refunds.
(B) A computer is able to analyze whether someone can claim an exemption.
(C) People fail to report exemptions and credits because they do not think they qualify.
(D) Either individuals or tax preparers may elect to file electronically.
(E) It is difficult to miscalculate tax owed when a computer does the math.

283. Wheaton Gun Factory closed in the 1960s, but recently a number of carcinogens in the soil surrounding the shuttered plant have been discovered. Walter Mann of Toxic Mapping described CTBs leaching into the soil as far as a quarter mile away, yet neighbors living closer to the plant, on Hilltop Road, had no contamination at all in their yards.

Which of the following is the most likely explanation for the discrepancy described?

(A) Hilltop Road is uphill from the plant, and CTBs flowed downhill with runoff.
(B) CTBs cannot leach into soil that is in residential neighborhoods.
(C) Toxins from the shuttered plant were also found in drinking water.
(D) Walter Mann failed to test farther than half a mile from the gun factory.
(E) CTBs are just one of the six toxins that Toxic Mapping found in the area.

284. At daycare centers in Israel where a fine was imposed on parents who picked up their children late, researchers found that parents responded not by arriving on time but by arriving even later, despite the fine. Economist Samuel Bowles posits that this is because the fine created a negative synergy between ethical behavior and economic incentives and allowed parents to consider lateness just another purchasable commodity.

Which of the following investigations is most likely to yield significant information that would help to evaluate the economist's hypothesis?

(A) Was the fine high enough to constitute a financial hardship for most parents?

(B) Did parents with more than one child in the daycare center tend to arrive later?

(C) Was the amount of the fine the same from one daycare center to another?

(D) How did teachers react to the inconvenience of having parents arrive even later?

(E) Did parents who once arrived on time begin arriving late with the advent of the fine?

285. Chelsea Clinton recently wrote about the older generation's portrayal of millennials as money-hungry, cell-phone-addicted, social-media-obsessed youngsters who want everything to happen now, now, now. Yes, Clinton admits, millennials are "all about the money," but they are about money as it related to opportunity—about sharing wealth and developing growth and fixing fiscal challenges. Yes, they love their phones and their Facebook, but many are using both to promote discourse on critical issues. Yes, they are impatient, but perhaps their impatience reflects the fact that progress has been too slow.

Clinton's argument is structured to lead to what conclusion?

(A) If their parents had accomplished what they should have accomplished, millennials would not be so impatient.

(B) The millennials have a lot to teach their elders about achieving prosperity and opportunity.

(C) Older generations have a lot to learn about the way that their children and grandchildren think.

(D) Millennials would be wise to put away their toys and address life as bona fide adults.

(E) The millennial habits that some perceive as selfish are often altruistic and beneficial to society.

286. Although people are buying more music than ever, the introduction of iTunes and other similar online music stores has meant that revenues have plummeted for the recording industry because no one is buying whole albums anymore. Supporters of the digital industry and lovers of downloaded singles say that the fact is, people never wanted to buy entire albums and would always have preferred to buy individual songs.

Which of the following questions would be most relevant to evaluating the preceding argument?

(A) What was the difference in revenues for the record companies when cassettes gave way to CDs in the 1990s and 2000s?

(B) How can musicians use touring and merchandise sales to make up the difference in lost album sales?

(C) To fit the definition of an "album," what is the least number of songs that can be included?

(D) When records were on vinyl, how did the sale of two-song 45s compare to the sale of long-play albums?

(E) How did Apple alter the original MP3 system it purchased to make iTunes more user-friendly?

287. The laboratory had indicated that if the patent came through by September, the new drug could be on pharmacy shelves by December. The lab received its patent on August 15, so pharmacies can expect to have their first orders filled before the end of the year.

Which of the following supports its conclusion in the same way as the preceding argument?

(A) Because the Qur'an is written in Classical Arabic, the language is considered sacred by most Muslims. Modern Standard Arabic differs in only a few ways from Classical Arabic, and both have much in common with Hebrew and Aramaic.

(B) Patent medicine, despite its name, is not patented. In the 1600s, medical elixirs that were favored by the Crown were issued letters patent endorsing them. Receiving a royal endorsement, however, was no indication that the medicine was worthy or even safe.

(C) Former Prime Minister Tony Blair declared that all profits from the sale of his 2010 memoir would be donated to the Royal British Legion, a charity that serves those who have served in the armed forces and their dependents. The book became one of the fastest-selling autobiographies in Britain, so it is safe to say that the charity received a hefty donation.

(D) Perhaps had all U.S. Allies endorsed Woodrow Wilson's Fourteen Points, Wilsonian idealism might have had a stronger and longer-lasting effect. However, Clemenceau, George, and Orlando were all skeptical, so the plan was doomed to fail.

(E) The experiment may succeed, or it may fail again. If it succeeds, we will proceed to step 2. If it fails, we will nevertheless skip ahead to step 2. In other words, no matter what results we obtain over the next few weeks, we will be launching step 2 soon.

288. Failure of citizens to participate in an election causes a number of injuries to democracy. First, elected officials cannot be said to represent the public, since a majority of the public had nothing to do with their election. Second, an apathetic electorate fails to provide oversight, so corruption becomes widespread.

If the previous statements are true, which of the following must be true?

(A) Public officials may be held accountable by the electorate.
(B) Citizens fail to vote because they do not like their choices.
(C) Corruption is not possible in a truly representative democracy.
(D) Democracy is not viable because people fail to take part in it.
(E) Elected officials represent only themselves and their families.

289. Dr. Rodriguez is an oral surgeon in Greensboro, and he is also board certified in cosmetic facial surgery. So at least one Greensboro oral surgeon is also a plastic surgeon.

Which of the following is most like the preceding argument in its logical structure?

(A) Writing nonfiction is quite different from writing fiction, in that the former requires more research, and the latter requires more creativity. So if you are a fount of creativity but don't much like research, try your hand at fiction writing.
(B) The newest Super Shamrock Store will be built either on Route 13 or Route 42. Since there is already a Super Walmart on Route 13, the likeliest choice is Route 42.
(C) Unless the manager calls, Ralph will work the overnight shift. Right now Ralph is working the day shift, so the manager must not have called.
(D) People who order fish rather than chicken at corporate events are considered to be risk-takers. So ordering fish is a great way to let management know that you are dynamic and adventurous.
(E) Since the manager and head stylist of Bigwig Hair Salon also co-owns two restaurants in town with her husband, there is clearly a minimum of one hairstylist in town who is also a restaurateur.

290. The sales manager of Green Apple Publishing reviewed sales figures for the past five years and discovered that the company's three highest grossing books were all test prep books by Katie Xerxes. The publisher has now issued a 10-book contract to Ms. Xerxes.

The conclusion drawn is based on which of the following assumptions?

(A) Test prep makes up the bulk of Green Apple's publishing list.
(B) The need for test prep will continue to grow.
(C) Test prep books are the only books that sell well.
(D) The author is the reason for the books' popularity.
(E) Ms. Xerxes can complete one book per year.

291. Senator Furman addressed the crowd to push for the pipeline's construction. He referred to it as a "job-creating" project, saying that it would bring the unemployment rate in the region down by several percentage points and create stability in the area for decades to come.

Which of the following, if true, casts the most doubt on the senator's assertion?

(A) The project would create hundreds of temporary construction jobs over two years, but only a few dozen jobs would be permanent.

(B) Several oil spills from the already-constructed part of the pipeline have led to massive cleanups involving hundreds of workers.

(C) Some of the pipeline-related jobs are low-skill, but many involve high levels of engineering expertise.

(D) The company building the pipeline underwrote a study indicating that the project would fund more than 100,000 jobs.

(E) A group of senators and representative are holding up passage of a transportation bill until the pipeline issue is resolved.

292. A handful of people on a flight from Chicago were injured when the full plane lurched forward unexpectedly near the gate. Although the captain had just turned off the seatbelt sign, only passengers in the front of the plane were affected; passengers in the back of the crowded jet were completely unharmed.

Which of the following, if true, would best explain the discrepancy described?

(A) Flight attendants were in the process of unlocking the front door.

(B) Passengers were less crowded near the rear of the plane.

(C) Families with young children were seated in the rearmost seats.

(D) Only passengers nearest the front door had left their seats already.

(E) The captain was making an announcement when the plane lurched.

293. Many people supplement their geothermal heating systems with solar panels as a means of defraying the cost of electricity to run the heat pump. After looking into setting up solar panels, one homeowner decided to hold off, because the breakeven point of 15 years was too far in the future to make the purchase worthwhile.

Which piece of additional information would be most useful in evaluating the argument?

(A) How much does the average home in the area spend on electricity?

(B) What size heat pump did the homeowner install with his system?

(C) How long does the homeowner expect to stay in his home?

(D) Would the homeowner need to install more than one solar panel?

(E) Does solar energy production fluctuate widely with the seasons?

294. Certain yoga styles use a form of meditation designed to quiet the mind, focusing on the breath rather than on those random thoughts that flood the brain and can cause stress. There are clear biochemical responses to yoga postures and movements that decrease levels of stress-causing neurotransmitters. Most yoga students in a recent study reported feeling happier immediately after taking a class.

The preceding argument depends on which of the following assumptions?

(A) Happiness is correlated to a reduction of stress.
(B) Feeling happy is a product of intense meditation.
(C) Yoga suppresses only unhappy thoughts.
(D) Focusing on your breath is the key to happiness.
(E) The effects of yoga are entirely temporary.

295. At the awards ceremony on Tuesday, 32 high school seniors walked away with anywhere from one to three awards apiece. In all, local businesses and state colleges issued 100 awards to the participants.

Which of the following, if true, would best explain the paradox described?

(A) Most recipients received three awards.
(B) More than half of the recipients received two awards.
(C) Some recipients got awards from different companies.
(D) Colleges gave 50 awards, and businesses gave the rest.
(E) Some of the awards were given to juniors.

296. The firm will relocate either to Vermont or to Maine. If it moves to Vermont, it will take over an existing plant near Burlington. If it moves to Maine, it will need to build new. Hence, either it will move to a site near Burlington, or it will build a new plant.

Which of the following is most like the preceding argument in its logical structure?

(A) Most early aircraft used a biplane design. Although the biplane structure offers better lift and more strength than a monoplane, it also causes more drag. Thus, when speed became an issue for plane travel, most biplanes were put out of service.

(B) If Tucker Industries moves to Vermont, it will give its 60 personnel the option to move and will pay their way. If it presents the option to move, the expectation is that 50 percent of the current workforce will move with the company. Therefore, if Tucker Industries moves to Vermont, it will bring 30 employees with it.

(C) For her new bakery, Lucinda must decide whether to hire two bakers or a store manager and a baker. If she hires two bakers, Lucinda will manage the store herself. If she hires a store manager and a baker, she will spend more time in the kitchen. Therefore, either Lucinda will work as a manager or she will work in the kitchen.

(D) When corn syrup is eliminated from most products for children, the cost of those products typically goes up. The cost of Yummy Juice has stayed stable for five years. Yummy Juice must still contain corn syrup.

(E) The light is still on in the inner office, meaning either that Sarah is working on the company's books or that Letitia is drafting a revised contract for the merger. Since Letitia went home at six, the late worker must be Sarah.

297. The Miller family routinely taps several maple trees on the property and collects sap from which to make maple syrup through a long boiling process. Paul Miller notes that the ratio of sap to syrup is approximately 40 gallons of sap to 1 gallon of finished product, and that this ratio rarely varies by more than a point or so from year to year. However, this year Paul's son tracked the results from five individual trees and found that the ratio for one was closer to 60 to 1, while the other trees remained at 40 to 1.

Which of the following, if true, would best explain the discrepancy described?

(A) Paul's son tested the trees around sunset, when the sap was not running.

(B) Paul had tested the trees in early March, and his son tested in late March.

(C) Paul's son boiled some sap on a wood fire and some on a gas grill.

(D) Much of the sap Paul's son boiled was lost through evaporation.

(E) One of the trees that Paul's son tested was a red maple, not a sugar maple as the others were.

298. After seeing how well his brother, a linebacker at the university, performed on a regimen of protein shakes and vitamins, Simon decided to follow the same plan himself. He felt certain that a few months of this would improve his standing as a tennis player.

Which of the following, if true, most clearly points to a flaw in Simon's reasoning?

(A) Simon's brother has been on the regimen for several months.

(B) Protein shakes may also contain potassium and carbohydrates.

(C) Vitamins play a crucial role in converting food to energy.

(D) Taking megadoses of some vitamins can harm your health.

(E) A linebacker typically requires a muscle-building regimen.

299. People who are fond of printed books rejoiced the other day when Arthur Frommer bought back his name brand travel book line from Google, which had purchased the line from John Wiley & Sons in 2012. To some travel fans' surprise, Google seemed ready to close out the popular series, using only Frommer's maps to update and elaborate on its own Google Maps. With Frommer's repurchase of the brand, however, _____.

Which of the following best completes the passage?

(A) John Wiley & Sons will refocus its marketing

(B) travelers will be able to use either kind of map

(C) Frommer's will operate its own travel website

(D) travel guides will continue to appear in print format

(E) the series will regain the reputation it had lost

300. Carl read a report claiming that sugary drinks were responsible for obesity in teens. As a slightly overweight 13-year-old, Carl resolved to reduce his consumption of sweetened soda and juice. To his surprise, after two months of this regimen, his weight had actually increased by a few pounds.

Which of the following best explains the apparent contradiction described?

(A) To lose weight, Carl would have had to cut his consumption completely.

(B) The report only dealt with teenagers older than Carl.

(C) Two months were not enough to show a decrease in weight.

(D) Carl's weight problem was caused by something other than juice and soda.

(E) The report claiming sugary drinks caused obesity was erroneous.

301. Retail sales rose more than 1 percent last month, largely due to an increase in the sale of gasoline. However, the spike in gas prices meant that consumers failed to visit malls or restaurants as much as might have been expected. In places like suburban New Jersey, restaurants are hard-hit whenever gas prices rise.

The preceding conclusion is based on which of these assumptions?

(A) Mass transit would be beneficial to restaurants.
(B) Restaurants everywhere depend on commuters.
(C) Gas price spikes affect the East Coast most.
(D) Gas prices are rising fastest in New Jersey.
(E) Suburban residents must drive to reach restaurants.

302. Customers at the Chicken Shack on South Street purchase full meals about 50 percent of the time. The rest of the time, they purchase what the franchise refers to as "parts," which is to say a salad, an order of fries, or a small box of chicken tenders. In contrast, customers at the Chicken Shack in the mall purchase "parts" around 80 percent of the time, sitting down for meals for only one in every five purchases.

If the previous statements are true, which of the following must be true?

(A) People who visit malls must not have time to eat full meals.
(B) The Chicken Shack on South Street must take in more money.
(C) Chicken Shacks do not exhibit consistent purchasing patterns.
(D) Buying a few "parts" at a Chicken Shack is cheaper than buying a meal.
(E) Purchasing fries and chicken tenders qualifies as buying a full meal.

303. Looking over the entering freshman class, the principal told his assistant that he could easily tell which students would succeed, and which would fail. "If someone has three or more incidents in middle school that result in detention or in-house suspension, that person is going to end up failing out or dropping out of high school," he said.

Which of the following, if true, would most seriously weaken the principal's conclusion?

(A) Teacher and administrator expectations of students often manifest themselves as a self-fulfilling prophecy.
(B) The principal's high school has a graduation rate of 79 percent, with 10 percent of dropouts being transfer students.
(C) This year, the middle school reported 15 in-house suspensions and 125 students in detention, some repeat offenders.
(D) Students in detention or in-house suspension are expected to use that time to make up classwork.
(E) Studies show that because of hormonal changes, middle school students have the highest incidence of behavioral problems.

304. How does the parent respond to the teenager in the following situation?

TEENAGER: I need a new phone, and this time it should be a smartphone. All of my friends have smartphones, and it's embarrassing to be the only one without one. It doesn't need to be a super-fancy one like Bridget's or Kerry's, but it should allow me to use the apps I like.

PARENT: I accept that you need a new phone, because your old one is certainly damaged. However, the argument that all your friends have one is not very convincing. You would do better to consider how having a smartphone would improve your communication or research abilities. If you were able to demonstrate a genuine need, I might be more supportive.

(A) By offering a counterargument that undermines the teenager's argument
(B) By revealing a fatal flaw in the teenager's assumptions about smartphones
(C) By demonstrating ways in which the argument might be strengthened
(D) By showing the teenager how to draw a more logical conclusion
(E) By rebutting the teenager's argument by unveiling a paradox

305. Visitors to the Majestic Theater in 1895 were titillated by the sight of the leading lady's ankles, which were delightfully revealed in the pegged skirt made especially for her by the leading costumier of the day. A reviewer at a matinee, however, remarked that he did not know what all the fuss was about, as the actress's ankles were well covered, and her skirt, although cunningly made and clearly a product of the renowned costumier, swept the floor.

Which of the following, if true, would best explain the discrepancy described?

(A) The reviewer watched the play from a box overlooking the stage.
(B) The costumier did not provide costumes for matinee performances.
(C) The underskirt of the costume was not pegged.
(D) A shorter understudy played the role in the matinee.
(E) The actress had only a few scenes where she stood up.

306. Twelve-year-old Ethan Duggan paraded through the Austin trade show, demonstrating his new LazyHusband app, which offers phrases such as "You look amazing today" to be called up on demand by lazy husbands. If Ethan's app does well, we can expect to see a flood of apps by preteens at the next trade show.

Which of the following is an assumption on which the argument depends?

(A) LazyHusband is guaranteed to make money.
(B) Lots of 12-year-olds have Ethan's ability and access.
(C) Most new apps are being created by young people.
(D) Men are the main consumers of unusual apps.
(E) Preteen apps often appeal to much older buyers.

307. Window damage, particularly to sliding glass doors, is often prevalent during a hurricane. Added to that, the cost of window replacement can be the highest single cost following a hurricane. People living in hurricane zones should refrain from installing sliding glass doors, no matter how pleasant they seem as an access to the beach or pool.

Which of the following, if true, would most weaken this conclusion?

(A) Sliding glass doors to a patio or deck add significantly to the resale value of a house.

(B) Window protection such as shutters or precut plywood performs very well in a hurricane.

(C) Double garage doors that deflect inward are another structural problem in cases of high winds.

(D) Homes can be uninhabitable for long periods of time following wind and rain damage in a storm.

(E) Sliding patio doors come in a wide configuration of styles, sizes, and custom designs.

308. A new theory about the extinction of Neanderthals blames their large eyes for their demise. It is certainly true that studies of skulls indicate that the eye sockets of Neanderthals are significantly larger than those of *Homo sapiens,* but their brains are not larger. With so much of the Neanderthal brain dedicated to vision, it seems to scientists that _____.

Which of the following best completes the passage?

(A) Neanderthals should have adapted easily to higher latitudes with low light

(B) the skulls of modern humans have eyes a quarter-inch smaller in diameter

(C) overall, Neanderthals also had bigger bodies than *Homo sapiens*

(D) less of the brain was available for high-level processing necessary for survival

(E) Neanderthals were akin to owls or hawks rather than to other mammals

309. Lacrosse is rapidly becoming a favorite high school sport, especially in the East. However, it is still comparatively rare compared to old standards such as football and basketball. Because popular college lacrosse teams are looking desperately for top recruits, it is also a sport that offers a fairly good chance at scholarships. Even small high schools that institute a lacrosse program will find that their students receive offers from top-notch colleges and universities.

The conclusion drawn cannot be true unless which of the following is true?

(A) Lacrosse begins to take hold in midwestern and western schools.
(B) Students from small schools are also offered academic scholarships.
(C) Colleges and universities generate more interest in lacrosse.
(D) Small high schools are able to field competitive lacrosse teams.
(E) Lacrosse becomes more popular than football or basketball.

310. Looking to save money, Clearview College is considering cutting those departments whose majors have the least relevance to today's job market. After comparing current employment figures from the government to the college's offerings, they have decided to eliminate Comparative Literature, Music, and Fine Art.

Which of the following, if true, most undermines the college's decision?

(A) A poll of employers found that students with a strong, varied liberal arts background are often better employees than those who specialize in college.
(B) Clearview College has three relatively undersubscribed programs in Anthropology, Economics, and Education.
(C) The founder of Clearview College gave money to build a large, architecturally renowned building that now houses the Conservatory of Music.
(D) Students in the Comparative Literature department often minor in one or more foreign languages.
(E) Students in the Department of Fine Art recently won several nation-wide competitions, bringing new prestige to Clearview College.

CHAPTER 3

Sentence Correction

The following questions present a sentence, part of which or all of which is underlined. Beneath the sentence, you will find five ways of phrasing the underlined part. The first of these repeats the original; the other four are different. If you think the original is best, choose the first answer; otherwise choose one of the others.

These questions test correctness and effectiveness of expression. In choosing your answer, follow the requirements of standard written English; that is, pay attention to grammar, choice of words, and sentence construction. Choose the answer that produces the most effective sentence; this answer should be clear and exact, without awkwardness, ambiguity, redundancy, or grammatical error.

311. The handshake, long used as a means of conducting business, is believed to date to ancient times, where it was a means of showing strangers that the extended hand held no weapon.

    (A) where it was a means of showing strangers
    (B) having been a means to show strangers
    (C) being a means to showing strangers
    (D) where it meant of showing strangers
    (E) used as means to show strangers

312. The Internal Revenue Service has issued a warning about a phony web page looking essentially identical to a real page that offers products for tax preparers.

    (A) looking essentially identical to a real page that offers products for tax preparers
    (B) that looks essentially identical to a real page that offers products for tax preparers
    (C) having looked essentially identical to a real page that offers products for tax preparers
    (D) it looks essentially identical to a real page that offers products for tax preparers
    (E) looking identical essentially to a real page that offers products for tax preparers

313. Because they may be contaminated with *E. coli* bacteria, several grocery stores are recalling Organic Spring Mix salads.
    (A) Because they may be contaminated with *E. coli* bacteria
    (B) In case they are contaminated with *E. coli* bacteria
    (C) Because *E. coli* bacteria may have contaminated them
    (D) Fearing the product's contamination with *E. coli* bacteria
    (E) After having been contaminated with *E. coli* bacteria

314. Compared to September of the previous year, overall economic activity was up 2.4 percent, as reported the College Index of County Economic Activity.
    (A) as reported the College Index of County Economic Activity
    (B) shown by the College Index of County Economic Activity
    (C) according to the College Index of County Economic Activity
    (D) recounted by the College Index of County Economic Activity
    (E) along with the College Index of County Economic Activity

315. Building permits typically being a very volatile indicator of growth or decline; for over two years, however, there has been little upward or downward trend.
    (A) Building permits typically being a very volatile indicator of growth or decline
    (B) Building permits are typically a very volatile indicator of growth or decline
    (C) Building permits being typically a very volatile indicator of growth or decline
    (D) Building permits have typically a very volatile indicator of growth or decline
    (E) Typically, building permits being a very volatile indicator of growth or decline

316. With nine scrap metal facilities in the New England States, most purchasing over the past few years, company president Wexler states that his company is poised to sell scrap to mills around the world.
    (A) most purchasing over the past few years
    (B) mostly purchasing over the past few years
    (C) most purchased over the past few years
    (D) most had been purchased over the past few years
    (E) most having purchased over the past few years

317. The Business and Education Committee of the Chamber of Commerce is soliciting students and business-leader mentors and participating in its ninth annual student mentoring program.

(A) The Business and Education Committee of the Chamber of Commerce is soliciting students and business-leader mentors and participating in its ninth annual student mentoring program.

(B) The Business and Education Committee of the Chamber of Commerce is soliciting students and business-leader mentors having participated in its ninth annual student mentoring program.

(C) The Business and Education Committee of the Chamber of Commerce is soliciting students and business-leader mentors who participate in its ninth annual student mentoring program.

(D) The Business and Education Committee of the Chamber of Commerce solicits students and business-leader mentors and participates in its ninth annual student mentoring program.

(E) The Business and Education Committee of the Chamber of Commerce is soliciting students and business-leader mentors to participate in its ninth annual student mentoring program.

318. The Standard & Poor's 500 fell as much as 8 percent during the five weeks following the 2000 election between George W. Bush and Al Gore.

(A) The Standard & Poor's 500 fell as much as 8 percent during the five weeks following the 2000 election between George W. Bush and Al Gore.

(B) The Standard & Poor's 500, during the five weeks following the 2000 election, fell as much as 8 percent between George W. Bush and Al Gore.

(C) During the five weeks following the 2000 election, the Standard & Poor's 500 fell as much as 8 percent between George W. Bush and Al Gore

(D) The Standard & Poor's 500 fell as much, during the five weeks following the 2000 election between George W. Bush and Al Gore, as 8 percent.

(E) Following the 2000 election between George W. Bush and Al Gore, the Standard & Poor's 500 fell as much as 8 percent after five weeks.

319. At the peak of the storm, the power company had nearly 120,000 customers without power, a tally that goes down to 60,000 by midday Thursday.

(A) a tally that goes down to 60,000 by midday Thursday

(B) a tally had gone down to 60,000 by midday Thursday

(C) a tally that been down to 60,000 by midday Thursday

(D) tallying down to 60,000 by midday Thursday

(E) a tally that was down to 60,000 by midday Thursday

320. Gas exploration and production companies, <u>adjoining midstream providers and manufacturers</u>, continue to make investments in the Marcellus Shale basin, despite the controversy.

(A) adjoining midstream providers and manufacturers
(B) along with midstream providers and manufacturers
(C) pertaining to midstream providers and manufacturers
(D) colluding midstream providers and manufacturers
(E) besides midstream providers and manufacturers

321. <u>Assuming that prices continue to rise, we can expect that farmers continuing to produce these crops at a steady rate.</u>

(A) Assuming that prices continue to rise, we can expect that farmers continuing to produce these crops at a steady rate.
(B) Assuming that prices continue to rise, we can expect that farmers are producing these crops at a steady rate.
(C) Assuming that prices continue to rise, we can expect that farmers will continue to produce these crops at a steady rate.
(D) Assuming that prices continue to rise, we can expect that farmers have continued to produce these crops at a steady rate.
(E) Assuming that prices continuing to rise, we can expect that farmers continuing to produce these crops at a steady rate.

322. Officials in the town mentioned late payments, reduced revenues, <u>and paying more to employees</u> as three factors leading to a deficit this year.

(A) and paying more to employees
(B) and paid more to employees
(C) and more paid employees
(D) and increased payroll
(E) and more employees to be paid

323. Of all of the many factors that improve office morale, <u>perhaps none is so important than</u> listening to and acting on workers' suggestions.

(A) perhaps none is so important than
(B) perhaps none is as important than
(C) perhaps nothing matters more as
(D) perhaps nothing so important as
(E) perhaps none is as important as

324. The newly opened crafts store will specialize in materials and tools for quilting, knitting, sewing, and embroidering.

    (A) quilting, knitting, sewing, and embroidering

    (B) quilting and knitting, also sewing and embroidery

    (C) both quilting and knitting and sewing and embroidery

    (D) quilting as well as knitting and sewing and embroidery

    (E) the following: quilting, knitting, sewing, embroidering

325. More than 150 Brazilian newspapers pulled out of Google News, this included many of the nation's largest papers.

    (A) More than 150 Brazilian newspapers pulled out of Google News, this included many of the nation's largest papers.

    (B) More than 150 Brazilian newspapers pulled out of Google News, which includes many of the nation's largest papers.

    (C) More than 150 Brazilian newspapers, this included many of the nation's largest papers, pulled out of Google News.

    (D) More than 150 Brazilian newspapers, including some of the nation's largest papers, pulled out of Google News.

    (E) Included with some of the nation's largest papers, more than 150 Brazilian newspapers pulled out of Google News.

326. The keyboard for the new tablet resembles a laptop; this useful accessory snaps onto the tablet to make typing faster and easier.

    (A) The keyboard for the new tablet resembles a laptop

    (B) The keyboard for the new tablet works like a laptop

    (C) The keyboard for the new tablet is like that of a laptop

    (D) The tablet's keyboard resembles a laptop

    (E) The keyboard of a new tablet and laptop are similar

327. The recent merger of two once-powerful publishing giants is thought of as an effort to create a megapublisher large enough to compete with online behemoth Amazon.

    (A) is thought of as an effort to create a megapublisher

    (B) is thought to be an effort to create a megapublisher

    (C) is thought through as an effort to create a megapublisher

    (D) has thought to be an effort to create a megapublisher

    (E) can be thought to become an effort to create a megapublisher

328. One of the top securities dealers at the company will retire next month, <u>effectively forced out after lost the three-way race to head the division.</u>

    (A) effectively forced out after lost the three-way race to head the division

    (B) effectively having been forced out after the three-way race to head the division was lost

    (C) effectively forced out after losing the three-way race to head the division

    (D) having been effectively forced out and losing the three-way race to head the division

    (E) having been effectively forced out after having lost the three-way race to have headed the division

329. Wall Street employees, <u>with paychecks that have recently seen cuts,</u> may actually receive small bonus increases this year.

    (A) with paychecks that have recently seen cuts

    (B) whose recent paychecks have seen cuts

    (C) with recently cuts in paychecks

    (D) whose paychecks have seen recent cuts

    (E) who recently have seen cuts in their paychecks

330. The CEO of Yahoo announced that she is looking at a variety of investments for the company, <u>mostly small acquisitions which align well with Yahoo's other businesses.</u>

    (A) mostly small acquisitions which align well with Yahoo's other businesses

    (B) mostly small acquisitions, which align well with Yahoo's other businesses

    (C) mostly small acquisitions that align well with Yahoo's other businesses

    (D) mostly small acquisitions aligning well with Yahoo's other businesses

    (E) small acquisitions, for the most part, in good alignment with Yahoo's other businesses

331. In contrast to the samba, a street festival dance that originated in Brazil, <u>Cuba is the origin of the popular dance called the mambo.</u>

    (A) Cuba is the origin of the popular dance called the mambo

    (B) the popular dance called the mambo originated in Cuba

    (C) the mambo, the popular dance that originated in Cuba

    (D) Cuba originated the popular dance called the mambo

    (E) the popular dance, the mambo, was originated in Cuba

332. Tempers are running high as Election Day nears, <u>and polls indicate that the distance between the two candidates are narrowing</u>.

    (A) and polls indicate that the distance between the two candidates are narrowing

    (B) with polls indicating the narrowing of distance between the two candidates

    (C) and polls indicate that the distance between the two candidates is narrowing

    (D) with indications in the polls of a narrowing of distance between the two candidates

    (E) and polls indicate that the distances between the two candidates are narrowing

333. <u>Having completed the online application and submitting his résumé, Jason began to assemble a list of possible references.</u>

    (A) Having completed the online application and submitting his résumé, Jason began to assemble a list of possible references.

    (B) Having completed the online application and having submitted his résumé, Jason began assembling a list of possible references.

    (C) After completed the online application and submitted his résumé, Jason began to assemble a list of possible references.

    (D) Having completed the online application and submitted his résumé, Jason begin to assemble a list of possible references.

    (E) After completing the online application and submitting his résumé, Jason began assembling a list of possible references.

334. <u>As opposed to the widespread use of optical scanners on Election Day</u>, the village of Cecilia remains committed to its old-fashioned lever machines.

    (A) As opposed to the widespread use of optical scanners on Election Day

    (B) Despite the widespread use of optical scanners on Election Day

    (C) Although there is a widespread use of optical scanners on Election Day

    (D) Without the widespread use of optical scanners on Election Day

    (E) Considering the widespread use of optical scanners on Election Day

335. Walking purposefully along the factory floor, <u>Mr. Monroe's eyes were in constant movement</u>, observing every machine and worker.

    (A) Mr. Monroe's eyes were in constant movement

    (B) Mr. Monroe's eyes moved constantly

    (C) Mr. Monroe's eyes constantly moved

    (D) Mr. Monroe constantly moved his eyes

    (E) the eyes of Mr. Monroe moved constantly

336. Manufactured in China out of recycled plastic that is unusually durable, children find that these toys last for years even with harsh treatment.

(A) Manufactured in China out of recycled plastic that is unusually durable, children find that these toys last for years even with harsh treatment.

(B) Manufactured in China out of unusually durable recycled plastic, these toys last, children find, for years, even with harsh treatment.

(C) Children find that even with harsh treatment, these toys, which are manufactured in China out of unusually durable recycled plastic, last for years.

(D) These toys, manufactured in China out of recycled plastic that is unusually durable, children find last for years even with harsh treatment.

(E) Children find that these toys, even with harsh treatment, last for years, being manufactured in China out of recycled plastic that is unusually durable.

337. The president pro tem of the Senate, among all duly elected senators, <u>is the senior official, although the vice president outranks him or her.</u>

(A) is the senior official, although the vice president outranks him or her

(B) are the senior officials, although the vice president outranks them

(C) holds the senior office, outranked by the vice president

(D) is the senior official, while being outranked by the vice president

(E) except for the vice president, who outranks him or her, be the senior official

338. The gray bat (*Myotis grisescens*), a glossy light-colored bat with long black ears, once resided in most of the southern states and as far north as Illinois; <u>they are now considered endangered in every region.</u>

(A) they are now considered endangered in every region

(B) in every region, they are now considered endangered

(C) now they are considered endangered in every region

(D) in every region where it is now considered endangered

(E) it is now considered endangered in every region

339. Although the company began in 1912 as a mom-and-pop operation, <u>by the mid-1950s it has been reinvented</u> as a worker-owned conglomerate.

(A) by the mid-1950s it has been reinvented

(B) by the mid-1950s it had been reinvented

(C) by the mid-1950s it is reinvented

(D) by the mid-1950s it reinvented

(E) by the mid-1950s it became reinvented

340. Field testing of the two products, whether across states, within rural or urban settings, or among age groups, <u>has proved remarkably inconclusive.</u>

   (A) has proved remarkably inconclusive
   (B) prove remarkably inconclusive
   (C) have proved remarkably inconclusive
   (D) are proving remarkably inconclusive
   (E) yet prove remarkably inconclusive

341. Saab was the first company to offer seat belts as standard in its automobiles; prior to that time, <u>Nash and Ford offer safety belts only as an option.</u>

   (A) Nash and Ford offer safety belts only as an option
   (B) Nash and Ford had offered safety belts only as an option
   (C) Nash and Ford did offer safety belts only as an option
   (D) Nash and Ford was offering safety belts only as an option
   (E) Nash and Ford would have offered safety belts only as an option

342. Running rapidly through the airport to catch a flight that was mere moments from taking off, <u>Liza's ankle was seriously sprained in a fall.</u>

   (A) Liza's ankle was seriously sprained in a fall
   (B) Liza's ankle fell and was seriously sprained
   (C) in a fall Liza's ankle was seriously sprained
   (D) Liza fell and seriously sprained her ankle
   (E) Liza had her ankle seriously sprained in a fall

343. Neither the speaker nor the head of the committee <u>were aware of the commotion in the hall</u> that erupted when several protestors staged a small demonstration.

   (A) were aware of the commotion in the hall
   (B) was aware of the commotion in the hall
   (C) notice the commotion the hall
   (D) were made aware of the commotion in the hall
   (E) awared of the commotion in the hall

344. John Deere, was an inventor and blacksmith whose name now graces a world-renowned manufacturing company, first developed a very successful cast-steel plow with a wrought-iron frame.

- (A) John Deere, was an inventor and blacksmith whose name now graces a world-renowned manufacturing company
- (B) John Deere, who was an inventor and blacksmith whose name now graces a world-renowned manufacturing company
- (C) John Deere, an inventor and blacksmith whose name now graces a world-renowned manufacturing company
- (D) John Deere, whose name now graces a world-renowned manufacturing company, was an inventor and blacksmith
- (E) Inventor and blacksmith John Deere, whose name a world-renowned manufacturing company now graces

345. The interns observed the administrative candidates interviewed with the hiring committee and meeting members of the board.

- (A) administrative candidates interviewed with the hiring committee
- (B) administrative candidates interviewing with the hiring committee
- (C) administrative candidates interviewed by the hiring committee
- (D) administrative candidates interview with the hiring committee
- (E) administrative candidates who interviewed with the hiring committee

346. The Panic of 1857 is believed by economists to have arisen due to an imbalance between the domestic and international economies.

- (A) The Panic of 1857 is believed by economists to have arisen
- (B) The Panic of 1857, economists believe, had arisen
- (C) Economists believe the Panic of 1857 to have arisen
- (D) The Panic of 1857 arose, believe economists,
- (E) Economists believe that the Panic of 1857 arose

347. The local political committees are working hard to get out the vote by telephoning constituents, sending postcard reminders, and some even hold up signs at intersections.

- (A) by telephoning constituents, sending postcard reminders, and some even hold up signs at intersections
- (B) by contacting constituents by telephone or postcard, and sometimes holding up signs at intersections
- (C) through telephoning constituents, sending postcard reminders, or some even hold up signs at intersections
- (D) in these ways: telephoning constituents, sending postcard reminders, holding up signs at intersections
- (E) by telephoning constituents, sending postcard reminders, and even at times holding up signs at intersections

348. The article praised Jasper Hewitt, noted philanthropist and <u>who built many high-tech housing developments</u>.

    (A) who built many high-tech housing developments
    (B) the one who built many high-tech housing developments
    (C) had built many high-tech housing developments
    (D) builder of many high-tech housing developments
    (E) someone who built many high-tech housing developments

349. Politicians noted that barring quick action on the floor of the House, the act could fail, ensuring that thousands of active-duty soldiers will live in shoddier conditions <u>after leaving the force than today</u>.

    (A) after leaving the force than today
    (B) after leaving the force than they do today
    (C) having left the force than today
    (D) after leaving the force as today
    (E) after leaving the force as they do today

350. Despite the excellent reputation it has attained, <u>the company had not yet received an influx of capital from investors</u>.

    (A) the company had not yet received an influx of capital from investors
    (B) the company is not yet in receipt of an influx of capital from investors
    (C) the company has not yet received an influx of capital from investors
    (D) the company has not yet have received an influx of capital from investors
    (E) the company have not yet received an influx of capital from investors

351. If the largest firms on Wall Street were to relocate to Connecticut, <u>they will take with them both important taxpaying entities and intellectual capital</u>.

    (A) they will take with them both important taxpaying entities and intellectual capital
    (B) they have taken with them both important taxpaying entities and intellectual capital
    (C) they will have taken with them both important taxpaying entities and intellectual capital
    (D) they would have taken with them both important taxpaying entities and intellectual capital
    (E) they would take with them both important taxpaying entities and intellectual capital

352. With this minimal increase in workers' contributions to their health coverage, the employees have not only retained a fine healthcare plan, <u>but they have shown willingness to negotiate in good faith.</u>

(A) but they have shown willingness to negotiate in good faith
(B) and they have shown willingness to negotiate in good faith
(C) as well as showing willingness to negotiate in good faith
(D) but they have also shown willingness to negotiate in good faith
(E) having shown willingness to negotiate in good faith

353. The laboratory technicians placed the vials in hot water overnight <u>to see did the cloudiness in the glass disappear.</u>

(A) to see did the cloudiness in the glass disappear
(B) to see if the cloudiness in the glass disappeared
(C) to see whether the cloudiness in the glass would disappear
(D) to see the cloudiness in the glass could disappear
(E) seeing if the cloudiness in the glass might disappear

354. People who eat several small meals a day appear to have fewer health issues overall <u>than do people with just three larger meals.</u>

(A) than do people with just three larger meals
(B) than people do with just three larger meals
(C) than people eating just three larger meals
(D) than do people who eat just three larger meals
(E) from people eating just three larger meals

355. <u>If the quarterback just passes the ball successfully once in a while, the Packers win against the strong Dallas defense.</u>

(A) If the quarterback just passes the ball successfully once in a while, the Packers win against the strong Dallas defense.
(B) If the quarterback would pass the ball successfully once in a while, the Packers win against the strong Dallas defense.
(C) When the quarterback passes the ball successfully once in a while, the Packers would win against the strong Dallas defense.
(D) Had the quarterback passed the ball successfully once in a while, the Packers won against the strong Dallas defense.
(E) If the quarterback passed the ball successfully once in a while, the Packers might win against the strong Dallas defense.

356. If the two companies were to merge successfully, they would represent one of the largest communications empires in South Asia.

(A) If the two companies were to merge successfully
(B) If the two companies would merge successfully
(C) If the two companies would have merged successfully
(D) If the two companies can merge successfully
(E) If the two companies have merged successfully

357. The store had planned a soft opening for last October, but unusual weather has kept that from happening on schedule.

(A) but unusual weather has kept that from happening on schedule
(B) but unusual weather will have kept that from happening on schedule
(C) but unusual weather keeps that from happening on schedule
(D) but unusual weather kept that from happening on schedule
(E) but unusual weather would have kept that from happening on schedule

358. As a source of inexpensive and easily accessible energy, many agree that geothermal heat is the alternative to consider.

(A) As a source of inexpensive and easily accessible energy, many agree that geothermal heat is the alternative to consider.
(B) As a source of inexpensive and easily accessible energy, many agree upon geothermal heat as the alternative to consider.
(C) Many agree that geothermal heat, a source of inexpensive and easily accessible energy, is the alternative to consider.
(D) Many agree that geothermal heat is the alternative to consider as a source of inexpensive and easily accessible energy.
(E) As a source of inexpensive and easily accessible energy, geothermal heat is the alternative to consider, as agreed by many.

359. Several prominent economists insist that low taxes on the wealthy do nothing to stimulate the economy; it is asserted that the extra income goes into savings or offshore investments.

(A) it is asserted that the extra income goes into savings or offshore investments
(B) it can be asserted that the extra income goes into savings or offshore investments
(C) they assert that the extra income goes into savings or offshore investments
(D) the extra income goes into savings or offshore investments, it is asserted
(E) that the extra income goes into savings or offshore investments is asserted

360. A major breakthrough in colleges of business occurred when its curricula expanded to include hands-on activities such as mock trading floors.

(A) when its curricula expanded to include hands-on activities
(B) when their curricula expanded to include hands-on activities
(C) when its curriculum expanded to include hands-on activities
(D) because its curricula expanded to include hands-on activities
(E) whenever the curricula expanded to include hands-on activities

361. Neither the teachers nor the administrative team take responsibility for the students' dreadful test scores.

(A) take responsibility for the students' dreadful test scores
(B) are responsible for the students' dreadful test scores
(C) bear responsibility for the students' dreadful test scores
(D) takes responsibility for the students' dreadful test scores
(E) were given responsibility for the students' dreadful test scores

362. The tractors, like most of the vehicles on the enormous farm, requires chains to move through the ice and snow in winter.

(A) requires chains to move through the ice and snow in winter
(B) moves through winter's ice and snow using chains
(C) requires chains for moving through the ice and snow in winter
(D) have chains that move through the ice and snow in winter
(E) require chains to move through the ice and snow in winter

363. Rashes, respiratory illnesses, and even nerve damage may result of working too closely with toxic agents such as certain heavy metals.

(A) may result of working too closely with toxic agents
(B) may prove consequential from working too closely with toxic agents
(C) may result from working too closely with toxic agents
(D) may be outcomes from working too closely with toxic agents
(E) may give rise to working too closely with toxic agents

364. That supervisor of Henrietta's is a very friendly person; he helped me enormously when I first considered working here.

(A) That supervisor of Henrietta's is a very friendly person
(B) That supervisor of Henrietta is a very friendly person
(C) Henrietta supervisor is a very friendly person
(D) A very friendly person is that supervisor of Henrietta
(E) A very friendly person is that Henrietta's supervisor

365. Because I took three months off to complete my thesis, <u>my income in 2013 was lesser than my income in 2012</u>.

(A) my income in 2013 was lesser than my income in 2012

(B) my income in 2013 was fewer than my income in 2012

(C) my income in 2013 declined by my income in 2012

(D) my 2013 income was lesser than my 2012 income

(E) my income in 2013 was less than my income in 2012

366. My English professor tried hard to convince me that <u>a degree in comparative literature was as good as a degree in accounting</u> when it came to finding future employment.

(A) a degree in comparative literature was as good as a degree in accounting

(B) a degree in comparative literature was good as in accounting

(C) a degree in comparative literature was no worse as a degree in accounting

(D) a degree in comparative literature was equally good with a degree in accounting

(E) degrees in comparative literature and accounting was equally good

367. After examining the options, Fred decided that <u>the course at the community college covered as much material as at the university</u> for a far smaller cost.

(A) the course at the community college covered as much material as at the university

(B) the community college course covered as much material as at the university

(C) the community college course covered as much material as the university

(D) the community college course covered as much material as the university course

(E) the course at the community college covered so much material as the one at the university

368. <u>To continue to support this candidate after all of his gaffes is ensuring defeat at the polls.</u>

(A) To continue to support this candidate after all his gaffes is ensuring defeat at the polls.

(B) After all of his gaffes, to continue to support this candidate is ensuring defeat at the polls.

(C) Continuing to support this candidate after all of his gaffes is to ensure defeat at the polls.

(D) To continue supporting this candidate after all of his gaffes is ensuring defeat at the polls.

(E) To continue to support this candidate after all of his gaffes is to ensure defeat at the polls.

369. A CEO of unquestioned ability, Margaret's realignment of the company earned praise from the board.

(A) A CEO of unquestioned ability, Margaret's realignment of the company earned praise from the board.

(B) A CEO of unquestioned ability, Margaret earned praise from the board for her realignment of the company.

(C) Margaret, a CEO of unquestioned ability, realigned the company while earning praise from the board.

(D) As a CEO of unquestioned ability, Margaret's realignment of the company earned praise from the board.

(E) A CEO of unquestioned ability, the board praised Margaret for her realignment of the company.

370. As soon as we have finished examining the paperwork and consulting with our lawyer, we will make an offer.

(A) we will make an offer

(B) we will have made an offer

(C) we will be making an offer

(D) we made an offer

(E) we have made an offer

371. Each of the students in my marketing classes have their own talents; some are excellent designers, and some are great wordsmiths.

(A) Each of the students in my marketing classes have their own talents

(B) Each of the students in my marketing classes have his own talents

(C) All of the students in my marketing classes have their own talents

(D) Each of the students in my marketing classes has their own talents

(E) Everyone of the students in my marketing classes has his own talents

372. She tried on endless prom dresses for her two friends, but she could not decide which of them to choose.

(A) she could not decide which of them to choose

(B) she could not decide which dress to choose

(C) she could not choose among them

(D) she could not decide which one to choose

(E) they could not decide which of them to choose

373. Dashing across the frozen pond as though followed by a pack of hounds, Marco pointed out the 10-point buck.

(A) Dashing across the frozen pond as though followed by a pack of hounds, Marco pointed out the 10-point buck.

(B) Dashing across the frozen pond as though followed by a pack of hounds, the 10-point buck was pointed out by Marco.

(C) As it dashed across the frozen pond as though followed by a pack of hounds, the 10-point buck was pointed out by Marco.

(D) Marco pointed out the 10-point buck dashing across the frozen pond as though followed by a pack of hounds.

(E) Marco pointed out the 10-point buck as though followed by a pack of hounds as it dashed across the frozen pond.

374. When they discuss their reasons for banning hydrofracking, town board members mention the increase in truck traffic, the danger to wetlands, and the intruding on the rural landscape.

(A) the increase in truck traffic, the danger to wetlands, and the intruding on the rural landscape

(B) the increase in truck traffic, the danger to wetlands, and the intrusion on the rural landscape

(C) the increase in truck traffic, danger to wetlands, and intruding on the rural landscape

(D) the increasing in truck traffic, the endangering to wetlands, and the intruding on the rural landscape

(E) the increase in truck traffic, the danger to wetlands, and the intruding of the rural landscape

375. It was difficult for the seniors to decide between AmeriCorps programs, graduate school, and the world of work.

(A) to decide between AmeriCorps programs, graduate school, and the world of work

(B) to decide between AmeriCorps programs, graduate school, or the world of work

(C) to decide between AmeriCorps programs, or graduate school and the world of work

(D) to make a decision from AmeriCorps programs, graduate school, and the world of work.

(E) to decide among AmeriCorps programs, graduate school, and the world of work

376. We had long been accustomed to the sounds of the city, but the construction in the building next door was beyond anything we had known before.
   (A) We had long been accustomed to the sounds of the city
   (B) The sounds of the city had long been customary to us
   (C) We had long been accustomed by the sounds of the city
   (D) We had long been accustomed for the sounds of the city
   (E) The sounds of the city had long been accustomed

377. The restoration of the old bed-and-breakfast was expensive; nevertheless, the owners considered it a worthwhile investment.
   (A) nevertheless, the owners considered it a worthwhile investment
   (B) despite the owners considering it a worthwhile investment
   (C) besides, the owners considered it a worthwhile investment
   (D) although the owners considered it a worthwhile investment
   (E) in particular, the owners considered it a worthwhile investment

378. The movement of suburbanites back into the city will effect everything from transportation to service industries.
   (A) will effect everything from transportation to service industries
   (B) has effect on everything from transportation to service industries
   (C) will affect everything from transportation to service industries
   (D) will have effected everything from transportation to service industries
   (E) will have an affect on everything from transportation to service industries

379. Not only is it the world's largest toy company, but Mattel is an enormous outsourcer of manufacturing to Asia.
   (A) but Mattel is an enormous outsourcer of manufacturing to Asia
   (B) but Mattel is also an enormous outsourcer of manufacturing to Asia
   (C) but Mattel outsources largely its manufacturing to Asia
   (D) but Mattel outsources enormous amounts of manufacturing to Asia
   (E) and Mattel is an enormous outsourcer of manufacturing to Asia

380. There was hordes of rats and a great deal of asbestos among the surprises found by the building contractors.

    (A) There was hordes of rats and a great deal of asbestos among the surprises found by the building contractors.

    (B) There was a horde of rats and a great deal of asbestos among the surprises found by the building contractors.

    (C) Among the surprises found by the building contractors including hordes of rats and a great deal of asbestos.

    (D) Among other surprises, the building contractors found hordes of rats and a great deal of asbestos.

    (E) Hordes of rats and a great deal of asbestos was among the surprises found by the building contractors.

381. Whether the mall is built in Shelburne or in Cardiff will be determined by studies of shopping habits and transportation patterns.

    (A) Whether the mall is built in Shelburne or in Cardiff will be determined by

    (B) If the mall is to be built in Shelburne or in Cardiff will be determined by

    (C) Whether the mall is built in Shelburne or in Cardiff will be determined with

    (D) Determination of whether the mall is built in Shelburne or in Cardiff will be by

    (E) It will be determined whether the mall shall be built in Shelburne or in Cardiff by

382. The pollsters noted that compared to four years ago, far less voters indicated that their lives were improving.

    (A) far less voters indicated that their lives were improving

    (B) far less voters indicated an improvement in their lives

    (C) a lesser number of voters indicated that their lives were improving

    (D) less voters by far indicated that their lives had improved

    (E) far fewer voters indicated that their lives were improving

383. After trying all 10 samples, Jason admitted that the mocha tasted far better to him than the other flavors.

    (A) the mocha tasted far better to him than the other flavors

    (B) the mocha tasted far better to him than the other flavors did

    (C) the mocha was the best flavor compared to the other flavors

    (D) the mocha tasted best out of the other flavors

    (E) out of all the other flavors, the mocha tasted better to him

384. The neighbors in the condominium found themselves <u>in a dispute with the assignment of responsibilities.</u>

(A) in a dispute with the assignment of responsibilities
(B) in a dispute having to do with the responsibility assignments
(C) in a dispute over the assignment of responsibilities
(D) in a dispute about the responsibility assignments
(E) disputing around the assignment of responsibilities

385. Although Jack considered himself well-versed in consumer trends, <u>he had a hard time predicting what they might be willing to spend on a vacation package.</u>

(A) he had a hard time predicting what they might be willing to spend on a vacation package
(B) he had a hard time predicting what he might be willing to spend on a vacation package
(C) he had a hard time making a prediction about what they might be willing to spend on a vacation package
(D) he had a hard time predicting what might be willing to be spent on a vacation package
(E) he had a hard time predicting what consumers might be willing to spend on a vacation package

386. The team members studied efficiencies on the factory floor for months; <u>even so, they felt perfectly well prepared to submit their report to management.</u>

(A) even so, they felt perfectly well prepared to submit their report to management
(B) as a result, they felt perfectly well prepared to submit their report to management
(C) similarly, they felt perfectly well prepared to submit their report to management
(D) for example, they felt perfectly well prepared to submit their report to management
(E) moreover, they felt perfectly well prepared to submit their report to management

387. The news about their unrelated accidents <u>strike us as both sad and oddly coincidental.</u>

(A) strike us as both sad and oddly coincidental
(B) strike us both as sad and oddly coincidental
(C) strikes us as both sad and oddly coincidental
(D) stricken us as both sad and oddly coincidental
(E) did strike us as both sad and oddly coincidental

388. Nearly two-thirds of the wood <u>were used in the framework of the building</u>.
- (A) were used in the framework of the building
- (B) was used in the framework of the building
- (C) used in the framework of the building
- (D) have been used in the framework of the building
- (E) was in use in the framework of the building

389. Before I depart for Haiti, my good friend Lionel <u>has agreed to tutor me in his native Creole dialect.</u>
- (A) has agreed to tutor me in his native Creole dialect
- (B) has agreed to tutor me with his native Creole dialect
- (C) agrees to tutor me in his native Creole dialect
- (D) is in agreement to tutor me in his native Creole dialect
- (E) has agreed to tutor me about his native Creole dialect

390. Very few employees plan to work over the Thanksgiving holiday; <u>consequently, even fewer will work over winter break.</u>
- (A) consequently, even fewer will work over winter break
- (B) instead, even fewer will work over winter break
- (C) correspondingly, even fewer will work over winter break
- (D) for instance, even fewer will work over winter break
- (E) furthermore, even fewer will work over winter break

391. <u>Have either of you taken Dr. Pendergrass's course on Applied Economic Theory?</u>
- (A) Have either of you taken Dr. Pendergrass's course on Applied Economic Theory?
- (B) Did either of you taken Dr. Pendergrass's course on Applied Economic Theory?
- (C) Are either of you taken Dr. Pendergrass's course on Applied Economic Theory?
- (D) Has either of you taken Dr. Pendergrass's course on Applied Economic Theory?
- (E) Had either of you took Dr. Pendergrass's course on Applied Economic Theory?

392. Every member of the committee except two, <u>him and her, was in attendance at the informal luncheon.</u>

   (A) him and her, was in attendance at the informal luncheon
   (B) he and she, was in attendance at the informal luncheon
   (C) him and her, were in attendance at the informal luncheon
   (D) he and she, were in attendance at the informal luncheon
   (E) he and she, attended the informal luncheon

393. It is increasingly evident that <u>Rae Ann is more competent than</u> the other members of the team.

   (A) Rae Ann is more competent than
   (B) Rae Ann is most competent of
   (C) Rae Ann has the most competence of
   (D) Rae Ann is more competent comparing
   (E) Rae Ann's competence is greater than

394. <u>As we departed, we thanked the conductor as we boarded the train who had directed us to our seats.</u>

   (A) As we departed, we thanked the conductor as we boarded the train who had directed us to our seats.
   (B) As we departed, we thanked the conductor who, as we boarded the train, he had directed us to our seats.
   (C) As we departed, we thanked the conductor who had directed us to our seats when we boarded the train.
   (D) In departing, we thanked the conductor who had directed us to our seats while boarding the train.
   (E) Thanking the conductor as we departed, we boarded the train and were directed to our seats.

395. My first job involved selling gift baskets <u>at a shop in the mall containing stuffed animals and small toys.</u>

   (A) at a shop in the mall containing stuffed animals and small toys
   (B) containing stuffed animals and small toys at a shop in the mall
   (C) at a shop containing stuffed animals and small toys in the mall
   (D) and stuffed animals and small toys at a shop in the mall
   (E) at a shop in the mall; they were containing stuffed animals and small toys

396. All employees, accepting those who are on 10-month contracts, receive a set number of paid days off.

- (A) All employees, accepting those who are on 10-month contracts
- (B) All employees with the acceptance of those who are on 10-month contracts
- (C) Except for employees who are on 10-month contracts, each of them
- (D) All employees, excepting those who are on 10-month contracts
- (E) All employees except employees who are on 10-month contracts

397. During the interview, the congresswoman responded to all the questions, even the silliest ones; she was patient about it.

- (A) responded to all the questions, even the silliest ones; she was patient about it
- (B) responded with patience to all the questions, silly or otherwise
- (C) responded in a patient manner to all the questions, even the silliest ones
- (D) was patient in her response to all the silliest questions
- (E) responded patiently to even the silliest questions

398. Our director of advertising neither attended art school or received any formal training, yet she has the eye of an artist.

- (A) neither attended art school or received any formal training
- (B) either attended art school or received any formal training
- (C) did not attend art school or received any formal training
- (D) neither attended art school nor received any formal training
- (E) neither attended art school, receiving any formal training

399. The combination of pumpkin and spice, which is used in everything from lattes to muffins, is incredibly popular in autumn.

- (A) pumpkin and spice, which is used in everything from lattes to muffins, is incredibly popular
- (B) pumpkin and spice that is used in everything from lattes to muffins is incredibly popular
- (C) pumpkin and spice used in everything from lattes to muffins is incredibly popular
- (D) pumpkin, and spice, which are used in everything from lattes to muffins, are incredibly popular
- (E) pumpkin and spice, used in everything from lattes to muffins, are incredibly popular

400. Dr. Strickland used the whiteboard, and he demonstrated the equation three different ways, but the class remained confused.

(A) Dr. Strickland used the whiteboard, and he demonstrated the equation three different ways, but the class remained confused.

(B) Despite having demonstrated the equation three different ways on the whiteboard, Dr. Strickland's class remained confused.

(C) Dr. Strickland used the whiteboard to demonstrate the equation three different ways, the class remained confused.

(D) Although Dr. Strickland used the whiteboard to demonstrate the equation three different ways, the class remained confused.

(E) Dr. Strickland's using the whiteboard to demonstrate the equation three different ways, the class remained confused.

401. We saw an imposing man standing in the lobby, and he later turned out to be the CEO of the company.

(A) We saw an imposing man standing in the lobby, and he later turned out to be the CEO of the company.

(B) The imposing man whom we saw standing in the lobby later turned out to be the CEO of the company.

(C) We saw an imposing man standing in the lobby that later turned out to be the CEO of the company.

(D) When we saw the imposing man standing in the lobby, he later turned out to be the CEO of the company.

(E) In the lobby we saw an imposing man; later he turned out to be the CEO of the company.

402. I did not give myself enough credit for completing the task in the short amount of time allotted.

(A) I did not give myself enough credit for completing

(B) I did not give myself enough credit for having to complete

(C) I did not give me enough credit for completing

(D) I gave myself not enough credit for completing

(E) I did not give myself enough credit after completing

403. Grant just received a phone call from Loretta Lenape; do you know whom she is?

(A) do you know whom she is

(B) do you know who she is

(C) do you know what that is

(D) do you know who they are

(E) do you know whom it is

404. Carlotta did poor on the exam, but from what I hear, Neville did more badly.

   (A) Carlotta did poor on the exam, but from what I hear, Neville did more badly.

   (B) Carlotta did poorly on the exam, but from what I hear, Neville did more bad.

   (C) Carlotta did poorly on the exam, but from what I hear, Neville did worse.

   (D) Carlotta did not do good on the exam, but from what I hear, Neville did worse.

   (E) Carlotta did bad on the exam, but from what I hear, Neville did worst.

405. The report is still in his in-box that he should have read and commented upon three weeks ago.

   (A) The report is still in his in-box that he should have read and commented upon three weeks ago.

   (B) The report in his in-box is one on which he should have read and commented upon three weeks ago.

   (C) The report that he should have read three weeks ago is still in his in-box to be commented upon.

   (D) The report, which he should have read and commented upon three weeks ago, is still in his in-box.

   (E) In his in-box remains the report that he should three weeks ago have read and commented upon.

406. To win allies during any prolonged power struggle at the workplace, petty criticisms should be avoided.

   (A) petty criticisms should be avoided

   (B) they should avoid petty criticisms

   (C) avoid petty criticisms

   (D) avoiding petty criticisms is best

   (E) to avoid petty criticisms

407. I suggest that you give the task of creating the slide presentation to Howard, who you can trust to do a creative, comprehensive job.

   (A) who you can trust to do a creative, comprehensive job

   (B) who you can trust to do a creative and comprehensive job

   (C) you can trust him to do a creative, comprehensive job

   (D) he will do a creative and comprehensive job

   (E) whom you can trust to do a creative, comprehensive job

408. After raising her hand to be called upon, the young woman raised from her chair to make her point.

- (A) After raising her hand to be called upon, the young woman raised from her chair to make her point.
- (B) After raising her hand to be called upon, the young woman risen from her chair to make her point.
- (C) After rising her hand to be called upon, the young woman rose from her chair to make her point.
- (D) After raising her hand to be called upon, the young woman rose from her chair to make her point.
- (E) After having risen her hand to be called upon, the young woman had risen from her chair to make her point.

409. Once this season ends in October, the team has completed their fourth trip in a row to the playoffs.

- (A) the team has completed their fourth trip in a row to the playoffs
- (B) the team has completed its fourth trip in a row to the playoffs
- (C) the team will have completed its fourth trip in a row to the playoffs
- (D) the team completed its fourth trip in a row to the playoffs
- (E) the team did complete their fourth trip in a row to the playoffs

410. Each of the men on the committee performed his duties with eager expertise.

- (A) Each of the men on the committee performed his duties with eager expertise.
- (B) Each man on the committee performed his or her duties with eager expertise.
- (C) Each of the men on the committee performed their duties with eager expertise.
- (D) The men on the committee each performed their duties with eager expertise.
- (E) Of the men on the committee, each one performed his duties with eager expertise.

411. The company's markets in East Africa are stronger than what they ever were; sales are up from Kenya to Mozambique.

   (A) The company's markets in East Africa are stronger than what they ever were
   (B) The company's markets in East Africa are stronger than they ever were
   (C) The company's market in East Africa is stronger than ever was
   (D) The companies markets in East Africa are stronger than they have been
   (E) The companies who market in East Africa are stronger than what they ever were

412. Tonight's featured speaker, the person who is the author of our textbook, hails from Chicago.

   (A) the person who is the author of our textbook
   (B) the person that authored our textbook
   (C) our textbook author
   (D) and author of our textbook
   (E) the author of our textbook

413. One of the lunchroom events my colleagues enjoy most is me telling stories about travels for the United Nations.

   (A) me telling stories about travels for the United Nations
   (B) my telling stories about travels for the United Nations
   (C) have me tell stories about travels for the United Nations
   (D) me to tell stories about travels for the United Nations
   (E) if I tell stories about travels for the United Nations

414. Three weeks is more than enough time to complete this simple project.

   (A) Three weeks is more than enough time to complete this simple project.
   (B) Three weeks is more than enough time for the completion of this simple project.
   (C) Three weeks are more than enough time to complete this simple project.
   (D) Three weeks are more time than enough to complete this simple project.
   (E) Three weeks is more time needed to complete this simple project.

415. In order so employees can receive professional development, the firm will be closed for business on Tuesday.
    (A) In order so employees can receive professional development
    (B) In order to receive professional development for employees
    (C) In order to provide professional development to employees
    (D) In order for employees can receive professional development
    (E) In order for providing professional development to employees

416. Unless it takes place over the weekend, my colleagues and I will attend the workshop.
    (A) Unless it takes place over the weekend
    (B) Barring that it takes place over the weekend
    (C) Except it takes place over the weekend
    (D) But for its taking place over the weekend
    (E) Exclusive of its taking place over the weekend

417. Interrupt a speaker, whether to ask a question or interject a remark, is never polite.
    (A) Interrupt a speaker
    (B) Having interrupted a speaker
    (C) To interrupt a speaker
    (D) Interruptions of a speaker
    (E) When you interrupt a speaker

418. The recent changes in the way companies size women's clothing make trying on dresses a difficult chore.
    (A) make trying on dresses a difficult chore
    (B) make the trying on of dresses a difficult chore
    (C) is making trying on dresses a difficult chore
    (D) makes trying on dresses a difficult chore
    (E) will be making trying on dresses a difficult chore

419. For the past several weeks, us employees have tried a new way of working together to solve problems.
    (A) us employees have tried a new way of working together
    (B) us employees has tried a new way of working together
    (C) we employees will try a new way of working together
    (D) we employees have tried a new way of working together
    (E) as employees, have tried a new way of working together

420. Beside the usual chicken dinners and diner visits, the candidates will have occasional home-cooked meals in supporters' homes.

 (A) Beside the usual chicken dinners and diner visits
 (B) Beside the usual chicken dinners and visits to diners
 (C) Plus the usual chicken dinners and diner visits
 (D) For the usual chicken dinners as well as diner visits
 (E) Besides the usual chicken dinners and diner visits

421. As soon as the mayor got teary-eyed over the slow progress of flood relief, he starts to win over the citizens.

 (A) he starts to win over the citizens
 (B) he started to win over the citizens
 (C) he starts winning over the citizens
 (D) the citizens started to be won over
 (E) citizens started being won over

422. Was there this much damaged buildings following the earthquake of 2005?

 (A) Was there this much damaged buildings following the earthquake of 2005?
 (B) Were there this much damaged buildings following the earthquake of 2005?
 (C) Were this much buildings damaged in the earthquake of 2005?
 (D) Were there this many damaged buildings following the earthquake of 2005?
 (E) Were there so much damaged buildings following the earthquake of 2005?

423. The chairman of the board congratulated three employees for their ongoing charity work at the annual meeting.

 (A) The chairman of the board congratulated three employees for their ongoing charity work at the annual meeting.
 (B) For their ongoing charity work, the chairman of the board congratulated three employees at the annual meeting.
 (C) Three employees at the annual meeting were congratulated by the chairman of the board for their ongoing charity work.
 (D) At the annual meeting, the chairman of the board congratulated three employees for their ongoing charity work.
 (E) The chairman of the board, at the annual meeting, congratulated three employees for their ongoing charity work.

424. Lucas <u>had ought to work shorter hours if he can</u>; his grueling schedule is affecting his family life.

    (A) Lucas had ought to work shorter hours if he can

    (B) Lucas had ought to work shorter hours if he could

    (C) If he can work shorter hours, Lucas ought to

    (D) Lucas ought to work shorter hours if he can

    (E) If Lucas can, he had ought to work shorter hours

425. By the end of his animated lecture, <u>the professor looked like he had been through a battle.</u>

    (A) the professor looked like he had been through a battle

    (B) the professor looked as though he had been through a battle

    (C) the professor looked like he had been battling

    (D) it seemed like the professor had been through a battle

    (E) the professor looked as he had been through a battle

426. It seems obvious that <u>the culinary staff must of forgot one of the key ingredients.</u>

    (A) the culinary staff must of forgot one of the key ingredients

    (B) the culinary staff must of forgot a key ingredient

    (C) a key ingredient was forgotten by the culinary staff

    (D) the culinary staff must have forgot one of the key ingredients

    (E) the culinary staff must have forgotten a key ingredient

427. Professor MacKinnon asked <u>him and I for our opinions of her presentation.</u>

    (A) him and I for our opinions of her presentation

    (B) he and I for our opinions of her presentation

    (C) him and me for our opinions of her presentation

    (D) me and him for our opinion of her presentation

    (E) he and I for our opinion of her presentation

428. The custodians quickly swept up all of the paper <u>that was laying on the floor of the conference room.</u>

    (A) that was laying on the floor of the conference room

    (B) laying on the floor of the conference room

    (C) that was lying on the floor of the conference room

    (D) that laid on the floor of the conference room

    (E) that was laid on the floor of the conference room

429. One of the pigeons had built its nest on the ledge outside my office window.

    (A) One of the pigeons had built its nest on the ledge outside my office window.

    (B) One of the pigeons had built her nest on the ledge outside its office window.

    (C) One of the pigeons had built their nest on the ledge outside my office window.

    (D) Of the pigeons, one had built its nest on the ledge outside my office window.

    (E) Outside my office window, one of the pigeons had built their nest on the ledge.

430. The supervisor suggested that we invite whoever we thought might benefit from the workshop.

    (A) whoever we thought might benefit from the workshop

    (B) whomever we thought might benefit from the workshop

    (C) anyone who we thought might benefit from the workshop

    (D) those whom might best benefit from the workshop

    (E) whoever might benefit from the workshop in our minds

431. Our office manager, like many people whose jobs involve juggling dozens of projects, must has a brain that resembles a filing cabinet.

    (A) must has a brain that resembles a filing cabinet

    (B) must has a brain that resemble a filing cabinet

    (C) have a brain resembling a filing cabinet

    (D) must have a brain that resembles a filing cabinet

    (E) has to has a brain that resembles a filing cabinet

432. I am feeling good about my presentation; the report is clear, and my visuals are terrific.

    (A) I am feeling good about my presentation

    (B) I am feeling well about my presentation

    (C) My presentation makes me feel well

    (D) About my presentation, I am feeling good

    (E) I am feeling good around my presentation

433. The small circuit was developed by Robert Litvak, <u>he is a physicist with ProRata, Incorporated.</u>

    (A) he is a physicist with ProRata, Incorporated.
    (B) a physicist with ProRata, Incorporated
    (C) who is a physicist of ProRata, Incorporated
    (D) that is a physicist for ProRata, Incorporated
    (E) is a physicist with ProRata, Incorporated

434. <u>Informally and delightfully, the riverfront restaurant is a favorite of ours</u> for brunches or early suppers.

    (A) Informally and delightfully, the riverfront restaurant is a favorite of ours
    (B) Informally and delightfully, the riverfront restaurant is ours favorite
    (C) Informal and delightful, the riverfront restaurant is a favorite of ours
    (D) Delightfully and informally, the riverfront restaurant is our favorite
    (E) The informal and delightful and riverfront restaurant is a favorite of ours

435. <u>To accidentally forget someone's name is not a crime</u>; do not be afraid to ask.

    (A) To accidentally forget someone's name is not a crime
    (B) To forget accidentally someone's name is not a crime
    (C) Is not a crime accidentally to forget someone's name
    (D) It is not a crime to accidentally forget someone's name
    (E) Accidentally forgetting someone's name is not a crime

436. <u>While transporting it from the gallery to the museum</u>, the bust of Napoleon lost its nose.

    (A) While transporting it from the gallery to the museum
    (B) While it was transported from the gallery to the museum
    (C) While workers transported it from the gallery to the museum
    (D) Having transported it from the gallery to the museum
    (E) From the gallery to the museum as it was transported

437. On days that he knew would be chaotic, <u>Durwood has often wrote himself reminders in the morning.</u>

    (A) Durwood has often wrote himself reminders in the morning
    (B) Durwood has often written himself reminders in the morning
    (C) Durwood often written himself reminders in the morning
    (D) Durwood often writes himself reminders in the morning
    (E) Durwood often wrote himself reminders in the morning

438. The researcher used the telephone <u>to ask people who their favorite candidate was</u>.

  (A) to ask people who their favorite candidate was
  (B) to ask people who was their favorite candidate
  (C) to ask people whom their favorite candidate was
  (D) to ask of people their favorite candidate
  (E) to ask about the favorite candidate of people

439. Nobody in the office <u>takes their work home or expects to stay later than five</u>.

  (A) takes their work home or expects to stay later than five
  (B) take their work home or expect to stay later than five
  (C) take his or her work home or expect to stay later than five
  (D) takes his or her work home or expects to stay later than five
  (E) is taking their work home or expecting to stay later than five

440. <u>A potential disaster was averted by the automobile company's speedy recall.</u>

  (A) A potential disaster was averted by the automobile company's speedy recall.
  (B) A disaster was potentially averted by the automobile company's speedy recall.
  (C) A potential disaster had been averted by the speedy recall of the automobile company.
  (D) The automobile company's speedy recall averted a potential disaster.
  (E) The speedy recall of the automobile company averted a potential disaster.

441. <u>Whenever Lucinda presented her side of the argument</u> to the committee members, she invariably wins them over.

  (A) Whenever Lucinda presented her side of the argument
  (B) Whenever Lucinda argued her side
  (C) Whenever Lucinda has presented her side of the argument
  (D) Whenever Lucinda was presenting her side of the argument
  (E) Whenever Lucinda presents her side of the argument

442. On April 12 of next year, <u>I shall been serving on the board for a decade</u>.

  (A) I shall been serving on the board for a decade
  (B) I have been serving on the board for a decade
  (C) I shall have been serving on the board for a decade
  (D) I will serve on the board for a decade
  (E) I will been serving on the board for a decade

443. The sun had just rose over the hilltops when the five travelers got under way.
  (A) The sun had just rose over the hilltops
  (B) The sun just had rose over the hilltops
  (C) The sun was just risen over the hilltops
  (D) The sun is just rising over the hilltops
  (E) The sun had just risen over the hilltops

444. Although Jason hates standardized tests and feels sorry for the other students who surround him, he feels confident that he can handle anything they ask.
  (A) he feels confident that he can handle anything they ask
  (B) he feels that he can confidently handle anything they ask
  (C) he feels confident that he can handle anything the tests ask
  (D) he feels confident that he can handle anything it asks
  (E) he feels confident that he can handle anything to be asked

445. The town placed a certain percentage of revenues in a rainy-day reserve every year; furthermore, it was able to cope with the unexpected expense after the ice storm.
  (A) furthermore, it was able to cope with the unexpected expense
  (B) consequently, it was able to cope with the unexpected expense
  (C) that is, it was able to cope with the unexpected expense
  (D) meanwhile, it was able to cope with the unexpected expense
  (E) even so, it was able to cope with the unexpected expense

446. Washing my car or gardening help me to unwind after a busy week.
  (A) Washing my car or gardening help me to unwind after a busy week.
  (B) Washing my car or gardening have helped me to unwind after a busy week.
  (C) Washing my car or gardening do help me to unwind after a busy week.
  (D) Washing my car or gardening helps me to unwind after a busy week.
  (E) Gardening or washing my car help me to unwind after a busy week.

447. The ledgers that were old and dusty after many years in the back room held several important secrets.

   (A) The ledgers that were old and dusty after many years in the back room held several important secrets.

   (B) The ledgers that, after many years in the back room, were old and dusty held several important secrets.

   (C) The ledgers holding several important secrets were old and dusty after many years in the back room.

   (D) The ledgers, being old and dusty after many years in the back room, held several important secrets.

   (E) The ledgers, which were old and dusty after many years in the back room, held several important secrets.

448. The hero of the play and my supervisor at work share a number of personality quirks.

   (A) share a number of personality quirks

   (B) shares a number of personality quirks

   (C) has several personality quirks in common

   (D) are sharing a number of personality quirks

   (E) have shared a number of personality quirks

449. Residential neighborhoods in the city vary geographically, historically, and in population.

   (A) vary geographically, historically, and in population

   (B) varies geographically, historically, and in population

   (C) vary geographically, historically, and demographically

   (D) vary in geography, historically, and demographically

   (E) are varied in geography, history, and demographically

450. I wish I would have given him more attention at the meeting.

   (A) I wish I would have given him more attention

   (B) I wish I would have paid him more attention

   (C) I wish I have given him more attention

   (D) I wish I had given him more attention

   (E) I wish I gave him more attention

451. Whenever we need a proofreader or someone who edits, we call on Carlotta or one of her freelance employees.
   (A) Whenever we need a proofreader or someone who edits
   (B) When needing a proofreader or editor
   (C) Whenever we need a proofreader or editor
   (D) When being in need of a proofreader or an editor
   (E) Having need of either a proofreader or someone who edits

452. Collecting every possible bit of state aid is critical to a district like ours, where nearly 70 percent of students is eligible for free or reduced lunch.
   (A) where nearly 70 percent of students is eligible for free or reduced lunch
   (B) in which nearly 70 percent of students is eligible for free and reduced lunch
   (C) given nearly 70 percent of students eligible for free or reduced lunch
   (D) where nearly 70 percent of students are eligible for free or reduced lunch
   (E) where free-or-reduced lunch eligibility is true of nearly 70 percent of students

453. Collecting his prize for the best essay, Jonas showed humility equal to Mother Teresa during an audience with the Pope.
   (A) equal to Mother Teresa during an audience with the Pope
   (B) equal to that of Mother Teresa during an audience with the Pope
   (C) equivalent to Mother Teresa's having an audience with the Pope
   (D) equal to Mother Teresa's audience with the Pope
   (E) that was equal to Mother Teresa when she had an audience with the Pope

454. Wishing to keep the information secret, the director set up a password-protected site from which hiring committee members received notifications as job candidates applied.
   (A) from which hiring committee members received notifications as job candidates applied
   (B) which hiring committee members could receive information from as job candidates applied
   (C) from which notifications go to hiring committee members as job candidates applied
   (D) as job candidates applied allowing hiring committee members to receive notification
   (E) giving hiring committee members a way to receive notifications as job candidates have applied

455. After sending thank-you notes to everyone who attended the reception in his honor, <u>it was time to enjoy his retirement.</u>

(A) it was time to enjoy his retirement
(B) his retirement was able to be enjoyed
(C) he had time to enjoy his retirement
(D) his retirement could begin enjoyably
(E) it allowed him to enjoy his retirement

456. <u>To complete the project on time and under budget, all of their weekends were devoted to on-site work.</u>

(A) To complete the project on time and under budget, all of their weekends were devoted to on-site work.
(B) In order to complete the project on time and under budget, all of their weekends were devoted to on-site work.
(C) Completing the project on time and under budget, all of their weekends were devoted to on-site work.
(D) To complete the project on time and under budget, they devoted all of their weekends to on-site work.
(E) To complete the project on time and under budget meant devoting to on-site work all of their weekends.

457. <u>The story in the newspaper shocked Dennis and I</u>; we were sure that the reporter had made a mistake.

(A) The story in the newspaper shocked Dennis and I
(B) The story in the newspaper shocked me and Dennis
(C) The story in the newspaper shocked Dennis and me
(D) The newspaper story was shocking to me and Dennis
(E) I and Dennis were shocked by the newspaper story

458. The sandwich shop that recently opened in the basement of the Fallwell Building offers sandwiches <u>that have a range of</u> traditional ham and Swiss to new age sprouts and fire-roasted tofu with a cranberry glaze.

(A) that have a range of
(B) ranging from
(C) ranged from
(D) in a range between
(E) of a range from

459. Maize, or corn, especially in its ground form, cornmeal, was a staple in Mexico <u>as it was of the Africans</u> following its introduction there by Portuguese traders.

(A) as it was of the Africans
(B) just like that of Africans
(C) as it was in Africa
(D) as did the Africans
(E) similar to Africa

460. Canberra, Australia's capital city, was built for that purpose in 1908 as a compromise when rivals Sydney and Melbourne <u>could not agree on which of them would be the seat of the Australian government.</u>

(A) could not agree on which of them would be the seat of the Australian government
(B) could not agree which one would be the seat of the Australian government
(C) disagreed on who would be the seat of the Australian government
(D) failed to agree who of them would be the seat of the Australian government
(E) could not agree on who would be the seat of the Australian government

461. <u>Politicians should listen to we ordinary citizens</u> instead of paying so much attention to biased polls.

(A) Politicians should listen to we ordinary citizens
(B) Politicians should listen to we, the ordinary citizens
(C) Politicians should listen to ordinary citizens like we are
(D) Politicians should listen to us ordinary citizens
(E) Politicians should listen to us as ordinary citizens

462. Although the bridge was scheduled to open in 2010, <u>problems involving soil stability, the flooding of the river, and damaged concrete forms delayed construction</u> for over a year.

(A) problems involving soil stability, the flooding of the river, and damaged concrete forms delayed construction
(B) problems involving the stability of the soil, the flooding of the river, and the damaging of concrete forms delayed construction
(C) problems involving soil stability, the flooding of the river, and damaged concrete forms has delayed construction
(D) problems involving soil stability, river flooding, and damaging to concrete forms delayed construction
(E) problems involving soil stability, river flooding, and damaged concrete forms delayed construction

463. Whereas butter is made from milk fat, margarine is made mostly from plant oils, although it may contain skimmed milk.

(A) Whereas butter is made from milk fat

(B) While milk fat is used to make butter

(C) Although milk fat is used to make butter

(D) Whereas butter is a product of milk fat

(E) Whereas we derive butter from milk fat

464. Being as the film version of Rodgers & Hammerstein's *Oklahoma!* was a huge hit, it made sense that the producers would choose another Rodgers & Hammerstein musical, *South Pacific*, to adapt for the screen next.

(A) Being as the film version of Rodgers & Hammerstein's *Oklahoma!* was a huge hit

(B) With the film version of Rodger & Hammerstein's *Oklahoma!* having been a huge hit

(C) Since the film version of Rodger & Hammerstein's *Oklahoma!* was a huge hit

(D) The fact being that the film version of Rodger & Hammerstein's *Oklahoma!* was a huge hit

(E) With the film version of Rodger & Hammerstein's *Oklahoma!* being a huge hit

465. The London Underground is the rapid transit system in the United Kingdom it serves most of Greater London.

(A) it serves most of Greater London

(B) that serves most of Greater London

(C) which serves most of Greater London

(D) having served most of Greater London

(E) and serving most of Greater London

466. There are several companies in the United States that provide broadband for private and commercial aviation; Aircell being just one of them.

(A) Aircell being just one of them

(B) Aircell just one of them

(C) Aircell is just one of them

(D) one of them being Aircell

(E) just one of them is Aircell

467. Purdue University, a six-campus system, is named for the Lafayette, Indiana, businessman <u>who donated the land and money to establish a college of science, technology, and the study of agriculture.</u>

(A) who donated the land and money to establish a college of science, technology, and the study of agriculture

(B) whom donated the land and money to establish a college of science, technology, and the study of agriculture

(C) who donated both land and money for establishing a college of science, technology, and the study of agriculture

(D) who donated the land and money to establish a college of science, technology, and agriculture

(E) donating the land and money to establish a college of science, technology, and agriculture

468. Thomas Eakins, the American realist painter, is best known for his <u>portraits of family and friends and prominent people in the arts, scientists, and doctors.</u>

(A) portraits of family and friends and prominent people in the arts, scientists, and doctors

(B) portraits of family, friends, and prominent people in the arts, scientists, and doctors

(C) portraits of family and friends as well as prominent people like artists, scientists, and doctors

(D) portraits of family, friends, and prominent people in the arts, sciences, and medicine

(E) portraits of family, friends, and prominent people in the arts as well as science and doctors

469. Many Yankees fans do not realize that their team was founded in Baltimore as the "Orioles" <u>and only moved to New York in 1903,</u> whereupon they took the name "Highlanders."

(A) and only moved to New York in 1903

(B) and moved to New York only in 1903

(C) moving only to New York in 1903

(D) having moved to New York only in 1903

(E) only in 1903 moving to New York

470. The television ratings known as the "Nielsens" are collected in one of two ways: using targeted viewer diaries, in which viewers record their own viewing habits, and with Set Meters, which are electronic devices connected to televisions.

(A) using targeted view diaries, in which viewers record their own viewing habits, and with Set Meters

(B) using targeted view diaries, in which viewers record their own viewing habits, and using Set Meters

(C) by targeted viewer diaries, in which viewers record their own viewing habits, as well as Set Meters

(D) targeted viewer diaries, in which viewers record their own viewing habits, and with Set Meters

(E) using targeted view diaries, which viewers record their own viewing habits, and using Set Meters

471. The director of the museum, Dr. Felicity Krumm, was kind enough to escort my classmates and I around the restoration facility.

(A) to escort my classmates and I

(B) escorting my classmates and me

(C) in escorting my classmates and I

(D) escorting me and my classmates

(E) to escort my classmates and me

472. There was a small building on the grounds of the boarding school that had been a hideout for soldiers in the French and Indian War.

(A) There was a small building on the grounds of the boarding school that had been a hideout for soldiers in the French and Indian War.

(B) On the grounds of the boarding school stood a small building that had been a hideout for soldiers in the French and Indian War.

(C) On the grounds of the boarding school from the French and Indian War stood a small building that had been a hideout for soldiers.

(D) A small building stood on the grounds of the boarding school that had been a hideout for soldiers in the French and Indian War.

(E) A small building stood on the grounds of the boarding school, once a hideout for soldiers in the French and Indian War.

473. In the whole, people tend to become disenchanted with products whose advertisements seem overproduced or poorly written.

(A) In the whole
(B) Mainly
(C) On the whole
(D) Each time
(E) Without a hitch

474. For his exciting and original work in particle physics, Professor Judah Wright consistently receives more federal funding than anyone at the university.

(A) than anyone at the university
(B) of anyone at the university
(C) than anyone else at the university
(D) than anyone at the university does
(E) than everyone at the university

475. After a brief pause, which was received with gratitude by all of the nearby residents, the jackhammer started up again even more louder than before.

(A) the jackhammer started up again even more louder than before
(B) the jackhammer started up again more louder than even before
(C) the jackhammer started up again even more loud than before
(D) the jackhammer started up again even more loudly than before
(E) the jackhammer started up again loudlier than ever before

476. On reaching my 18th year in the spring of 2010, my parents and grandparents pooled their resources and bought me the very car I am still driving today.

(A) On reaching my 18th year in the spring of 2010
(B) Reaching my 18th year in the spring of 2010
(C) Having reached my 18th year in the spring of 2010
(D) When I reached my 18th year in the spring of 2010
(E) In the spring of 2010, turning 18 years of age

477. Henry Ford, the most famous of all American industrialists, founded the automobile company that bears his name and was the one who perfected the assembly line, a means of production still in use today.

(A) founded the automobile company that bears his name and was the one who perfected

(B) founded the automobile company that bears his name and was the man who perfected

(C) not only founded the automobile company that bears his name and also perfected

(D) founded the automobile company that bears his name and perfected

(E) founded the automobile company which bears his name and perfected

478. Adam Smith's supposition that an individual who pursues his own self-interest is promoting the good of society is an underpinning of certain political and economic philosophies up to the present day.

(A) is promoting the good of society

(B) promotes the good of society

(C) promotes society's good

(D) is promoting the good of the society

(E) would be promoting the good of society

479. Dubai, hitherto known for its oil wealth, enormous construction projects, and thriving economy, has recently become a major airline hub for Western travelers moving back and forth to South Asia and the Middle East.

(A) hitherto known for its oil wealth

(B) henceforth known for its richness in oil

(C) subsequently known for its oil wealth

(D) accordingly known for its oil wealth

(E) nonetheless known for its rich oil fields

480. In 1970, following the passage of the 1967 Public Broadcasting Act, being signed into law by President Johnson, National Public Radio began as a national production center for news and cultural programming.

(A) being signed into law

(B) having been signed into law

(C) which was signed into law

(D) that was signed into law

(E) who signed into law

481. Company representatives watched in dismay as a phalanx of police officers handcuffed and led away their chief executive on the monitors.

- (A) Company representatives watched in dismay as a phalanx of police officers handcuffed and led away their chief executive on the monitors.
- (B) In dismay, company representatives watched a phalanx of police officers handcuff and lead away their chief executive on the monitors.
- (C) As a phalanx of police officers handcuffed and led away their chief executive, dismayed company representatives watched on the monitors.
- (D) Dismayed company representatives watched as a phalanx of police officers on the monitors handcuffed and led away their chief executive.
- (E) A phalanx of police officers handcuffed and led away the chief executive of company representatives watching on the monitors in dismay.

482. The accident could of been prevented if only the town had insisted on overriding the railroad's rule of requiring one flashing signal for every four blocks.

- (A) could of been prevented if only
- (B) could only of been prevented if
- (C) might of been prevented if only
- (D) might have been prevented when
- (E) could have been prevented if only

483. Between the defense budget, so-called "entitlement" programs, and the deficit, Congress has its fiscal work cut out for it in the next session.

- (A) Between the defense budget, so-called "entitlement" programs, and the deficit
- (B) From the defense budget, so-called "entitlement" programs, and the deficit
- (C) Between the defense budget and so-called "entitlement" programs, and including the deficit
- (D) From the defense budget to so-called "entitlement" programs to the deficit
- (E) Among the defense budget and so-called "entitlement" programs, plus the deficit

484. Reduction in airline service to small, rural regions has resulted in a variety of declines in those areas; among them are a decline in new businesses, a decline in college populations, and fewer tourists.

- (A) among them are a decline in new businesses, a decline in college populations, and fewer tourists
- (B) among these are declines in new businesses, college populations, and tourism
- (C) including declines in new businesses, declines in college populations, and declines in numbers of tourists
- (D) for example, new businesses, college populations, and tourists
- (E) showing declines are new businesses, college populations, tourists

485. Small business owners interested in this type of loan are required either to submit a complete application by the deadline or that they appear in person before the governing board of the foundation.

- (A) that they appear in person
- (B) appearing in person
- (C) a personal appearance
- (D) making a personal appearance
- (E) to appear in person

486. Advertisements lead consumers to purchase name-brand products, but a little research proves that store brands are cheaper and often fresher than purchasing better-known brands.

- (A) store brands are cheaper and often fresher than purchasing better-known brands
- (B) purchasing store brands costs less and is often fresher than better-known brands
- (C) to purchase store brands is cheaper and often fresher than to purchase better-known brands
- (D) store brands are cheaper and often fresher than better-known brands
- (E) store brands are cheaper than better-known brands and often fresher as well

487. Ambassador Munter, he being recently retired from the embassy in Pakistan, will spend several months as a visiting professor of law and foreign policy.

(A) Ambassador Munter, he being recently retired from the embassy in Pakistan

(B) Ambassador Munter, who recently retired from the embassy in Pakistan

(C) Ambassador Munter, who was recently retired from the Pakistan embassy

(D) Recent retiree from the embassy in Pakistan Ambassador Munter

(E) Being recently retired from the embassy in Pakistan, Ambassador Munter

488. The working of 12-hour shifts, common for many nurses today, has been found to contribute to medical errors and substandard care.

(A) The working of 12-hour shifts, common for many nurses today, has been found to contribute to medical errors and substandard care.

(B) Working 12-hour shifts, as many nurses today does, has a chance of contributing to medical errors and substandard care.

(C) Medical errors and substandard care may be the result of the working of 12-hour shifts, as are common for many nurses today.

(D) The 12-hour shifts common for many nurses today may contribute to medical errors and substandard care.

(E) Twelve-hour shifts, which are common for many nurses today, are contributors for medical errors and substandard care.

489. The term *factory farm* is typically used to describe industrial agriculture that raises large quantities of livestock in high-density conditions.

(A) is typically used to describe industrial agriculture that raises

(B) typically is used when describing the kind of industrial agriculture who raise

(C) may typically describe industrial agriculture raising

(D) is typically a term that describes industrial agriculture to raise

(E) may be used in describing industrial agriculture and raising

490. The FDA's responsibility surrounds promoting public health by the regulation and oversight of safe foods, medications, medical devices, and many other products.

(A) The FDA's responsibility surrounds promoting public health by the regulation and oversight

(B) The FDA is responsible for promoting public health through the regulation and oversight

(C) The FDA's responsibility for public health is the regulation and oversight

(D) The FDA is responsible for public health with the regulating and overseeing

(E) Through regulation and oversight, the FDA fulfills its responsibility to promote public health

PART 2

Analytical Writing Assessment

CHAPTER 4

Analysis of an Argument

For each of the following items, you will be asked to write a critique of an argument. You are not being asked for your opinion; instead, you must read the argument and the instructions that follow it, which involve considering questionable assumptions, providing alternative explanations or counterexamples, or suggesting ways to strengthen the argument presented.

Write your response on a separate sheet of paper or type it on a computer. Observe the 30-minute time limit for each response.

491. The following appeared in a school district bulletin:

"In order to vote in school elections in Lowville, you need only be a citizen, have lived in the district for 30 days, and be over the age of 18. Concerned that the turnout at recent school elections has been quite low, with only about 20 percent of eligible voters coming to the polls, school officials have discussed changing the regulations to require that voters be registered with the board of elections, as they must be for a general or municipal election. They posit that voters who are registered are already committed to the electoral process and thus are more likely to come to the polls for school elections as well."

Discuss how well reasoned you find this argument. In your discussion be sure to analyze the line of reasoning and the use of evidence in the argument. For example, you may need to consider what questionable assumptions underlie the thinking and what alternative explanations or counterexamples might weaken the conclusion. You can also discuss what sort of evidence would strengthen or refute the argument, what changes in the argument would make it more logically sound, and what, if anything, would help you better evaluate its conclusion.

492. The following appeared on a town website:

"To get a better sense of the recreational needs of the community, the Lowville Town Board sent a questionnaire addressed to the 'head of household' in every home in the town. The board asked a series of questions designed to zero in on residents' recreational preferences, in hopes of finding three they might fund in the upcoming year. The board was gratified to get a reasonable return rate of nearly 40 percent of all questionnaires. Based on that response, the board was able to recommend that the following top vote-getters be added to the town budget: a snowmobile trail, a skeet-shooting range, and a putting green."

Discuss how well reasoned you find this argument. In your discussion be sure to analyze the line of reasoning and the use of evidence in the argument. For example, you may need to consider what questionable assumptions underlie the thinking and what alternative explanations or counterexamples might weaken the conclusion. You can also discuss what sort of evidence would strengthen or refute the argument, what changes in the argument would make it more logically sound, and what, if anything, would help you better evaluate its conclusion.

493. A resident of Coburn sent the following letter to the editor of the weekly newspaper:

"I strongly object to the proposed placement of walking trails in Coburn. Although the trails will use land that belongs to the railroads, it is land that adjoining neighbors are accustomed to using for their own purposes. In addition, it is clear that people bent on nefarious purposes such as robbery will be able to use the trails to access the houses that back onto that land. Walking trails that steal land and protect criminals have no place in Coburn."

Discuss how well reasoned you find this argument. In your discussion be sure to analyze the line of reasoning and the use of evidence in the argument. For example, you may need to consider what questionable assumptions underlie the thinking and what alternative explanations or counterexamples might weaken the conclusion. You can also discuss what sort of evidence would strengthen or refute the argument, what changes in the argument would make it more logically sound, and what, if anything, would help you better evaluate its conclusion.

494. The state school board association sent this note to its constituent school board members:

"It is clear that the proposed 10 percent cuts to state aid affect poor districts more than wealthy districts. If the statewide average cut per student is $500, wealthy districts' cuts are far below that average, whereas the poorest upstate districts will receive cuts that are nearly twice that average. Since state aid is distributed now in a way that gives more to the poor districts than to the wealthy districts, shouldn't cuts in state aid be similarly equitable?"

Discuss how well reasoned you find this argument. In your discussion be sure to analyze the line of reasoning and the use of evidence in the argument. For example, you may need to consider what questionable assumptions underlie the thinking and what alternative explanations or counterexamples might weaken the conclusion. You can also discuss what sort of evidence would strengthen or refute the argument, what changes in the argument would make it more logically sound, and what, if anything, would help you better evaluate its conclusion.

495. Senator Winston Diehard recently delivered a speech at West Point, from which this is excerpted:

"I could not disagree more with Senators Weeks and Bland, who are lobbying Congress day and night to dismantle the Triton Missile Program. Yes, at $10 billion spent so far in research and development, Triton is expensive, but what price freedom? Would your tax dollars really be better spent propping up a variety of social programs than in defending our nation from the enemy abroad? Furthermore, why would you simply throw that $10 billion down the drain?"

Discuss how well reasoned you find this argument. In your discussion be sure to analyze the line of reasoning and the use of evidence in the argument. For example, you may need to consider what questionable assumptions underlie the thinking and what alternative explanations or counterexamples might weaken the conclusion. You can also discuss what sort of evidence would strengthen or refute the argument, what changes in the argument would make it more logically sound, and what, if anything, would help you better evaluate its conclusion.

496. The following paragraph appeared in a local newspaper:

"Presented with a serious deficit, the county administrator in Kindle County suggested reducing sanitation workers' pay by 1 percent to avoid layoffs. The union balked and called for a raise, as in previous years, of 4 percent. The county board decided it would be only fair to split the difference and agreed to a 2.5 percent increase in wages along with a slight increase in the county's share of health benefits."

Discuss how well reasoned you find this argument. In your discussion be sure to analyze the line of reasoning and the use of evidence in the argument. For example, you may need to consider what questionable assumptions underlie the thinking and what alternative explanations or counterexamples might weaken the conclusion. You can also discuss what sort of evidence would strengthen or refute the argument, what changes in the argument would make it more logically sound, and what, if anything, would help you better evaluate its conclusion.

497. The following is excerpted from a library bulletin:

"In an attempt to clear space for our proposed media room, we anticipate ridding the library of nonfiction materials with a copyright date before 1980. Note that this applies only to nonfiction; we will not be eliminating classic literature of the 18th, 19th, and 20th centuries. However, because the fields of science and history tend to evolve over time, most of our old nonfiction texts contain information that is outdated and supplanted by more current facts and details, whether those are found in more recent print texts or online."

Discuss how well reasoned you find this argument. In your discussion be sure to analyze the line of reasoning and the use of evidence in the argument. For example, you may need to consider what questionable assumptions underlie the thinking and what alternative explanations or counterexamples might weaken the conclusion. You can also discuss what sort of evidence would strengthen or refute the argument, what changes in the argument would make it more logically sound, and what, if anything, would help you better evaluate its conclusion.

498. This argument appeared in an industry newsletter:

"For too long, fringe environmental groups have tried to divide communities through fear. Now is the time to speak truth to hysteria. The fact is that if we do not pursue horizontal drilling for shale gas, we will continue to be slaves to Middle Eastern oil. A recent report by the Energy Institute at the University of Texas determined that the kinds of contamination ascribed to horizontal drilling (fracking) are common to most gas and oil operations, and that pollution of groundwater, when it occurs, is due to above ground spills or mishandling of wastewater, not to the drilling per se."

Discuss how well reasoned you find this argument. In your discussion be sure to analyze the line of reasoning and the use of evidence in the argument. For example, you may need to consider what questionable assumptions underlie the thinking and what alternative explanations or counterexamples might weaken the conclusion. You can also discuss what sort of evidence would strengthen or refute the argument, what changes in the argument would make it more logically sound, and what, if anything, would help you better evaluate its conclusion.

499. Congressman Bud Jett included this argument in a recent speech:

"So-called 'trickle-down economics' has served this country well. The accumulation of capital and the health of our overall economy depend on people's ability to save and invest, which depends in turn on reducing taxes and regulations. Excessive taxes, as you know, in fact reduce potential revenue, because they lower incentives to produce and grow. This 'trickle-down' plan worked beautifully in the 1980s to grow our economy, and any growth we see in the future will be due to the tax cuts we impose today."

Discuss how well reasoned you find this argument. In your discussion be sure to analyze the line of reasoning and the use of evidence in the argument. For example, you may need to consider what questionable assumptions underlie the thinking and what alternative explanations or counterexamples might weaken the conclusion. You can also discuss what sort of evidence would strengthen or refute the argument, what changes in the argument would make it more logically sound, and what, if anything, would help you better evaluate its conclusion.

500. The following is excerpted from a letter to Senator Ann T. Bellum's constituents:

"Some of you have written with your concerns about our efforts to wage the war on terror. I have no qualms about using lengthy periods of detention, hate-speech laws, wiretapping, and even, in certain cases, behaviors not sanctioned by the Geneva Conventions as we defend ourselves against those who would do us harm. Terrorism is evil, and terrorists do not follow the rules of war, so those who wage war against them cannot be bound by those rules. The proof of the pudding is in the eating: We have not experienced a serious foreign terrorist action on our shores in recent years, and we have eliminated many of the leaders of the movements, so our tactics, ideal or not, are working."

Discuss how well reasoned you find this argument. In your discussion be sure to analyze the line of reasoning and the use of evidence in the argument. For example, you may need to consider what questionable assumptions underlie the thinking and what alternative explanations or counterexamples might weaken the conclusion. You can also discuss what sort of evidence would strengthen or refute the argument, what changes in the argument would make it more logically sound, and what, if anything, would help you better evaluate its conclusion.

ANSWERS

Chapter 1: Reading Comprehension

1. (A) According to the first paragraph, the victory "ensured America's sovereignty over the Louisiana Territory," implying that America's ownership was not a sure thing before that victory.

2. (C) Draw conclusions based on what is presented, not on guesses. The writer states, "Like all good historical restorations and most of our national historical parks, this one conjures up the history it celebrates," indicating that this is a desirable feature of historical sites.

3. (B) The opening paragraph explains what the battle was and why it was important.

4. (E) The battlefield has sights of interest to tourists of all kinds (B) and also to historians and lovers of history (A), but it also houses the tombs of those killed in World Wars I and II and Vietnam, making it appropriate for veterans of foreign wars as well.

5. (A) The author appears to appreciate the site, as evidenced in the comparison to "all good historical restorations."

6. (B) The author does indicate that choice (A) is a possibility; however, just because this detail is included does not make it the central thesis. Although the major threat is to equatorial amphibians (C), it is not true that "only" those species are in danger, nor is that the main idea. There is no support for choice (D). The main idea, instead, revolves around choice (B). The new study indicates that previous anecdotal evidence was correct: Amphibians really *are* a barometer of environmental health.

7. (D) The answer may be inferred from the opening paragraph, which thanks the scientists involved for offering "proof of this hypothesis" through their "concerted, Internet-based effort." The assessment did not set forth the hypothesis (A); that had already been done via anecdotal evidence. It certainly did not eliminate the need for more study (B); nor did it refute the contention (C). It proved it (D).

8. (C) Paragraphs 2, 3, and 5 do not mention the Caribbean at all. Paragraph 4 includes the information "the highest percentages of threatened species are in the Caribbean," followed by three examples: "In Haiti, for example, 9 out of 10 species of amphibians are threatened. In Jamaica, it's 8 out of 10, and in Puerto Rico, 7 out of 10." Because the evidence appears in paragraph 4, the best answer is choice (C).

9. (B) The author is not providing background on the assessment study (A). This particular paragraph does not contain a list of amphibians that are most at risk (C). Nor does it give examples of dangers (D); instead, it explains why certain environmental factors (clean water, clean air) are especially important for amphibians. It does not supply an action plan (E). The point of the paragraph is to indicate what qualities amphibians have that put them at risk, so choice (B) is the best answer.

10. (D) The Bering Land Bridge is described as connecting Siberia to what is now Alaska. If humans walked across from Siberia, the first ones in North America would have emerged into Alaska.

11. (A) According to the passage, you could drive across the bridge, if it still existed, in about an hour. Based on that information, you can infer that the bridge was about as long as a typical mileage per hour, which would put it at choice (A), between 50 and 75 miles.

12. (A) A land bridge is a piece of land with water on either side that connects two larger pieces of land. That makes it equivalent to an isthmus (A). A bay (B) is a body of water, a strait (C) is a channel of water connecting two pieces of land, a pass (D) is a narrow piece of land between mountains, and an island (E) is a landmass entirely surrounded by water.

13. (D) The third paragraph begins with a description of the ecology of the mammoth steppe and ends by explaining that the movement of large mammals across the Bering Land Bridge led to the movement of human hunters across that same bridge. Since the main topic of the passage is the Bering Land Bridge, the author's reason for including this information is to show how the bridge was used to move animals and then human hunters. There is no information about animal growth (A), the author does not emphasize the need for toughness in animals (B), the author does not contrast the two climates (C), and the animals described are certainly not domesticated (E). The only possible answer is choice (D).

14. (A) Although the paragraph mentions geologists and ethnologists (B), it does not compare their methodology. Nor does it list reasons for migration (C), contradict a theory (D), or show a change in focus (E). The paragraph primarily puts forth a theory about migration across the land bridge, supporting the theory with discoveries made by ethnologists, from shared religions to similarities in tools and food preservation. The best answer is choice (A).

15. (B) According to the passage, some Native Americans object to the theory because "it contradicts most native teachings on the origins of the people" and "it seems to undermine the notion that they are truly 'native' to the North American continent." In other words, it challenges their history and status.

16. (C) According to the second paragraph, "Bulldozers remove the topsoil, and excavators or other types of power machinery are used to remove the underlying layer of bauxite." In other words, a layer of bauxite lies underneath the layer of topsoil. Although clay is then often removed from the bauxite, there is no indication that bauxite is found wherever clay is found (B), and the first paragraph stated directly that aluminum is *in* Earth's crust, not *below* it (D).

17. (C) The third paragraph describes the process of refinement and its by-products. Those that are mentioned in the paragraph include choices (A), (B), (D), and (E). There is no mention of choice (C), which is an alloy of aluminum and an element not involved in this refining process.

18. (A) A quick scan of the second, third, and fourth paragraphs indicates that the second is about mining, the third about refining, and the fourth about smelting. All three are steps in the process of making aluminum, so choice (A) is correct.

19. (B) The three-step process that produces aluminum is described as involving mining, refining, and smelting. It is typical of the process that results in most metal products that we use, so it is parallel to copper production (B). None of the other three products results from the same three-step process.

20. (B) Choice (A) is true, but it has nothing to do with the protests. There is no evidence to support choice (D). Choices (C) and (E) may or may not be true; they are implied, but they are not a major point. The mention of protests mainly indicates choice (B), that working people are beginning to question the dangers of mining.

21. (A) There is nothing to support choices (B), (C), or (E), and the author is completely objective when it comes to the discussion of Karl Bayer (D). In the final paragraph, the author states, "As with all mining of metals, bauxite mining presents certain hazards," indicating that choice (A) is the best answer.

22. (A) George Thomson was J.J.'s son, and his work followed that of his father. Hertz and Lenard are described as working with waves but not as particles. Of the choices, only Johnstone Stoney is mentioned as having described the particle he called the *electron*.

23. (C) Return to the passage and look for information on Thomson's first experiment. "The first experiment determined that the negative charge of cathode rays could not be separated from the rays themselves using magnetism." The negative charge (A) was discovered earlier by Jean Perrin. Thomson diverted the rays (B) in his second experiment, not the first, and he determined the tiny size and huge charge of the particles (D) in his third experiment. The fact that the charge could not be removed from the rays indicated that it was a property of particles. The answer is choice (C).

24. (B) Corpuscles are mentioned as a term of Isaac Newton's, which he used to describe particles of light long before his theories were proved. The same term was used by Thomson to describe the particles he found in cathode rays. The best answer is choice (B).

25. (E) Following this opening, the author goes on to name the variety of scientists whose work led to this important discovery. Even if you did not understand the opening sentence, you could tell that this was not a straightforward discovery but rather one that depended on many people's discoveries. The author never, however, goes so far as to imply that the discovery could never have been made by a single scientist (C)—only that it was not.

26. (A) The author calls J. J. Thomson's experiments "elegant" and credits him with determining "the existence of a subatomic particle with a negative charge." There is no support in the passage for the other choices.

27. (C) An electron microscope uses streams of electrons to allow us to view things smaller than a beam of light. It relies on the connection between particles and waves in electrons. Although the other inventions mentioned rely on waves, they do not depend on the connection between those waves and the particles that make up those waves.

28. (D) Hunting and habitat destruction are the only reasons mentioned for the depopulation of elk prior to the 20th century.

29. (D) According to the passage, in 1913, 50 elk were moved from Yellowstone to Pennsylvania. Two years later, 95 more were moved. The total shipped in those years comes to 145.

30. (D) "At present," says the passage, "new herds are established in Arkansas, Kentucky, Michigan, and Wisconsin, in addition to Pennsylvania." There is talk of moving herds to Tennessee (A) and the Adirondacks (C) in the future. Georgia (B) is mentioned only as the original southernmost range of eastern elk; it is not a place where they might be seen today, and Ohio (E) is not mentioned at all.

31. (B) As the passage states clearly, "All of the eastern subspecies are now extinct." The reintroduced subspecies is the western subspecies, the one found in Yellowstone. It is a different subspecies from the original Pennsylvania elk.

32. (C) The author claims positive things about the reclamation of land (A) and the reintroduction of elk (D), and there is no support for choices (B) and (E) in the passage. Because reintroduction now includes careful monitoring of species and more concern about the animals' welfare, the author states, "today reintroduction is vastly improved." (C).

33. (B) A central thesis is a main idea. Although choice (C) may be inferred from the passage, it is not the main idea. Choice (A) is belied by the fact that the depression in Holland ended up moving across Europe, and choices (D) and (E) are incorrect, since the Stock Exchange already existed at the time of tulipomania. The passage primarily shows the damaging effects of a craze (B).

34. (A) You must make this prediction based on what the author has said in the passage. The author implies that the "people's exchange" was less safe than the Stock Exchange, so choice (B) is unlikely, but there is still no indication that trading stocks is "risk-free" (C). The author does not generalize about flowers as an investment (E). There is no opinion given about the wisdom of trading at auctions (D); certainly it does not work well in tulipomania, but generalizing from that to the world at large is not possible. It is more viable to generalize that trading in futures may be ill-advised (A), especially since the answer includes the qualifying word *may*.

35. (A) There is no example given of sales transacted in pubs and town squares (II), nor is there an example to show how Holland fell into a depression (III). The assertion that tulips have a built-in rarity (I) is supported by two examples: "It takes years to grow one from seed, and most bulbs produce only one or two bulb clones annually." Since only (I) is correct, the answer is choice (A).

36. (E) The so-called "people's exchange" was neither fair (A) nor efficient (D), and it certainly did not hold prices down (C). It was an informal trading structure outside the realm of the traditional Stock Exchange.

37. (B) "Speculation on prospective tulip growth" equals trade in commodities futures, which today takes place in exchange trading on the mercantile exchange.

38. (C) This question gives you a fact about the present and asks you to apply it to your understanding of the past. If Holland continues to trade tulips at auction, the auction system cannot be dead (A), and agricultural products must still be part of the Dutch economy (D).

Choice (B) in no way corresponds to the fact from today, and choice (E) seems very unlikely, given the Dutch experience with exotic commodities in the form of flowers. Choice (C), on the other hand, is a reasonable question. Now that Holland appears to be successful at the bulb trade, something must have happened to change the way things worked.

39. (B) The author uses the word *incredibly* to describe the fact that nearly every ape on the planet appears on the Red List. Her tone is that of someone who is shocked at this information. She surely does not feel that this is inevitable (A) or accepted (E), or she would not blame it so straightforwardly on human behavior. Nor does she think it is impossible (D); it is clearly happening. There is nothing to indicate that she thinks it is intentional (C); it is more a side effect of human behavior and not entirely deliberate, except in the case of poaching.

40. (B) According to the third paragraph, in areas with Ebola, it wipes out 90 percent of the gorillas. That leaves 1 in 10.

41. (C) The only way to answer this question is to refer back to the sentences indicated. Sentence 1: "The western lowland gorilla moved from 'endangered' to 'critically endangered' in 2007." Sentence 2: "'Critically endangered' indicates that its population and range are shrinking, and it is in imminent danger of extinction." Sentence 2 defines the term *critically endangered* that is used in sentence 1. The correct answer is (C).

42. (C) The main point of the passage will be the point around which every paragraph in the passage is centered. The author never states that gorillas are not designed for survival (A). Although conservation does not seem to be working at present, the author never suggests that it is an unrealistic goal (B). Choice (D) may be a tacit conclusion one may draw from the passage, but it is not overtly suggested and is not the main point. Choice (E) is never implied. Every part of the passage indicates that human behavior is harming the great apes in general and gorillas in particular. The best answer is (C).

43. (A) Return to the fifth paragraph and compare it to the answer choices. The author begins with the statement: "The number-one threat to gorillas, however, is human greed." The other sentences in the paragraph give examples of this, including the burning of forests for fuel and the killing of gorillas for meat and medicine. Although indignities are mentioned (B), the author does not "compare" them. Nor does the author list reasons for extinction of species (C); the list gives examples of harm done to gorillas but does not imply that they have caused extinction. The fifth paragraph does not contradict what has come before (D) or provide examples based on the previous paragraph (E); it confirms the hypothesis and adds examples, making choice (A) correct.

44. (E) The best answer will be clearly supported by the information in the passage. Choice (A) is contradicted by the fact that African rangers are trying to protect gorillas. Choice (B) is not suggested anywhere in the passage. Choice (C) is again contradicted by the fact that conservationists and rangers are doing their best. The only conclusion that is supported is choice (E). The author ends with the grim assessment: "Some give these vegetarian cousins of *Homo sapiens* no more than a decade before all wild specimens are eradicated."

45. (C) Ether's run is described as "brief but important," implying that despite its short reign as the anesthetic of choice, it was an effective choice. There is no support in the passage for any of the other answer choices.

46. (B) Choice (A) is far too broad for the four-paragraph passage given here, which really focuses on a single anesthetic (B). Choice (C) is not relevant to the passage, which focuses more on how anesthetics have been similar from century to century than on how they have changed. Although the passage opens with a reference to ancient physicians (D) and mentions some dangers (E), neither of these is the main idea of the passage.

47. (E) Your answer will be the statement that *least* indicates that ether was important. To find it, you must read each statement with that key idea in mind. Statement (A) supports the idea by showing how one doctor used ether. Statement (B) supports the idea by showing that doctors were eager to learn about ether. Statement (C) supports the idea by showing that artists of the day captured the important event. Statement (D) shows the interest of doctors and dignitaries. Only statement (E) does not fit; it states only that the usefulness of ether had not been discovered for many years.

48. (A) "Supposed to have discovered" means that Lullus is "said to have discovered." It implies that there is not a lot of corroborating evidence; if there were, the author would have simply said "discovered." Choice (B) may be true, but for the time being, the author is implying that Lullus may or may not have made the discovery.

49. (C) The fourth paragraph is a narrative that tells about Morton's demonstration, followed by his attempts to win a patent. It is told in story form, in the order in which events occurred.

50. (A) The inclusion of information about Long may in part be a cautionary tale about the importance of publishing results (B), but since Morton himself died in penury, it is not a very good cautionary tale. Choice (C) is true, but it is not the primary reason the author included this information. There is no evidence to support choice (D); in fact, the author makes clear that Long's being overlooked was largely his own fault. Long's mention has nothing to do with the safety of the procedure (E). The best answer is choice (A); Long performed an operation using ether before Morton did.

51. (E) Reread the entire sentence and compare it to the answer choices. The only choice that is supported by the sentence is choice (E)—Baffin Island is part of a geological shield that extends down into the northern United States, meaning that it shares physical traits with those northern states.

52. (D) The information cited comes from hunters and trekkers, making it anecdotal rather than scientific or historical.

53. (A) The second paragraph uses direction words and adjectives to provide a description of the island.

54. (C) Although the author names a few heroes of the sport (D), that is not the primary purpose of the passage, which is far more general and descriptive, without being historical (E).

55. (D) A score of 0 means the rider fell off. A score of 50 indicates great balance and control. A score in between means the rider may not have had one or more of those skills but still maintained his seat on the bull.

56. (A) The first sentence mentions certain bulls who have attained fame; the other sentences give examples of those.

57. (A) The Viking was a "heathen," making him inappropriate as a husband for a good Christian woman.

58. (C) You are asked to find another reason why Sunniva's body might have been intact when it was discovered by King Olav. Therefore, choice (B) cannot be correct. Choices (A) and (D) are irrelevant to the condition of her body, and choice (E) does not make sense. Only choice (C) provides a logical explanation.

59. (B) The first paragraph introduces Sunniva and ends by announcing the legend. The following paragraphs detail that legend.

60. (D) *La Solidaridad* was published in Spain, not the Philippines (A), and Rizal worked in Europe, not in the Philippines (C). There is no support for choice (B), and the revolution (E) came late in the decade. The best inference is choice (D).

61. (C) Choices (A), (B), (D), and (E) would not foment revolution among Filipinos, but descriptions of abuses (C) might.

62. (A) Paragraph 1 introduces the Propaganda Movement, and paragraphs 2 and 3 present two examples, one an organization and newspaper, and the other a key leader of the movement.

63. (E) The paragraph primarily discusses the purpose of GreenBiz, which is described in choice (E).

64. (A) The database contains a list of green business practices. Those might be useful for any new company.

65. (D) The sentence contrasts relatively new corporations, Cisco and Microsoft, with older ones, Ford and General Electric.

66. (E) The passage as a whole is about Lee and the various companies and institutions for which he worked.

67. (C) Rockefeller needed a publicity agent to reestablish his name following the dreadful mine strike disaster.

68. (C) The movement from disgrace to heroism is what is important here.

69. (A) You must find the one that Lee would probably *not* do. The author states that Lee "did not believe in covering up but rather in controlling the release of the truth."

70. (E) Although monetarism largely failed in modern times, the author concedes that it succeeded in helping today's authorities better understand the role of money in the stability of economies.

71. (D) A monetarist believes that fluctuations in the marketplace are due to the existence or lack of money.

72. (C) The passage is about monetarism, although some reference to Keynesian thought is made (A). Friedman (B) is not the focus, and the author does not make judgments about the proper or improper role of money (D) or about other policies (E).

73. (E) "In the 1970s," says the author, "this theory seemed to gibe with the inflation spikes that were occurring. . . ." Yet "inflation in the 1990s was unrelated to monetary policy."

74. (E) Monetarists, like libertarians, believe in a minimal role for government; whereas Keynesians, like statists, believe in a measure of government control of policy.

75. (C) Regarding acronyms, the author says only that leadership must clarify and define terms as they are intended to be used.

76. (E) Calls in a huddle are in a shorthand that is understood by all the participants and used to initiate an action, just as shared vocabulary in an organization should be.

77. (D) "Are they all on the same page when they talk about success or excellence?" asks the author. In other words, does everyone share the same definition of *success*? The author is using the term as an example of a simple word that might need a common definition.

78. (B) The author's main point is that shared vocabulary is necessary in any sort of institution.

79. (C) While any of the choices may be true, the only one the author focuses on is choice (C).

80. (C) Although AzPro's past practices apparently led to current problems, the author does mention that "its recent practices are considered state-of-the-art when it comes to public health and safety." Today's AzPro, in other words, is viewed positively.

81. (A) The third paragraph is entirely focused on arsenic as a cause of various health problems. It does not mention any other disease-causing agents (B).

82. (C) In the final paragraph, the author notes that the accepted levels of ppb have dropped recently, and that the discovered levels of arsenic around AzPro do not come near old levels once considered safe. The problem exists, but perhaps it is not as critical as some residents believe.

83. (E) MCLs, or maximum contaminant levels, would only be used to measure contaminants, and effervescence, although it may indicate some kind of gaseous contamination, is not itself a contaminant.

84. (D) Although the mention of the old standards does show how standards change over time (A), that is not the author's primary purpose. This inclusion in the passage shows that the AzPro reading would once have been well within acceptable standards and, therefore, may not be as distressing as some citizens might think.

85. (A) The author might possibly agree with choice (E), but there is no indication anywhere in the passage that this is important to him. Choice (A), on the other hand, is well supported by the information in the passage.

86. (C) The key word in this question is *primarily*. Although the author does promote the benefits of geothermal heat (B) and (E), the passage primarily describes the process and costs.

87. (D) The ground loop is described in the second paragraph. It "circulates water or another liquid, which absorbs the heat from the Earth and transports it to the heat pump." Later, "the heat pump removes heat from the hot air and transports it through the ground loop into the Earth." In other words, the ground loop conveys, or transports, heat via water or another liquid.

88. (E) The passage indicates that some people use solar panels to generate their own electricity, thus saving on the high cost of running the heat pump.

89. (B) Although its cost may look better as oil prices rise, the passage does not indicate that costs of geothermal will drop (A). However, more people may turn to geothermal, making choice (B) correct.

90. (B) William I abdicated, but his son and grandson did not. Like Queen Wilhelmina, William I relinquished the throne to his child, in his case, a son, not a daughter. Choice (B) is correct.

91. (E) It would seem logical for Willem-Alexander to cede his throne to his eldest daughter, but in fact, all of the female monarchs mentioned in the passage became queen because they were the only children or were the eldest of all girls. There is no mention of a rule of succession in the passage, so it is impossible based on the passage to know whether the new king would pass the throne to his eldest daughter or to any son he managed to have.

92. (D) "Clinging to their ceremonial roles for life" is not a very complimentary description of the British monarchy; the author seems to be rather critical of their methods.

93. (C) Hitler Youth is one thing that made Beatrix's marriage controversial among her people. It was an obstacle to be overcome, and it was overcome, apparently due to her husband's strong personality.

94. (A) In essence, Beatrix resigned her position and handed the reins to her child. She did not die first (E), and she did not retain her position while giving her daughter a job of her own (C). Choice (A) is best.

95. (D) The first paragraph defines the term *clawback*.

96. (B) The main idea is that these clawbacks are a new regulation with a specific purpose. Although choices (A) and (C) may be true, they are not the main focus of the passage as a whole.

97. (B) Although the mention of UnitedHealth does point up a particular scandal (C), its discussion in this context is meant to show how clawbacks were famously used.

98. (C) Cassidy writes that clawbacks may be more of a public relations tool than a reform with teeth, meaning that he is skeptical about their value.

99. (C) Paredes fears that executives may be penalized for mistakes that were honestly made rather than deliberately intended to defraud.

100. (E) Look back at the final sentence: "Some even swear that they work, either because they see immediate results and do not look for more long-term success, or because the results they see are due to any number of other, unrelated factors." If buyers believe that the devices work because they don't bother to look for long-term success, the assumption is that such devices really do not offer long-term success—they don't work in the long term.

101. (B) Choices (D) and (E) are stronger than the author's premise, and there is no support for choice (A) or (C). The author certainly suspects that some consumers will be disappointed because the devices offer no long-term relief.

102. (A) The FTC is now "requiring that efficacy claims be supported by scientific evidence." In other words, if a manufacturer makes a claim about the product's ability to eradicate pests, that claim should be backed up by proof.

103. (D) The author does not go so far as to issue a call to action (E), but the passage certainly expresses a negative opinion about ultrasonic pest control devices.

104. (C) Since the devices may work in the short term, and work better in open spaces than where walls may block the signals, choice (C) is the best bet.

105. (C) Sicker's central thesis is that without impediment, a classic love story could not exist.

106. (D) The final paragraph is about characters for whom romantic love is self-destructive, where a barrier may exist between character and reader. Edward in choice (D) is an example of such a character.

107. (A) Although barriers may indeed elongate the narrative (E), that is not their crucial role. Sicker speaks of the need for an impediment to love that ratchets up desire and conflict.

108. (A) The quote in the fourth paragraph essentially restates Sicker's central thesis.

109. (D) The legend is referred to as "one prototype for the love story."

110. (A) The passage does not discuss the disparity between rich and poor (B), nor does it suggest a migration of high-income earners (C). Choice (D) is not supported by the passage, and choice (E) is a wild surmise. The passage as a whole discusses the concentration of wealth in suburbs around large cities.

111. (E) Santa Barbara is referred to as "posh" and held up as an example of a surprise to the author—that Santa Barbara held less concentrated wealth than did Boulder, Colorado, was surprising. Santa Barbara, then, is a place with a reputation for wealth.

112. (B) The author does not suggest that income is irrelevant (D) or that the Census Bureau should have considered cost of living (A); she simply says that the study did not count cost of living, which can have an effect on real wealth or buying power.

113. (A) The author states that "office work became a goal for working women," not because it paid so much more, but because it was clean and pleasant.

114. (C) In the third paragraph, the reader learns that the status of women, even in office jobs, was lowly and restricted.

115. (D) The paragraph states: "The need for children to aid with planting and harvesting is the reason our antiquated school calendars still include a summer vacation." In other words, the current school calendar is traditional but outmoded.

116. (A) While Columbia freshmen and sophomores are immersed in a Core Curriculum, students at Princeton explore many disciplines.

117. (C) Princeton allows students to supplement their major with a certificate program that may be completely unrelated.

118. (E) The paragraph compares and contrasts two Ivy League undergraduate programs.

119. (D) The opening paragraph refutes the idea that an Ivy League education is homogenous, leading to paragraphs that provide examples to support that refutation.

120. (C) The author's premise is that the Ivies are different, and that what appeals to one student may not appeal to another. There is no indication that students should never apply both to Columbia and to Princeton (B), but rather that they should look for the school that fits their natures and needs (C).

121. (B) The focus of the paragraph is on the saving of Asian tigers by collaborative conservation programs.

122. (D) If a poacher can make nearly half a year's income for a single tiger pelt, the incentive is great to poach.

123. (B) Lao PDR, it seems, cannot even control the illegal deforestation that is decimating the environment. The implication is that one might expect that tiger conservation might not succeed there, either. It is succeeding in India, which has a strong and active government.

124. (D) By referring to deforestation as a "national disgrace," the author expresses some contempt for the leadership in Lao PDR.

125. (A) The description of Tigers Forever indicates that outsiders train local officials to enforce existing regulations. The most similar situation is U.S. soldiers training the Afghan army.

126. (B) It is certainly possible that hackers' work is enabling consumers to avoid paying for content (E), but that is not part of the passage. Hackers are described in paragraph 3 as providing open source software that allows for the conversion of content to more accessible modes.

127. (D) The area behind the walled garden appears to be quite easy to use and pleasant, but there is no question that it is limited. Choice (E) is only true in certain cases, as when children are protected from outside sources that might be disturbing.

128. (D) The author suggests that walled gardens offer ease of use to those consumers for whom a wholly open system might be too chaotic. There is no support for the other choices; the author never takes so firm a stand.

129. (A) The author defines the term and then offers a variety of examples—AOL, Kindle, iPad, and Facebook

130. (E) The author seems sympathetic with the sort of consumer who prefers to avoid chaos.

131. (C) The passage as a whole is about *Uncle Tom's Cabin* and its impact on U.S. history and culture.

132. (C) The author does not pass judgment on Harriet Beecher Stowe at all, but the passage does mention that she "received a classical education rarely available to girls at the time."

133. (C) It was the audience of women readers who "built the novel's reputation and spread its message," leading some who would not read political tracts to join the abolitionists.

134. (A) The author seems distressed that Stowe's readers had never before considered the perils of slave life. The readers were ignorant or obtuse about the realities of slavery, but they were certainly easily swayed by Stowe's descriptions.

135. (E) Unlike any of the other examples, the work of Arab Spring bloggers and videographers led directly to a change in history and culture, as readers and viewers became aware of conditions they might have dismissed in the past.

136. (B) The description of termite consumption is presented in a matter-of-fact tone, making choices (C), (D), and (E) unlikely. The writer says, "They are said to have a nutty taste and to be rich in protein," which indicates that she has not tasted them herself (A). Only choice (B) fits here.

137. (A) The third paragraph begins with a statement of opinion ("Termites are important in other ways") and goes on to list examples that support that opinion.

138. (B) The writer is not biased toward (D) or against termites (A), and she certainly does not approve of termites' destructive habits (C). She can see good as well as bad in the insects, making (B) the correct choice.

139. (A) Termites are described as breaking down wood products quickly, "releasing hydrogen as they do so."

140. (C) The rest of the passage stresses the positive qualities of termites, but this final paragraph reminds the reader of their harmful behaviors and gives some suggestions for homeowners.

141. (C) It is not the reflective surface (A) nor the antennae (E) that the author finds remarkable; rather, it is the size of that surface (C). Neither choice (B) nor (D) is supported by the paragraph.

142. (B) The three typical courses of study at Arecibo are described in the second paragraph. They include radio astronomy (C), atmospheric science (A and E), and radar astronomy (D). Since you are asked to find the exception, the correct answer is choice (B).

143. (D) To answer this kind of question, simply return to the paragraph in question and think about its main idea. The main idea of the fourth paragraph is established in the initial topic sentence: "Arecibo has been the site of hundreds of fascinating discoveries." The author then proceeds to list a few of these. The correct answer is choice (D).

144. (B) There is no way to predict whether the command center will succeed (A) or fail (C). The passage states that it will be used to study pulsars, not for atmospheric studies (D). There seems to be no logical connection between the remote-control center and expansion of the site (E). The best answer is choice (B)—the remote-control command center will mean that scientists in Texas need not travel to Puerto Rico to use the telescope.

145. (B) The author never indicates that Arecibo is anything other than a useful tool for scientists. All of the passage seems dedicated to that theme. There is no support for the other choices.

146. (C) Skim to locate mention of four out of five assertions. The underground system (A) appears in the second paragraph, rural and urban settings (B) are mentioned in the fourth paragraph, the fact that purple loosestrife is not native (D) appears in the first paragraph, and the eradication of competition (E) is in the third paragraph. The fifth paragraph says that it is "impervious to burning," making choice (C) the best answer.

147. (A) Gardeners (B) don't really object to purple loosestrife, as the second paragraph makes clear. Although many plants migrate, the passage is concerned only with one, making choice (C) too broad a title. Only the final paragraph has to do with largely unsuccessful attempts at controlling purple loosestrife, so (D) is not correct, either. Herbicides (E) are barely mentioned. The best title is choice (A)—the entire passage deals with a floral invader.

148. (B) This question indirectly asks you to locate an author's reasons for including a detail. Returning to the passage will help you see that the mention of the St. Lawrence refers to a type of wetland where purple loosestrife does well. The only answer supported by the text is choice (B).

149. (A) All five details are facts about purple loosestrife, but only its easy adaptability is a fact that "adds to its power of endurance," so the answer is choice (A).

150. (C) The answer appears in the second paragraph: "The same long growing season that makes it so beloved by gardeners makes it a seed-making machine." It is the long growing season (C) that gardeners like.

151. (D) You must infer the answer based on what you have learned about purple loosestrife from the passage. Because it thrives in wetlands and along rivers, the places it would *most* easily thrive include swamps (A), wetland meadows (B and E), and along inland waterways (C). By process of elimination, then, choice (D) is the best answer.

152. (B) Mayer's decision was away from the norm for Yahoo, which like other similar industries had always had a culture of telecommuting.

153. (C) There is nothing in the passage to support the idea that Yahoo had once had everyone in the office (B), but certainly there were data indicating that people were no longer working to capacity.

154. (E) Although the author mentions the reactions of others to Mayer's decision, the author's own suggestion is that "time will tell," and "we might all check back in a year's time to see where things stand."

155. (A) The author does not take a pro or con stance on the issue of telecommuting *vs.* office attendance. Instead, the author's attitude might be described as neutral, or detached.

156. (D) Although the author does suggest some motivations (A) and does explore some politics (C), the main point of the article is to show the various reactions once the decision was made. Choice (D) is the best answer.

157. (B) The author states that the drop is troublesome because it indicates stress on the part of consumers. In other words, the situation perturbs, or worries, the author.

158. (D) Because corporations paid out dividends in advance of a tax hike, the income levels in December were unnaturally high, leading to a larger-than-natural drop in January.

159. (C) Personal income is revealed to be in a decline, but the drop in January is also shown to be unnatural. It would be reasonable to expect a slight drop in February, but not one as severe as the one in January.

160. (A) In the last paragraph, the author warns the reader not to conflate the unnatural drop in income in January with the real and gradual drop in income for all middle-class workers.

161. (C) Haydn and Mozart enter the discussion as examples of classical composers who adopted the forms and characteristics of martial music. This does not mean that Janissary music came from Europe (B), and since Haydn and Mozart were musicians, not painters, choice (D) does not apply.

162. (C) Skim the passage to find whether examples are given to support each assertion. Looking first at assertion I, you can see that the author mentions the "Jingling Johnny" as an example of unusual percussion. Since I is a "yes," you can immediately eliminate answer choices (B) and (D). The only question remaining is whether the answer is choice (A), (C), or (E), so you must look for examples to support assertion III. The first sentence in paragraph 4 mentions "The Stars and Stripes Forever" as an example of Sousa's beloved marches. Since I and III are both "yes" responses, your answer could be choice (C) or (E). However, no example of martial music at a funeral is given, so only choice (C) is correct.

163. (A) This is a "what if?" question: What if the author included this particular piece of information? The fact that it refers to the 18th century means that it has no relation to the Civil War (C), and the use of drums preceded Janissary music (D). The best answer is choice (A); it would help support the idea that martial music was a key part of the military at that time.

164. (B) The author compares the Pentagon's expenditure on music to the government's comparatively paltry expenditure on K–12 music education. Although the information is fascinating (A), the shock value involved in the comparison makes it most likely to have been included as a critical remark.

165. (D) The entire passage is about a type of martial music, Janissary music, that was popular and influential for a while and then fell out of favor.

Chapter 2: Critical Reasoning

166. (B) Your choice must weaken the argument that purple loosestrife is best eradicated by digging it up, plowing it under, and reseeding. Choice (A) suggests another means of eradication but does not weaken the original argument. Choices (C) and (D) do not weaken or strengthen the argument, although both may suggest benefits of the eradication plan. Choice (E) shows the expense of such a plan, which is negative but not the best answer. Only choice (B) throws a monkey wrench in the works: If a new strain of purple loosestrife is growing up where it was once eliminated, then this form of eradication does not really work.

167. (D) Your challenge is to find the response that *best* supports the idea that the continents were once connected. Choice (A) affects only North America. Choice (B) affects only Siberia. Choice (C) is possible, but it does not provide the unambiguous evidence that choice (D) does. Choice (E) is really irrelevant.

168. (C) The paragraph never says either that biblical scholars don't accept evolution (D) or that evolutionary theory negates anything other than the age of the Earth in the Bible (E). It does imply that people understand the world through metanarratives, making choice (C) the best answer.

169. (D) If ether were truly important to the history of medicine, it would be nice to see some examples of its use that support that. Of the suggestions given, only choice (D) provides such examples. Ether's chemical makeup (A) has nothing to do with its importance. The names and occupations of patients (B) are unlikely to offer evidence of this kind— unless they proved to be famous historical figures. Since there is no evidence that they were, choice (B) is not the best option. A comparison of two other anesthetic agents (C) would not add or subtract useful evidence about ether's importance, and neither would lists of other compounds (E). The best answer is choice (D).

170. (A) If an answer is to challenge the assertion that gorillas will die out in a decade, the answer must give gorillas hope for a longer existence. Of the answer choices given, choice (B) would potentially end Ebola in humans, but it is not clear that this would assist gorillas. Choice (C), the breeding of different subspecies, might help gorillas, but it would not help those "in the wild," as the question demands. Twin babies (D) might indicate better odds for survival, but it is not as clear a benefit as choice (A), which would keep all humans from getting near the gorillas to harm them by hunting, clearing land, or passing on diseases. This would be a stronger challenge than choice (E) would be.

171. (A) The argument is that because the United States has not ratified, even countries that have ratified have now softened their commitment. The only assumption that supports this is choice (A).

172. (B) It does not matter what the cause of the repairs was or what the customer expectations are if the intensity of testing was such that a result of $\frac{19}{20}$ of machines in functioning condition is suitably viable for the market.

173. (B) Bowdler was indeed untrained, but the excerpt does not claim that his editing was clever (A). Nor was he a better doctor than he was a man of letters (E); the paragraph says he "never really practiced" medicine. His editing involved removing what might give offense; in other words, he was a critic and censor, making choice (B) correct.

174. (C) To solve a problem of this sort, find the phrase that follows logically from what has come before. The sentence begins with the causal transition word *since*, meaning that the phrase will be an effect of the fact that H7N9 is rarely or never transmitted from person to person. There is no evidence supporting choice (D), making choice (C) the only logical answer.

175. (D) The writer's conclusion is that nodal development is problematic. Her reasons include that the rural towns do not have the critical mass of population needed to support such development. The boldfaced sentence provides specific evidence to support the writer's premise.

176. (D) One would assume that John's A in one course would bring up his average, but it did not. Something must have stood in the way of John's receiving the predicted 3.25 GPA. If his writing course were worth double (A), his GPA would have been even higher than 3.25. If he took German pass/fail, that would have increased his GPA. Choices (C) and (E) would have no effect. However, an additional course with a grade of C would have kept his GPA at 3.0, making choice (D) correct.

177. (C) Something happened to improve Arrow's market share. Was it the ads? It is at least conceivable that Arrow's competitors changed their approach (B), but a better question is the one in choice (C). Knowing that Arrow's customers choose products based on radio ads would help you to ascertain that the radio ads did the trick.

178. (B) The reasoning in the paragraph is a form of syllogism. It can be expressed in the language of logic thusly: *P* or *Q*. *Q*. Therefore, not *P*. Choice (B) is similar: Charter schools or public schools. Charter schools. Therefore, not public schools.

179. (A) The athlete claims he did not use marijuana, and he could not have failed the drug test due to casual contact with the smoke. The explanation for the failed drug test must come from another source, and only choice (A) would provide justification for the result.

180. (A) The EPA has concluded that alternatives should be used. This is supported by the toxicity of mercury and the possibility, though minuscule, of ingesting or inhaling it.

181. (B) When the spots first appear, they are not cause for alarm (A), but when they form patterns, a doctor may call for a needle biopsy.

182. (E) What makes Google the best company to work for? According to this, it has to do with the perks provided. This means that perks must equate to happy workers, making choice (E) correct.

183. (D) The village government must respond to villagers' concerns in order to achieve a "satisfactory" rank. If villagers have said they want mail, e-mail, and a website as forms of communication, and that is what the government is providing, villagers should be satisfied.

184. (A) The paragraph delineates the strikes against Al Smith as a candidate: He was the wrong religion, from the wrong city, and held the wrong opinions. Choice (A) sums that up. None of the other choices can be directly inferred from the paragraph.

185. (D) This is a hypothetical syllogism, which may be expressed this way: If *P*, then *Q*. If *Q*, then *R*. Therefore, if *P*, then *R*. Of the choices, only choice (D) follows this pattern: If it rains, Doward turns off the sprinkler. If he turns off the sprinkler, it won't reset for 24 hours. Therefore, if it rains, the sprinkler won't reset for 24 hours.

186. (E) The school board needs to know whether people voted no on the budget because they disliked the number of administrators. They can only determine this by asking the voters directly.

187. (B) Three out of four batches came out just fine, and the same timing and ingredients were used. Only choice (B) would result in a different result for one of the batches.

188. (C) This pattern of reasoning is known as *modus tollens* and may be expressed this way: If *P*, then *Q*. Not *Q*. Therefore, not *P*. Choice (C) follows this pattern: If Lionel is in the theater, then he sits in center orchestra. Tonight Lionel is not in center orchestra. Therefore, he must not be in the theater.

189. (D) The conclusion is that the county must attend to the roads. The accident involving the neighbor is presented as evidence.

190. (B) The author concludes that the village department is a luxury because the county sheriff and state police are so close by. This is only valid if those departments have the personnel and the authorization to patrol the village, making choice (B) the best answer.

191. (E) The manufacturer heads back to the drawing board to improve the drug because one-quarter of test subjects saw spikes in blood sugar. Was this the right conclusion? Not if test subjects could not be trusted, as in choice (E). The fact that other drugs went to market with only three-quarters effectiveness (D) might change the company's mind, but it would not actually weaken its conclusion.

192. (C) This problem asks only for support for the final sentence in the passage, which states that "middle school tends to be the time when children most require their parents' attention and oversight." Choice (A) would not support it, and choice (B) would belie it. Choices (D) and (E) are irrelevant. Choice (C), on the other hand, explains the author's conclusion by providing a reason.

193. (D) The thought to be completed is that it is not surprising that three of the five cities friendliest to small business are in Texas. What would make that true? The state's low taxes and minimal bureaucratic controls (D) would do so. The other choices may be attractive, but they are not specifically attractive to small business owners.

194. (A) The author concludes, based on the need for multilingual workers, that removing another foreign language from the curriculum will be harmful.

195. (B) Only choice (B) is supported by evidence in the paragraph; the other choices are beyond the scope of what is presented here.

196. (E) The publisher's conclusion is to publish in print on Wednesdays and Saturdays, most likely because those days feature coupons and therefore high readership. None of the other choices would support such a decision.

197. (D) Your answer must directly support the contention that elk repopulation is carefully monitored. Choices (A) and (C) have nothing to do with repopulation; they deal with animals in confined conditions. Choices (B) and (E) deal with wild elk but not with monitoring of the population. Choice (D) shows an example of monitoring that is taking place today.

198. (B) Although any of the pieces of evidence might be used to counter Jake's conclusion, only choice (B) is likely to have an effect. If increasing the wages proportionally does not really cause Jake to have to lay people off—because his income is great enough to cover it—his argument is weakened.

199. (A) The conclusion is that the cost of farmland will continue to grow, mostly because it is rare. Thus an increase in rarity will correlate with an increase in value.

200. (D) Which answer choice means that cities might *not* continue to grow despite a slowing of migration from the countryside? Only if population growth were slowed in some other way would the cities cease to grow. Choice (D) provides that other method of slowing growth.

201. (D) The conclusion is that herbal remedies should be controlled by the FDA, and the only choice that supports that argument is choice (D), which indicates a potential harm from unregulated herbs.

202. (A) Instead of leaping to the conclusion that diet and exercise don't work but medicine will, the doctor counters with the suggestion that the diet and exercise plan needs another three months to work. The patient has ignored the time element in developing his argument.

203. (B) The question is: Why did children become ill if there were no problems with the chicken casserole? The answer must be that the children became ill in some other way—in this case, by eating something else that did, in fact, contain disease-causing bacteria.

204. (A) The critics blame the outflow of rural doctors on the shrinking of Medicare reimbursements. To evaluate the validity of that argument, it makes sense to determine how those rural doctors are affected by the shrinking of reimbursements, and such a study might begin with the numbers of rural patients who rely on Medicare.

205. (E) To follow logically, the end of the sentence must continue to demonstrate ways in which the Shakers were "firmly inclusive." Only choice (E) shows this.

206. (C) Opponents of the town's plan must show why complete closure of the treatment plant is a problem. Of the choices given, only choice (C) does this. If the treatment plant is closed completely, how will sewage be dealt with in the meantime?

207. (C) The author's conclusion is that because they are not mentioned at Ellis Island, her great-grandparents must have originally landed in Canada. Support for that might include the records of their arrival in Canada, making choice (C) the best answer.

208. (A) The conclusion is that negative campaigning turned off the electorate. That presupposes that negative advertising *can* affect the electorate, which makes choice (A) the best answer.

209. (A) The paragraph is about the migration of rural workers to cities in China to find jobs, creating megacities. The only conclusion that can be drawn from this is that megacities are a product of economic realities, in this case, the need to find work.

210. (C) The author concludes that it should be easy to find a healthy chocolate lab pup now that breeders are more cautious. This would be supported by findings that allergies in chocolate labs have declined.

211. (B) Although all of the answers have a bit of relevance to the value of the poll, answer (B) is most useful. If the congressman plans to vote based on the wishes of the majority, pollsters must reach either all voters or a representative sample of voters.

212. (D) The premise is that the PC market declined due to dislike of the new operating system, but the fact that buyers can bypass the new system seems to belie that. The paragraph calls the old system "popular," making choice (A) incorrect. Choices (B) and (E) would not explain the discrepancy, and choice (C) just confuses the issue. However, if former PC buyers were suddenly moving over to tablets (D), the market would decline with or without any problems with the operating system.

213. (D) The premise that the employee has done great work may be correct, but it is immaterial because he is not eligible for promotion at present.

214. (B) Wendy's story is a hypothetical syllogism: If P, then Q. If Q, then R. Therefore, if P then R. Danielle's story follows the same pattern: If the landlord agrees, she will get a rescue dog. If she gets a rescue dog, it will be female. Therefore, if her landlord approves, Danielle will adopt a female dog.

215. (D) Since 40 percent of the students at Boylston chose math teachers regardless of how well they did in math class, the only logical conclusion is that success in *math* class is not an indication of affection for a teacher—unless you assume that the pattern is similar in other classes as well. Only then can you conclude that "success in *a class* is not an indication of affection for a teacher."

216. (B) The road at present is 28 feet across with 2-foot shoulders on either side, meaning that the lanes themselves are just 12 feet wide. If speed increases only at 15 feet, traffic should already be relatively calm even without the road's painted shoulders.

217. (D) The argument is that Asia must be buying New Jersey wine and wine from all other states where the industry is fast-growing. This is supported by the fact that even beloved California wines are having a profitable experience marketing to Asia.

218. (A) The points made in the paragraph lead most naturally to the conclusion in choice (A).

219. (E) Beef prices have gone up, the price of a hamburger has stayed the same, and profits have stayed the same. More consumers (B) would not balance this equation, but reduced serving sizes (E) would.

220. (E) This type of question asks the reader to draw the most likely conclusion from the facts given. The logical conclusion is choice (E).

221. (C) To be of any use, Sara's poll of her friends must reach out to friends who know something about both Sara and the jobs. The most useful advice would come from friends who not only live in the same location (A) but who work in the same field (C). Of the two, a similar job understanding is probably the more useful trait in an adviser.

222. (C) If competent applicants are not flocking to small, rural schools, it might simply be that they don't want to work in small, rural schools. For the conclusion to be reasonable, an assumption must be made that salary is the only thing keeping competent applicants away, and the only answer that makes that assumption is choice (C).

223. **(D)** The author's conclusion is that "beavers were an asset to the community." This is supported by the boldfaced material, which indicates that the beavers had kept overgrowth trimmed back. An assumption (B) is never directly stated in a passage.

224. **(C)** Choices (A) and (D) are too much of a stretch, and choices (B) and (E) have no support in the passage. Choice (C), on the other hand, is supported by the fact that foster care correlates with prison time and abuse.

225. **(C)** The argument is that looking at women as the caretakers of children limits the possibility of workplace parity, so you must look for the statement that supports that. The only example here is choice (C). By framing Yahoo's decision as affecting women specifically, the media bought into the notion that telecommuting is meant just for women rather than for all workers equally.

226. **(D)** Kalinda's travel story could be broken down like this: If Route 51, 63 miles. If 522N, 80 miles. Distance traveled = 63 miles; therefore, Route 51. The only scenario that fits that same *modus ponens* structure is choice (D): If brownies, 350. If cake, 325. Temperature: 350; therefore, brownies.

227. **(D)** The problem asks for the question that is least relevant to the developer's choice. It would be useful to know how many people rent (A), how many similar housing options exist (B), how much the move will cost (C), and how much could be recouped (E). The position of each apartment (D) is irrelevant.

228. **(A)** If the studies define "small" in a way that is not applicable to the situation described, the studies themselves cannot be considered relevant.

229. **(E)** Although choice (A) supports the conclusion, it is not a presupposition that guides the argument. Choices (B) and (D) are a stretch, and choice (C) is unsupported. Choice (E), whether it is true or not, would explain the author's argument that sending both to MIT is incorrect.

230. **(A)** The environmentalist does not just indicate a single oversight (B); he adds information that leads to an opposite conclusion.

231. **(C)** Only if Stuart obtained a different insurance policy would the percentage of his cost be just 20 percent. Choices (D) and (E) might reduce the total but not the percentage for which Stuart was responsible.

232. **(D)** The question asks you to find the one that is *least* relevant in evaluating the argument. Knowing the number of current personnel (A), the need for oversight (B), the quality of staff (C), and the level of satisfaction (E) would all help Donnelly School District make a decision. Although the number of districts within the consortium (D) might be useful in determining how much attention Donnelly might receive, it is low on the list of critical factors.

233. (A) This is a simple *modus ponens* argument: If *P*, then *Q*. *P*. Therefore, *Q*. Choice (A) is similar in structure: If the pH is less than 7, then the solution is acidic. Skin has pH less than 7. Therefore, it is acidic.

234. (B) As you read an item like this, end your reading with the word *therefore*, and see which of the choices follows logically. In this case, the new software can pull out obvious errors, but it can't tell students how to fix them. Therefore, it is no replacement for direct discourse with a professor, making choice (B) correct.

235. (A) Teens are switching to quick, snappy apps that appeal to their short attention spans because Facebook no longer appeals to their short attention spans; it is slower and stodgier.

236. (B) To bolster the argument, you need specific evidence that supporting lifestyle changes that prevent diseases saves money. Choice (B) provides exactly that.

237. (D) Which of the choices follows logically from the passage? There is only vague support for choices (A), (C), and (E) and none at all for choice (B). Choice (D), however, is clearly true—when the British imposed their plan on Cetshwayo's kingdom, chaos ensued.

238. (B) First, identify the two clauses: "Although the present mall has a small footprint compared to other local malls" and "its size is adequate for the population." The author's conclusion is that expanding the mall is the wrong decision. The first clause gives a counterargument—that the mall might be considered too small. The second clause counters that with the argument that the size is fine for the population.

239. (E) For tourists to cancel their cruises presupposes that the illness was contracted on board ship rather than in Havana or another port. The passage does not say that only cruises through the Gulf of Mexico or the Caribbean lost money, as choices (B) and (D) might indicate.

240. (D) If the current workers are salaried employees who are on call 24/7, and they are to be replaced by a 24/7 service with hourly workers, the savings could easily be eaten up by emergencies that take place on weekends or before and after normal work hours.

241. (E) Any piece of evidence that supports the idea that staying on the tarmac in hot or cold weather is harmful to pets would support the conclusion. The piece of evidence that does this best is choice (E).

242. (E) First, identify the discrepancy: Spring cleanup involves little trash. Fall cleanup involves lots of trash. Next, find the fact that explains it. There might be little trash in spring because people don't throw trash from cars in winter, but trash might accumulate over the summer when people drive with their windows down and toss trash out into the ditches.

243. (A) The correct answer will help to prove that adding a gym leads to higher productivity. Choice (A) would do that directly; the other choices would not.

244. (D) To help prove that Thomson's work on wave-particle duality was critical to quantum mechanics, you need to show a link between the two. Choice (D) provides that link.

245. (C) The developer's claim that the complex will increase taxes by increasing population is belied by the fact that the increased population will not pay taxes.

246. (E) The change in food did not cure the allergies, which could mean that the new food was allergenic as well or that the dog's allergies came from another source.

247. (E) The word *but* indicates a contrast, so the correct and logical answer will contrast with the start of the sentence. Choice (A) could be correct if "outlaw art" were art made in prisons, which is never suggested. Choice (C) could be correct if the previous sentence did not refer to graffiti murals as an "art form." Choice (E) is best—graffiti began as a sort of illegal expression of ideas and evolved to become acceptable public art.

248. (A) The passage indicates that if only smartphones had the same protection as work computers, cyber-scams would not be such a problem. This presupposes that mobile devices are not protected.

249. (C) The conclusion is that signs do nothing to capture votes, but if voters really need to see a name seven times before they retain it, signs, ubiquitous as they are, would work better than a single or even multiple meetings with constituents.

250. (B) The author concludes that York is the better burial place because Richard was unconnected to Leicester. Choice (A) would contradict this conclusion, and choices (C), (D), and (E) would be ineffective as support. Choice (B), on the other hand, would provide a strong reason to bury the king in York.

251. (D) Think: What would the next logical step in this discussion be? The main idea of the argument is that wrestling is being removed, possibly at the expense of those small nations for whom it is a source of pride and success. The most logical conclusion is choice (D).

252. (C) The facts in the passage lead a reader to understand that at one time, the townsfolk were considered ignorant by the country gentry. In other words, people in the country were of a higher class and worldlier than people in town.

253. (A) The prediction is that no more than two number 1 teams will make it to the Final Four. If choice (B) or (C) were true, you might expect all four number 1 teams to make it. If choice (D) were true, predictions would be impossible. Choice (E) might or might not be true, but it is not vital to the prediction, which can be made simply based on the assumption that what has happened in the past is enough to predict the future.

254. (B) If Dawn and her husband called only families the preschool recommended, the results would likely be biased in favor of the preschool.

255. (B) The argument is that the weather must have been less tropical. Drought conditions would mean far drier weather, which would not be suitable for mosquito breeding.

256. (A) The conclusion drawn by the students presupposes that on Earth, humans have more than trace amounts of zinc in digestive products. If that is not true, their conclusion cannot be correct.

257. (A) You must find the phrase that follows logically from the material in the passage. If Cranmore is looking for students who are geographically diverse, they may not want two very similar students from the exact same location.

258. (B) If in doubt, draw a Punnett square—but you should not have to. Black labs come in four possible genotypes, and yellow come in three. Yellow labs always have a genotype that ends in ee, meaning that choices (C) and (D) are impossible. Choices (A) and (E) are impossible because BBee and bbEe are not options for black labs. That leaves choice (B), which could result, although very rarely, in a litter of yellow labs with bbee genotypes.

259. (E) The editorial director bolsters the marketing manager's argument by adding information about a similar, successful move the company had made in the past.

260. (B) The argument is that since community college graduates are getting jobs at higher salaries than four-year college graduates, working at "middle-skills" jobs, all high schoolers should consider going to community college. That argument only makes sense if all of those high schoolers hope to end up in "middle-skills" jobs.

261. (C) Although the playground is now plastic, children are getting splinters. Why? If the splinters were plastic, choice (A) or (D) might make sense, but the splinters are wooden. Therefore, only choice (C) explains the discrepancy.

262. (E) The amount of income is never stated, making choices (A), (C), and (D) unsubstantiated. All we know from the passage is that most of the income comes from the sale of medical supplies, and 5 percent comes from consulting, making choice (E) correct.

263. (E) The pet carrier is too small for Sam's Great Danes, but they do not hold someone else's pet. Therefore, they must hold another pet of Sam's.

264. (C) Moving to Europe would not benefit U.S. retirees' healthcare unless they were guaranteed benefits similar to those of Europeans.

265. (C) What is the main idea of the writers' remarks? Because "sound biting" is already happening, and because the majesty of the hearings is educational, the members of the think tank imply that camera coverage would be mainly beneficial.

266. (B) The yogurt example is an invalid argument. There is no direct correlation drawn between the eating of yogurt and the lack of gastric diseases—the overall healthy diet may be the contributing factor. In addition, there is no indication that someone who already suffers from gastric diseases will benefit from eating yogurt, since the original study did not mention those with preexisting conditions. Choice (B) is similar—just because many wealthy citizens live in the east, it does not mean that moving east will make you wealthy.

267. (D) To evaluate whether capping the property tax levy will in fact lower property taxes, it's especially useful to know whether it has actually done so.

268. (C) You would expect 24-karat gold jewelry to be 100 percent gold. The fact that it is not may only be explained by choice (C)—that there is some reason it cannot appear in pure form.

269. (C) The argument is that fewer people attend the other races than attend the Derby because they lose interest. To undermine that argument, you must find another reason for attendance to be higher for the Derby and then drop off. Of the choices given, only choice (C) provides a reason—people may be attending the Derby for its pomp and pageantry.

270. (E) This is a form of argument known as a "dilemma." In this particular dilemma, both potential results are the same—Marcos will start an internship. In symbolic form, the problem may be stated this way: P or Q. If P, then R. If Q, then R. Therefore, R. The only choice that follows this pattern is choice (E): Vote for or against Proposition A. If for, the water project goes forward. If against, the water project goes forward. Therefore, the water project will go forward.

271. (D) Before completely revamping all products, the soft drink company may wish to make sure that the new sweetener works with other products besides cola.

272. (D) You are asked to find the *least* relevant question. It would be useful to know whether the park will incur additional expenses (A), whether juveniles can actually do the work (B), whether there are other options for savings (C), and whether the hiring is legal (E). Knowing the location of the work (D) is largely irrelevant to the Parks Department's decision.

273. (C) This is an example of *modus tollens*: If P, then Q. Not Q. Therefore, not P. Choice (C) matches the structure: If Bridget had CAD training, she would be eligible. She is not eligible. Therefore, she must not have CAD training.

274. (E) The problem is that IT directors are leaving. The CEO's plan is to increase pay. That makes sense only if the IT directors are leaving for more lucrative positions. Studying the perks (A), plans (B), materials (C), and duties (D) of the position makes sense to do before a new hire is made, but to prove the CEO right or wrong, you need to know whether the IT directors are making a change based on their paychecks.

275. (B) If cystic fibrosis typically killed patients in six months, Chopin would have been unlikely to survive to age 39.

276. (A) This is one form of disjunctive syllogism: P or Q. Not Q. Therefore, P. Choice (A) offers a similar structure: Spandex or new fabric. Not new fabric. Therefore, spandex.

277. (E) The worker is claiming that older workers end up on disability because they are not retrained. To evaluate this claim, you need to know whether the reason behind their high disability rates is lack of training. Choice (E) would explore that question.

278. (B) What is it that is "as expected"? Based on the preceding information, you would expect that investors would defect from stocks and rush to safer havens—such as gold and Treasury bonds.

279. (E) The conclusion of scientists is that the man-made lake will damage the ecosystem. This could be supported by an example of damage to the ecosystem by the lake, as in choice (E).

280. (C) The author's conclusion is that the number of female winners will grow because the number of female architecture school graduates is growing. Since the prize goes to practicing architects, that conclusion would be countered by the fact that the number of practicing architects is still largely male.

281. (B) The conclusion is that the credit downgrade was due to political instability rather than recession. For that to be true, the raters must assume that stability bolsters economic growth.

282. (E) There is no evidence that better math on the part of taxpayers equals faster refunds on the part of the IRS (A). However, the conclusion that it is hard to make errors when a computer is figuring your math (E) leads logically from the passage.

283. (A) The discrepancy is this: CTBs were found a quarter mile away, but Hilltop Road, closer than a quarter mile away, had none. This can be explained if there was some reason CTBs could not leach onto Hilltop Road, and choice (A) gives such a reason. Choice (B) gives an explanation, but it is extremely unlikely.

284. (E) If lateness is a purchasable commodity, then anyone can purchase it, including people who demonstrated ethical behavior in the past.

285. (E) Clinton posits that millennials' obsessions with money and social media and impatience all have potential upsides, making choice (E) the logical conclusion.

286. (D) If people *always* wanted to buy songs rather than albums, sales of two-song 45s would have exceeded sales of long-play albums back in the vinyl days. Determining whether that was true would help you to evaluate the argument.

287. (C) This *modus ponens* argument may be stated symbolically as if *P*, then *Q*. *P*. Therefore, *Q*. Choice (C) follows the same pattern: If Blair's memoir were profitable, profits would go to the charity. The memoir was profitable. Therefore, profits went to the charity.

288. (A) If the failure of the electorate to provide oversight results in corruption, it follows that an alert and active electorate may prevent corruption. This is not the same as choice (C), which is too broad a generalization.

289. (E) In this statement, the writer presents a specific illustration based on one example. Choice (E) does the same thing, using the example of the Bigwig manager to illustrate that a hairstylist may also be a restaurateur.

290. (D) The publisher has made the assumption that Katie Xerxes is the reason for the books' profitability, rather than, say, the popularity of the particular subject areas that Ms. Xerxes' books are testing.

291. (A) The assertion is that the pipeline will create jobs that will create stability for decades. If the jobs are not permanent, that assertion cannot be accurate.

292. (D) The discrepancy has to do with injuries to people in the front of the plane while people in the back were unharmed. Choice (B) could be correct if it weren't for the fact that the plane is described as "full." Choices (A), (C), and (E) would have no effect on one part of the plane over another. Choice (D), on the other hand, could explain the problem—if people in the front were standing, they could more easily be injured.

293. (C) The argument is that a breakeven point of 15 years is too long to be cost effective. This is especially true if the homeowner plans to sell or move within that 15-year period. However, if he expects to stay there for 25 years, the purchase might indeed be worthwhile. Since the breakeven point is given, the average expenditure (A), size of pump (B), number of panels (D), and fluctuation of energy production (E) are largely irrelevant to assessing the argument.

294. (A) The mention of happiness in the final sentence relies on a presupposition that happiness is connected to stress reduction. Clearly, yoga is not the only path to happiness, as choices (B) and (D) suggest.

295. (E) Even if all 32 seniors had received the maximum number of awards, there would only have been 96 awards issued. Therefore, for 100 awards to be given out, others must have received some of those awards.

296. (C) This is a "dilemma" construction, which may be written symbolically as P or Q. If P, then R. If Q, then S. Therefore, R or S. Lucinda's dilemma is similar and may be broken down in this way: P = Lucinda hires two bakers. Q = Lucinda hires a store manager and a baker. R = Lucinda manages the store. S = Lucinda works in the kitchen.

297. (E) Although the typical ratio is 40 to 1, and four out of five trees tested at 40 to 1, one tree tested at 60 to 1, which is far enough off the average to suggest a real anomaly. None of the answer choices would account for this except for choice (E). If one of the trees were a different species from the norm, it would likely have a different sap-to-syrup ratio than the norm.

298. (E) Simon's mistake is to assume that a regimen for a linebacker and a regimen for a tennis player are naturally equivalent.

299. (D) Follow the passage to its logical conclusion. Google was ready to close out the book line, but to the rejoicing of people who are fond of printed books, Frommer's repurchase means that the guides will still appear in print.

300. (D) Thinking that sugary drinks are causing his weight problem, Carl reduces his consumption of those drinks and is surprised when he continues to gain weight. If Carl's weight had declined a little or evened out, choice (A) or (C) might be feasible, but since it actually increased, the best answer is choice (D). Something else must be contributing to Carl's weight.

301. (E) A correlation between gas prices rising and suburban restaurant patronage declining must mean that people in the suburbs drive to get to restaurants.

302. (C) The difference between purchases at South Street and the mall has to do with the percentage of people who buy full meals rather than "parts." Based on the information given, the only conclusion you can reach without stretching beyond the limits of the passage is choice (C)—that different Chicken Shacks exhibit different purchasing patterns.

303. (E) The principal is making a prediction that depends on consistent bad behavior from middle school through high school. If bad behavior is in fact more prevalent in middle school, you can assume that at least some middle schoolers calm down and behave well in high school, making the principal's prediction unjustified.

304. (C) Instead of rejecting the teenager's argument, the parent kindly provides suggestions for a better argument. The conclusion, that the teenager needs a new phone, does not change, making choice (D) incorrect.

305. (D) The paradox lies in the fact that the ankles are revealed in the evening performance and covered at the matinee that the reviewer attended. Viewing the scene from above would not cause the dress to sweep the floor, as in choice (A). The dress is "clearly a product of the renowned costumier," making choice (B) incorrect. If the underskirt were not pegged (C), or if the actress rarely stood up (E), no viewers would have seen the ankles. However, if a different actress wore the costume, it might have been longer on that actress, meaning that choice (D) is the best response.

306. (B) If Ethan's app does well, the writer expects to see more preteen apps. However, that presupposes that many preteens have ideas for apps and can design and produce them.

307. (B) If window protection can prevent window damage, people may continue to use sliding glass doors with that protection.

308. (D) Scientists think that the amount of Neanderthal brain dedicated to vision somehow harmed Neanderthals. To complete that thought, the passage must end with a reason for that harm. Choice (D) provides that—the brain had too much room for vision and not enough for high-level processing.

309. (D) The conclusion is that even small schools with lacrosse will find that their students receive scholarship offers. This will only be true if those small schools can field competitive teams—poor players from inferior teams are not likely to receive offers. Colleges want "top recruits" from the schools they approach.

310. (A) Clearview has concluded that Comparative Literature, Music, and Fine Art have the least relevance to today's job market and should be cut. However, if those courses assist in the kind of strong, varied liberal arts program that forms better employees, Clearview's decision may be misguided. Choices (B), (C), and (E) may also contribute to a rethinking of the policy, but none of those choices directly address the marketability of majors that led to Clearview's decision in the first place.

Chapter 3: Sentence Correction

311. (A) Reading this sentence aloud and substituting the other answer choices should convince you that the original sentence is structured best.

312. (B) Although the repeated *that* is awkward, this is the best choice. Choice (D) would need to be introduced with a semicolon. Choices (C) and (E) are even more convoluted than the original sentence.

313. (D) Choices (A), (B), (C), and (E) imply that the stores themselves are contaminated. Only choice (D) makes the connection clear—the product (salad) is potentially contaminated and has therefore been recalled.

314. (C) If choice (A) read "as reported by," it might be correct. The best substitute for "as reported by" is "according to," in choice (C).

315. (B) The semicolon in the original sentence requires that both halves of the sentence be independent clauses. Choices (B) and (D) fulfill this need, but only choice (B) is grammatically correct.

316. (C) The phrase between the commas refers back to the nine scrap metal facilities. They are not doing the purchasing, they were purchased.

317. (E) Break down the sentence into parts. Whom is the committee soliciting? It is soliciting students and business-leader mentors. Why is it soliciting them? It is soliciting them to participate in its program.

318. (A) None of the other options puts the events in logical order.

319. (E) The rest of the sentence is in the past tense, so the underlined section should be in the past tense, too.

320. (B) You do not need to know what "midstream providers" are to choose the correct construction here.

321. (C) The sentence is predictive, so the present-tense verb in the first clause should be paired with a future-tense verb, in this case, *will continue.*

322. (D) The sentence contains three factors separated by serial commas. The three factors in the series should be parallel. Since *late payments* and *reduced revenues* are nouns preceded by adjectives, look for the answer choice that is equivalent: *increased payroll.*

323. (E) The correct idiomatic expression is *none is so important as*, or as in choice (E), *none is as important as*. Choice (C) would be correct if it used *than* rather than *as*.

324. (A) The items in a series should be parallel, and they are in the original sentence.

325. (D) For choice (A) to be correct, the comma would need to be replaced by a semicolon. Of the other choices, only choice (D) retains the logic of the sentence.

326. (C) Does the keyboard resemble a laptop? No, it resembles the keyboard on a laptop. Choices (A), (B), and (D) fail to make this comparison. Choice (E) is awkward; choice (C) is better.

327. (B) Although choice (A) is not completely illogical, choice (B) is clearer.

328. (C) Choice (A) is ungrammatical. Choice (B) is passive. Choice (D) mixes up the sequence of events. Choice (E) is not wrong, but it is terribly clunky. Choice (C) presents the causation, the sequence, and the correct verb usage that make the sentence meaningful and grammatical.

329. (E) The employees have seen the cuts. The paychecks have seen nothing at all.

330. (C) Use *which* if the clause is not part of the main meaning of the sentence—in other words, with nonrestrictive clauses that simply tell you something interesting about the subject or object. In this case, the fact that the acquisitions align well with Yahoo's other business is critical to understanding the CEO's planned investments. It belongs in a restrictive clause, one that uses the word *that*.

331. (B) The two parts of the sentence should be parallel. In the original sentence, *the samba* seems to be juxtaposed to *Cuba* rather than to *the mambo*. Choice (B) corrects this error.

332. (C) The only error here is in subject-verb agreement. The distance *is* narrowing. Matching the plural form of the verb to a plural subject, as in choice (E), is simply confusing. There is only one distance between the candidates.

333. (E) Read all of the choices aloud if you have trouble here. Only choice (E) has verbs that are in both the correct form and the correct tense.

334. (B) The sentence creates an opposition, but the contrast is best expressed in choice (B).

335. (D) All of the other choices make it seem as though the man's eyes were "walking purposefully along the factory floor." The modifying phrase must be as close as possible to the word being modified.

336. (C) Again, the original sentence contains a misplaced modifier. It is not the children who are manufactured in China out of durable recycled plastic, it is the toys. Of the choices that place the modifier close to the word being modified, choice (C) is clearest.

337. (A) The original sentence has correct subject-verb agreement and is logical. It might be better if it started "Among all duly elected senators," but that is not one of the choices.

338. (E) Up until the semicolon, the bat is referred to with a singular noun or pronoun. It should not suddenly become plural.

339. (B) The opening of this sentence is in the past tense, so the second half should not suddenly change to present perfect progressive. The past perfect progressive of choice (B) is correct.

340. (A) This is a simple subject-verb agreement problem. Remove all the excess verbiage, and you can see that the subject is *field testing*, and the verb is, correctly, *has proved*.

341. (B) The sentence refers to a time in the past, so the verb chosen should indicate that meaning. Of the responses given, choice (B) is clearest and simplest.

342. (D) When in doubt, pick the answer that is active rather than passive. In this case, too, it is not Liza's ankle that was running through the airport, it is Liza.

343. (B) The construction *neither . . . nor* calls for a verb that agrees with the closer of the two subjects. Examples might be *Neither my sisters nor my brother **speaks** Spanish* and *Neither my brother nor my sisters **speak** Spanish.* In this case, both subjects are singular, so the verb form should be singular, too.

344. (C) The commas in this sentence help you to understand that the words between the commas should form an appositive phrase that describes John Deere. The clearest and simplest version is choice (C).

345. (B) Whom did the interns observe? They observed the administrative candidates. What were the candidates doing? They were interviewing and meeting. Only choice (B) contains verbs that are parallel.

346. (E) Look for the choice that is active and simple.

347. (E) Choice (E) is the only construction that is both parallel and mechanically correct. Choice (B) would be fine without the comma.

348. (D) Who is Jasper Hewitt? He is a noted philanthropist and builder of developments. Choice (D) makes the two descriptors parallel.

349. (B) The clarifying phrase *they do* makes it clear that you are comparing the way soldiers live at two times in their lives.

350. (C) The verbs *has attained* and *has received* should be in the same tense; in this case, the present perfect.

351. (E) The word *If* at the beginning of the sentence defines the mood as subjunctive: If X were to happen, Y would or could happen.

352. (D) The correct grammatical pairing is *not only . . . but also*. Only choice (D) contains the critical word *also*.

353. (C) Typically, *if* introduces a condition, and *whether* indicates a choice. Here, the technicians are determining whether or not the cloudiness will disappear; there is an implied choice, so choice (C) is the best answer.

354. (D) It may seem overly wordy, but choice (D) correctly presents the parallel *people who eat/people who eat* construction.

355. (E) *If . . . then* constructions come in many forms. The sportscaster form, which is grammatically incorrect, is shown in choice (A). The word *would* is needed in choice (B), and choice (D) should read *might have won* or *would have won*. Choice (E) shows one correct form of several.

356. (A) The sentence is correctly written in the subjunctive mood.

357. (D) Reading the selections aloud in place of the underlined clause should help you to see that only choice (D) makes sense. Part one of the sentence is in past perfect tense, so part two needs to be in the past as well.

358. (D) The problem with the original sentence is that the modifying phrase that precedes the comma seems to modify *many* rather than *geothermal*. Of the choices that are clearer, only choice (D) retains the meaning of the original.

359. (C) The original subject is *economists*, so keeping *they* as a subject in the second clause makes sense. The other choices are all passive rather than active.

360. (B) The pronoun in the original sentence does not match its antecedent, *colleges*. The possessive pronoun must be plural, as it is in choice (B).

361. (D) In a *neither . . . nor* construction, the verb must agree with the subject nearer to it. In this case, that subject is *team*, used as a singular noun, so the verb must be in a singular form.

362. (E) The subject is *tractors*, so the verb must be in a plural form. Choice (D) implies that the chains are moving, rather than the tractors. Choice (E) is clearer.

363. (C) Something *results from* or *is the result of* something else. In the first case, *result* is a verb. In the second case, *result* is a noun. Choice (C) uses the correct idiom.

364. (B) *That supervisor of Henrietta's* is a common spoken construction, but it is considered a double possessive. You may say "Henrietta's supervisor" or "That supervisor of Henrietta."

365. (E) Because *income* is a singular word, it takes *less* rather than *fewer* (choice B); the proper comparative adjective is *less*, not *lesser*.

366. (A) The original sentence is clearest and most idiomatic.

367. (D) The problem with the original sentence is a lack of clarity. Fred is comparing two courses, not a course and a university. Choice (D) eliminates the confusion.

368. (E) You can improve this sentence by making the verbs parallel. *To continue* and *to ensure* are parallel; *to continue* and *ensuring* are not.

369. (B) Choices (A), (D), and (E) contain misplaced modifiers. Choice (C) makes it seem as though Margaret's realignment and praise from the board were simultaneous. Choice (B) places the modifying phrase close to *Margaret*, the subject being modified, and it retains the meaning of the original.

370. (A) Although there is nothing grammatically wrong with choice (C), the original sentence is crisper and clearer.

371. (C) *Each* is singular and takes a singular form of the verb as well as a singular pronoun. Choice (E) would be correct if it said "Every one of the students" rather than "Everyone of the students." The rewrite in choice (C) maintains the original meaning while solving the problems of verb and pronoun agreement.

372. (B) Is she choosing dresses or picking between friends? If there's any confusion, it's worth repeating the word *dress*, as in choice (B).

373. (D) Marco is not dashing across the frozen pond, the buck is. Choice (D) clarifies that. Choices (B) and (C) do, too, but both are passive constructions. Choice (E) is simply confusing.

374. (B) All three items in the series should be parallel, but right now, they are not. Changing the verb form *intruding* to a noun, *intrusion*, solves that problem.

375. (E) You choose *between* two things. You choose *among* three or more things.

376. (A) You may be *accustomed to* something, not *accustomed by* or *for* it.

377. (A) *Nevertheless* conveys the correct level of contrast—even though it was expensive, the owners considered it a good investment. The words *despite* and *although* convey contrast as well, but neither choice (B) nor choice (D) would be correct following a semicolon.

378. (C) You may *effect* change or *have an effect* on events, but you *affect* events. Choice (C) uses the correct verb.

379. (B) *Not only* calls for *but also*. Only choice (B) completes the construction correctly.

380. (D) Choices (A), (B), and (E) mismatch subjects and verbs. Choice (C) is not a complete sentence because it lacks a verb to go with its subject. Choice (D) rewrites the sentence to be grammatically correct without losing its basic meaning.

381. **(A)** The word *whether* correctly introduces a choice, and *will be determined by* is the correct construction.

382. **(E)** *Less* is used with singular words. The plural word *voters* requires the modifier *fewer*.

383. **(B)** Comparisons should state clearly what is being compared. If there is a chance of confusion, repeat or add words to clarify. Choice (D) would be better if it said "the mocha tasted best out of all the flavors."

384. **(C)** You can be in a dispute over something or in a dispute with someone. You cannot be in a dispute with something, as the original sentence indicates.

385. **(E)** The problem here is that the antecedent for *they* is unclear—who are the *they* that might be willing to spend some amount on a vacation package? Choice (E) may seem wordy, but it eliminates any confusion.

386. **(B)** *Even so* (A) implies that the team members have qualms about submitting the report after studying efficiencies for months. The sentence requires a phrase that indicates their readiness to report, which choice (B) does.

387. **(C)** *News* is a singular noun and requires the verb *strikes*, not *strike*.

388. **(B)** A word that states an amount or measurement is considered as one item and takes the singular form of a verb. If the fraction named individual pieces, as in "two-thirds of the cookies," it would require the plural form of the verb.

389. **(A)** The departure is in the future; the agreement is ongoing. *Has agreed* is correct, and to tutor someone *in* a subject is correctly idiomatic.

390. **(E)** *Consequently* implies that the lack of people working over winter break is the result of few working over Thanksgiving. A better word is *furthermore*, which indicates an additional event that may or may not be connected to the first.

391. **(D)** *Either* is singular, so *has taken* is correct. *Did taken* (choice B) and *had took* (choice E) are ungrammatical.

392. **(A)** Start at the beginning. The subject is *member*, so the correct verb is *was* (A and B). The sentence calls for object pronouns; this is clear if you think "except for _____ instead of "except _____." The original sentence is correct.

393. **(A)** She is not "most competent of the other members" (B), because she is not one of the other members. Instead, she is being compared to the other members. The original sentence is clearest and most succinct.

394. (C) Find the sentence that places all phrases in a logical order, with modifiers closest to the words they modify. Reading the sentences aloud may help you to select the best response.

395. (B) Did the shop in the mall feature stuffed animals and small toys? Possibly, but it is more likely that the gift baskets contained these items. Therefore, the choice that places the descriptive phrase *containing stuffed animals and small toys* closest to *gift baskets* is the best response. Choice (E) would be correct if it were not so awkwardly constructed.

396. (D) *Accepting* means "approving." *Excepting* means "not including." Choice (E) is correct but repetitive, and the comma would not be needed for that construction.

397. (E) The original sentence is not incorrect, but it is not the clearest or most succinct way to say that the congresswoman was patient in her response. In cases like this, look for the shortest answer—as long as it is grammatical and logical.

398. (D) The correct construction is *neither . . . nor.*

399. (A) It is the combination that is incredibly popular. The fact that the combination is used in everything from lattes to muffins is not required to make the sentence meaningful. For that reason, setting that nonessential (nonrestrictive) clause off with commas and *which* is correct.

400. (D) Again, the original sentence is not incorrect, but neither is it concise. The best restatement of the sentence appears in choice (D), which combines elements of the original sentence while retaining the meaning.

401. (B) Choice (C) would be correct if it used the word *who* rather than *that*. Again, look for the most concise sentence that retains the meaning of the longer and less precise original.

402. (A) The original sentence is both grammatical and idiomatic.

403. (B) Although you might think, "Do you know *him*?" and therefore choose choice (A), the operating clause is "who she is." Mixing this up gives you "she is who," a subject followed by a linking verb and a predicate nominative, which must be in the subjective case.

404. (C) *Poorly* is an adverb that modifies the verb *did*. *Worse* is the comparative form of *badly*. Choices (A) and (E) use an adjective rather than an adverb. Choice (B) uses the wrong form of *badly*. Choice (D) uses an adjective, *good*, rather than the adverb *well*.

405. (D) He should have read and commented upon the report, not the in-box (A). Choices (B) and (C) are convoluted, and choice (E) is awkward. Choice (D) removes the clause about reading and commenting and makes it nonrestrictive, placing the key part of the sentence before and after the commas.

406. (C) To correct items of this sort, use the active voice.

407. (E) Can you trust Howard? Yes, you can trust him. The pronoun must be in the objective case, making *whom* the correct choice. Choice (C) would be correct if it were preceded by a semicolon.

408. (D) *To rise* is to move oneself in an upward direction. *To raise* is to move something in an upward direction. The past tense of *rise* is *rose*.

409. (C) The action at the beginning of the sentence takes place in the future. Therefore, the action at the end of the sentence must take place in the future as well.

410. (A) *Each* is singular, so it agrees with a singular pronoun, *his*. All of the committee members described are men, making choice (B) incorrect. Choice (E) is not wrong, but it is not as clear as the original.

411. (B) The correct idiom is "than they ever were." Choice (D) looks correct at first glance, but it replaces the correct possessive form of *company* with a plural form.

412. (E) Find the appositive phrase that is cogent without being confusing.

413. (B) The original sentence is nearly correct, but a gerund (a verb form used as a noun, as *telling* is) must be modified by a possessive pronoun, not an object pronoun.

414. (A) Yes, *weeks* is plural, making choice (C) seem most reasonable. However, in this case, the sentence uses *three weeks* as a single measurement of time. The verb should therefore be singular, making the original sentence correct.

415. (C) The firm will be closed to provide professional development to employees. Choice (C) is the clearest indication of this.

416. (A) Sometimes the simplest construction is best. The other choices use phrases that are similar in meaning but neither clearer than nor superior to the original.

417. (C) You might also say "Interrupting a speaker," but that choice is not given.

418. (A) The correct verb must agree with *changes* and be in the present tense. Choice (B) adds unnecessary verbiage.

419. (D) Eliminating the word *employees* from the sentence should help you to see which choice works best.

420. (E) *Beside* means "next to." *Besides* means "in addition to."

421. (B) The introductory clause is in the past tense, so the main clause must be in the past tense as well. Choices (D) and (E) are in the passive voice.

422. (D) Use a plural verb to agree with *buildings*. In addition, since buildings can be counted, the adjective that describes them must be *many* rather than *much*.

423. (D) The charity work did not take place at the annual meeting, as the original sentence suggests. Moving the prepositional phrase from the end of the sentence to the beginning eliminates any confusion in the simplest way possible.

424. (D) Choice (D) is idiomatic and clear. *Had ought to* is always incorrect.

425. (B) In formal English, *as though* is preferable to *like* in this kind of construction.

426. (E) *Must of* is never correct; the construction should be *must have*. The correct past participle of *forget* is *forgotten*.

427. (C) The pronouns receive the action, so they must be object pronouns. It is traditional in English to name oneself last; therefore, choice (C) is better than choice (D).

428. (C) The verbs *lie* and *lay* are often misused. *Laying* means "placing" or "putting." *Lying* means "resting" or "being placed." In this case, the paper is not active; it is in a lying position.

429. (A) Choice (D) is not wrong, but it is not as clear as the original sentence. Choices (B), (C), and (E) use incorrect pronouns.

430. (A) This is a tricky sentence that you might wish to rephrase entirely. If you simply looked at "we invite whoever/whomever," the choice would be easy—*whomever* would be the correct object of *invite*. However, the noun clause is really "whoever/whomever might benefit," meaning that *whoever* is the subject. The words *we thought* may cause additional trouble. Think: "We thought she/her might benefit." In that case, the choice is obviously the subject pronoun.

431. (D) The helping verb *must* is used with the participle *have*.

432. (A) You feel *good* about something; you feel *well* if you are healthy.

433. (B) The original run-on sentence contains unnecessary words. Choice (B) replaces the run-on with a grammatical sentence that contains an appositive phrase.

434. (C) The words *informal* and *delightful* are adjectives that modify the noun *restaurant*.

435. (E) The original sentence splits an infinitive; it places the adverb between the two parts of the infinitive form of the verb, *to* and *forget*. Although this is acceptable in speech, it is considered inappropriate for formal writing. Choice (E) eliminates the split infinitive while retaining the meaning of the original.

436. (C) The original sentence does not make clear who is transporting what. Choice (B) is passive. Choice (C) fixes the confusion while remaining active.

437. (E) The beginning of the sentence is in the past tense; the second half does not need to be past perfect (choice B) but can be simple past (choice E) as well. It cannot be present tense (choice D). Choices (A) and (C) are ungrammatical.

438. (A) To determine the correct noun clause, think: Who was their favorite candidate? The subject pronoun is correct.

439. (D) *Nobody* is singular and requires the singular form of both verbs: *takes* and *expects*. As an antecedent, it also must agree with the singular form of a pronoun. Since the gender is unspecified, *his or her* is correct.

440. (D) The original sentence is passive, as are choices (B) and (C). Choice (E) makes it seem as though the company itself might have been recalled.

441. (E) The second clause in the sentence is in the present tense, so the first should be as well.

442. (C) The action is continuous and will resolve at some time in the future; the future perfect progressive tense is required.

443. (E) The participle that goes with the past perfect construction here is *risen*, not *rose*. Since the action in the second clause is in the past, choice (D) is incorrect.

444. (C) Who is doing the asking? Only the addition of *the tests* in choice (C) clarifies the statement.

445. (B) *Furthermore* implies additional information, but the fact that the town was able to cope with an unexpected expense is more of a cause-and-effect situation; the ability to cope is a result of careful establishment of reserve funds. The word that best addresses this connection between action and consequence is *consequently*.

446. (D) The existence of the conjunction *or* means that the verb must agree with the subject that is nearer to that verb. *Gardening helps* me to unwind after a busy week, so washing my car or *gardening helps* me to unwind after a busy week.

447. (E) Reading these sentences aloud may help you to determine which one is best. Placing the least important information in a nonrestrictive clause results is the clearest construction.

448. (A) The compound subject and plural form of the verb agree in the original sentence.

449. (C) The original sentence lacks parallel construction. Choice (C) makes all the words in the series into adverbs.

450. (D) "I wish I would have" is common in speech, but it is ungrammatical. Choice (D) corrects the error while maintaining the hypothetical or conditional aspect of the original sentence.

451. (C) Someone who edits is an editor, and using the word *editor* corrects the lack of parallel structure in the original sentence.

452. (D) Although *percent* is singular, *70 percent of students* is an amount that can be thought of as individual parts of a group, making the plural form of the verb correct.

453. (B) Jonas's humility is equal to Mother Teresa's humility, not to Mother Teresa herself, as the original sentence seems to indicate. Choice (B) eliminates the confusion.

454. (A) It is not a simple construction, but the original sentence surpasses the replacement choices in understandability and consistency of tense.

455. (C) Who sent the thank-you notes? He did. Choice (C) places the word *he* close to the clause modifier.

456. (D) The original sentence is passive, as is choice (B). Choice (C) is both passive and confusing, and choice (E) is syntactically awkward. Choice (D) corrects the sentence by making it active.

457. (C) The story shocked Dennis, and the story shocked me. It shocked Dennis and me. Naming oneself last in compound subjects and objects is considered proper in English grammar.

458. (B) The correct idiomatic expression is *ranging from.* You might also say "that range from," but that choice does not appear here.

459. (C) To make the construction parallel, *in Africa* should echo *in Mexico.*

460. (A) *Who* choices (C), (D), and (E) properly refer to people rather than cities. The cities could not agree *on* an issue, so choice (A) is better than choice (B).

461. (D) Eliminate *ordinary citizens* and test each clause in turn to determine which choice is best.

462. (E) The last choice is the best in terms of parallelism—each item in the series consists of a noun and a modifier.

463. (A) The original sentence is parallel: A is made from B, and C is made from D.

464. (C) *Being as* (A) is ungrammatical. The correct word to replace it is *since*, choice (C).

465. (B) The original sentence is a run-on. Choice (B) corrects that by placing the information in a modifying clause.

466. (C) Given the structure of the sentence, choice (C) is the simplest and most grammatical choice.

467. (D) "The study of" is understood in a college situation, and the inclusion of those words removes parallel structure from the original sentence. The series in choice (D) contains just three nouns separated by commas.

468. (D) First correct the parallelism of the series—*prominent people in the arts, sciences, and medicine* is a better construction than any of the other choices. Choice (D) also eliminates the awkwardness in the other series—*family and friends and prominent people* becomes *family, friends, and prominent people.*

469. (A) The original sentence indicates that the team did not move to New York until 1903. Choice (B) might indicate a single move, one that took place in the year 1903. Choice (C) might imply that there were various choices of cities, but that the team moved just to one of those choices. Choice (D) changes tenses, and choice (E) is awkward.

470. (B) Choices (A), (C), and (D) lack the parallelism of choice (B). Choice (E) is ungrammatical.

471. (E) The sentence requires an object pronoun (*me* rather than *I*), and the first person singular pronoun should appear last in the compound object.

472. (B) Presumably the small building and not the boarding school was a hideout for soldiers. Only choice (B) corrects this confusion.

473. (C) The idiom is *on the whole* or *in the main*, not *in the whole.*

474. (C) Because the professor *is* at the university, he cannot receive more funding than anyone at the university. He can, however, receive more than anyone *else* at the university.

475. (D) The correct comparative adverb is *more loudly.* An adverb is required to modify *started up.*

476. (D) Who reached age 18? It was not the parents and grandparents, as the original sentence suggests. Choice (D) is the best revision of the sentence because it eliminates the misplaced modifier.

477. (D) The sentence is better when it maintains parallel structure. *That bears his name* is a restrictive clause and correctly begins with *that*, making choice (E) incorrect.

478. (B) Simplifying the sentence so that both parts of the clause contain present-tense verbs clarifies the meaning.

479. (A) *Hitherto* means "until now" and is appropriate in this sentence, which contrasts Dubai's previous reputation with a more recent turn of events.

480. (C) *Which was signed into law by President Johnson* is a nonrestrictive, or nonessential clause, correctly set apart from the rest of the sentence by commas. Choice (D) would make it into a restrictive clause and require the deletion of the commas.

481. (C) The representatives watched an event on the monitors; the event did not literally take place on the monitors. Choice (C) places the misplaced modifier closer to the words it modifies.

482. (E) *Could of been* is never correct; the correct construction is *could have been* or *might have been*. *If only* correctly introduces the conditional statement: If this had happened, the accident could have been prevented.

483. (D) There are a few possible ways to construct this underlined phrase, but of the choices, only choice (D) works. The original statement uses *between* to compare more than two things; the correct word would be *among*.

484. (B) It is fine to repeat the word *decline*, but it does not need to be repeated endlessly, as in choice (C). Choice (B) makes the point while establishing parallelism in the series of examples.

485. (E) The second choice after the word *or* should be parallel to the first choice prior to the word *or*. Think: Small business owners are required either to X or to Y.

486. (D) Store brands are not cheaper and fresher than purchasing anything; they are cheaper and fresher than better-known brands. Choice (D) makes this clear in the simplest way.

487. (B) Select the choice that is clearest and most concise. Typically, a person retires; he or she does not get retired by outside forces, as choices (C) and (E) suggest.

488. (D) "The working of," as in choice (A), is an awkward construction. Choice (D) does not use many of the same words as in the original, but it retains the meaning of the original while being active and clear.

489. (A) Reading each choice aloud should prove that the original sentence is clearest.

490. (B) "The FDA's responsibility surrounds" is one of those phrases that indicates fuzzy thinking. Far better is the direct statement found in choice (B). Choice (C) moves away from the idea of promotion of public health and is therefore somewhat vague.

Chapter 4: Analysis of an Argument

Readers for the Analytical Writing Assessment (AWA) will consider four separate areas when scoring essays, as shown in the following table. Scores for the AWA range from 0 to 6 in half-point intervals. Use this rubric to assess your own writing or to have a partner analyze your work.

Analytical Writing Assessment Rubric

Score	6	5	4	3	2	1	0
Quality of ideas	Ideas are complex, clever, and well-reasoned.	Ideas are reasonable, well-stated, and thoughtful.	Ideas are sound but unremarkable.	Ideas make sense but lack originality.	Ideas indicate a lack of serious thought.	Ideas show confusion about the topic.	The essay does not respond to the prompt.
Organization and development	Ideas are presented in a balanced and logical order; transitions are logical.	Ideas are presented logically with clear transitions.	Ideas are presented logically; most transitions are clear.	Ideas are presented logically, but transitions may be confusing.	Ideas may appear haphazard; transitions are lacking.	Ideas appear random; no transitions connect ideas.	Ideas are unconnected and fail to relate to the prompt.
Supporting ideas and reasoning	Reasons and examples are coherent, relevant, and plentiful.	Reasons and examples are coherent and relevant.	Reasons and examples are clear, but some seem unconvincing.	Reasons and examples are weak.	Few reasons are given for the writer's opinion.	The essay does not support the writer's opinion.	No reasons or examples exist.
Grammar, usage, and mechanics	Few or no errors in syntax, vocabulary, punctuation, or spelling exist; vocabulary and sentence structure are sophisticated.	Few or no errors in syntax, vocabulary, punctuation, or spelling exist; sentence structure is varied.	Occasional errors in syntax, vocabulary, punctuation, or spelling exist; sentence structure is varied.	Several errors in syntax, vocabulary, punctuation, or spelling exist; sentence structure may vary.	Multiple errors in syntax, vocabulary, punctuation, or spelling exist; sentence structure is basic.	Errors in syntax, vocabulary, punctuation, or spelling interfere with meaning; run-ons and fragments may appear.	The essay is rendered unreadable by a great number of errors.

The following are sample top-scoring essays. Compare these essays to your own to get a sense of where yours might stand along the continuum presented in the AWA rubric.

491. This essay is fluent and coherent. It addresses the prompt directly by dissecting the key flaws in the argument and then suggesting sensible alternatives to the proposal. There are no real errors in English usage or mechanics.

> The school officials in Lowville are earnestly trying to find a way to improve their election turnout, but their proposal is flawed. By requiring voters to be registered, they presume that they will attract an electorate that is already committed to regular voting. However, they come to this conclusion based on assumptions rather than evidence.
>
> It is logical to assume that the current electorate at Lowville school elections consists both of registered voters and of voters who merely come out for school elections rather than municipal elections and therefore have not bothered to register with the Board of Elections. Let's assume for a moment that those groups are about equal in number. So 10 percent of eligible voters vote in school elections and are registered, and 10 percent of eligible voters vote in school elections and are not registered, for a total of 20 percent.
>
> If registered voters are that much more dedicated to voting, why would they not come out to the school polls in greater numbers? Does it make sense to assume that only 10 percent of the entire electorate is registered, and that they all vote in school elections? Even if that number were closer to the total of 20 percent, it would still be extremely low. The Lowville school officials need to look closely at the turnout in municipal elections to know whether they would gain anything at all by forcing their voters to register. Do 100 percent of all registered voters typically vote in Lowville's municipal elections? It's doubtful, so the school officials' premise is flawed.
>
> In addition, it is certainly possible that requiring registration would have a reverse effect and would in fact suppress the vote. If half of the existing vote came from people who were not registered, or even if the percentage were less than that, it's still clear that some unregistered voters thought the school election important enough to come out to vote.
>
> There are probably good reasons to require all voters to be registered, but the assumption that registration promotes a higher turnout is unsupported by the few facts provided. Lowville school officials might look at changes in the accessibility of their polls, the date of the election, and/or their own promotion of the election through the media or other means as more plausible ways of increasing turnout.

492. This essay is short but comprehensive. The writer locates a possible error in data gathering that may have led to a biased conclusion and goes on to explain how that might have happened and how it might be corrected. There are no real errors in English usage or mechanics.

> The oddball, rather macho trio of recreational activities that the Lowville Town Board recommended derives from the fact that their initial sample was biased. This bias led to an unrepresentative response.
>
> The town made the simple mistake of addressing its questionnaire to the "head of household." Although households today are very likely to be "headed" by women, the response received makes it fairly clear that most people who responded to the questionnaire were the traditional "man of the house" respondents. This may be because the town is small and rural, or there may be some other reason that is unclear from the information given.

The questions used to derive the response are unknown, but they seem to have been personalized for the individual answering the questionnaire rather than focused on (for example) the entire family in the household. For that reason, no activities appropriate for young children are in the final three. One would hope that a town's recreation plan would be more inclusive.

If Lowville is entirely composed of middle-aged, middle-class men, then the recommendation of the board is reasonable and proper. If, however, it is a typical small town, with women and girls, men and boys, all seeking recreational outlets, then the mailing should be redone, with questions that incorporate all family members for a truly representative response.

493. This essay is well organized and cogent. The writer notes distortions and assumptions that detract from the letter's persuasive argument. There are no real errors in English usage or mechanics.

The Coburn resident is obviously extremely concerned about the proposed placement of walking trails. However, he or she shows the dangers of making unfounded assumptions, and the conclusion, which describes the institution of trails as something that "steals land and protects criminals," is a distortion of the situation.

First, the trails will use land that belongs to the railroads. This being true, only the railroads can determine that land use. Just because the neighbors are accustomed to using that land "for their own purposes" does not make it their land, no matter how long that state of affairs has existed.

Second, people bent on robbery or other "nefarious" deeds are presumably already able to access the houses from the rear—or from the front, for that matter. The railroad beds already supply a means of access, as do the roads that run in front of the houses. Suggesting that robbery is a natural by-product of trail building is illogical. If the writer had proof that criminal activity was common in other places where trails had been established, this argument might be more believable. As it is, the robbery issue seems more like a red herring designed to spread fear and distract readers from the real issue.

The final sentence is a gross exaggeration. The trails do not "steal land"; the land does not belong to the neighbors. There is no evidence given that supports the idea that the trails "protect criminals." This writer would do better to think of a few realistic reasons for his or her position—perhaps the noise factor of having a walking trail, or concerns that the neighbors might have to provide upkeep—and write a letter that expresses genuine concerns rather than overstated fears.

494. This essay is short but complete. The writer uses a comprehensible mathematical example to point out a possible flaw in the original reasoning and follows up with a suggestion about future study. No errors in English usage or mechanics detract from the argument.

The state school board presents an impassioned argument in favor of modifying state cuts to schools to make them more equitable. Since the cut per student is less at rich schools than at poor schools, they argue, the cuts are harmful to poor schools.

The problem is that as things stand, the state already gives less per student to wealthy districts, who presumably then make up that difference using their own existing wealth. So a rich district might receive $2,000 per student from the state, while an average district gets, say, $5,000 per student. A cut of 10 percent to that rich district's aid then limits its payment to $1,800 per student, while the average district still gets $4,500. Yes, the cut to the rich district is only $200 per student, while the cut to the average district is $500. However, the result is still a 2:5 ratio of aid—exactly the same ratio as before the cut was made.

Despite this, the school board is not entirely wrong in its supposition that poor schools will be harmed. They will be harmed not because of an inequitable aid cut but because they do not have the money to supplement state aid. The state school board would be better off addressing that fundamental inequity. If school districts have to make up the difference through property taxes, or if they are simply unable to make up the difference at all and therefore have less to offer their students than wealthy districts do, that's a real problem that warrants everyone's immediate attention.

495. This essay is solid and well organized. The writer dissects the speaker's claims one by one and then suggests ways of making his argument stronger. There are practically no errors in English usage or mechanics.

Senator Diehard toes the party line in standing up for an expensive missile program, but as he does so, he manufactures a flood of fallacies with which to bamboozle his listeners.

"What price freedom?" cries the senator. Well, most of us would nod and agree that freedom is in fact, priceless. However, that begs the question of whether the $10 billion spent so far on Triton is a reasonable price for freedom—or, more important, whether Triton represents freedom at all. The senator's emotional appeal is a red herring, pulling his listeners' attention away from the facts at hand.

The senator goes on to ask, "Would your tax dollars really be better spent propping up a variety of social programs than in defending our nation from the enemy abroad?" Here the senator presents his listeners with a false dilemma—you may have either social programs or defense but not both. There is absolutely nothing to indicate that if the Triton Missile Program were cancelled today, its funding would switch over to support Medicare or housing in the inner cities. The only reason to present such a dichotomy is to sow confusion and fear.

The senator concludes with the suggestion that to stop the program now would be to throw $10 billion "down the drain." This is a very common argument from Washington or our state capital. However, just as two wrongs don't make a right, so throwing good money after bad doesn't correct a situation that is possibly wrong-headed to begin with.

Instead of appealing to fear and ridicule, the senator would do better to present what he sees as the positive values of the Triton Missile Program. What advances has the funding provided? What is the role of the program in our overall defense? Can costs be controlled and a deadline met? Standing up for his beloved program with facts and figures might prove more successful than covering up the program's faults with swaggering, fallacious obfuscation.

496. This essay is clear and compelling. The writer points out the county board's faulty reasoning and the pitfalls of such reasoning, ending with a strong admonishment. The argument contains no errors in English usage or mechanics.

Caught between the county administrator's call for a 1 percent reduction in wages and the union's call for a 4 percent increase, the county board compromised on 2.5 percent increase, halfway between the two, as well as a slight take back by the county in health costs. Although the county board was well-meaning, a compromise like this is no compromise at all.

The union's position was unreasonable from the start. It is not reasonable to expect what you have received in past years if the money is no longer there. Nevertheless, the union probably started at that place in order to open negotiations.

Unfortunately, the county board fell into a classic middle-ground fallacy, assuming that the middle ground between the two extremes must be the correct place to be. This would only work if the county administrator called for a reduction knowing that it would never fly and hoping that some middle ground would be reached. There is no evidence that this is the case. The county board, and the union, would have to assume that the county administrator's numbers, as suggested, were the numbers required to avoid layoffs. The county administrator called for the reduction because of the existing budget deficit. Any amount tacked on above that reduced level would, presumably, necessitate layoffs.

By compromising on a 2.5 percent increase, the county board ensured a need for sanitation worker layoffs. By agreeing as well to a take back in health costs, the board ensured an even greater impact to their budget in years to come. Since they do represent the county taxpayers, they would have done better to work a bit longer to negotiate a figure closer to the county administrator's figure.

We are used to assuming that the point precisely between A and B is the best compromise between A and B. Children negotiate that way all the time, splitting the difference to avoid hard feelings. Our representatives are not children, and we should require more from them than a simple acceptance of a middle-ground solution.

497. This essay is specific and personal. The writer uses examples to counteract the questionable assumption of the original bulletin and includes suggestions for better solutions. There are no errors in English usage or mechanics.

The library's unfortunate contrast of nonfiction with "classic literature of the 18th, 19th, and 20th centuries" indicates that it is starting with a biased premise—the assumption that only fiction can be "classic." If library administrators follow their own guidelines, they will eliminate patrons' access to truly classic tomes of nonfiction, from Darwin's *Voyage of the Beagle* to de Tocqueville's *Democracy in America*. While it may be true that the fields of science and history evolve over time, it is equally true that without understanding where we have been, we cannot hope to recognize the significance of where we are now.

The library has an established problem: It lacks space for a proposed media room. Assuming that there is no money to expand, the library must rid itself of some material to make room. However, there are clearly better ways to do so than by eliminating an entire genre.

Would it not be better, for example, to search the checkout information for the current library holdings, and perhaps to get rid of those books that have not been checked out in a decade? That way, the likelihood that someone might miss the removed books is diminished.

Another possibility might be to determine which of the current holdings could be accessed electronically, and to provide e-readers preloaded with those materials. Readers of young adult novels might prefer to read them on e-readers, or the library might remove its magazines and present them electronically instead, thus freeing up some space.

The dangers of the library's proposed path are many and include the potential removal of critical research materials that may not be available in any format other than print. When I wrote my senior thesis on the Great Depression, for example, I needed access to many obscure books that held copyrights from the late 1800s and early 1900s. Without those critical primary and secondary sources, my paper would have read more like a Wikipedia article than like a scholarly work. We depend on our libraries to house materials from all genres and all eras. I would certainly hope that the library changes its plan.

498. This essay is well reasoned and convincing. The writer identifies fallacies in the original work and suggests changes that would improve the argument as a whole. There are no significant errors in English usage or mechanics.

Amusingly, the author begins by pointing to groups that try to divide us through fear and then goes on to present his own appeal to fear: the vision of us all as "slaves to Middle Eastern oil." Fighting fire with fire, in this case, results in an argument of manipulation, not of facts.

The facts that the newsletter does present, that the kinds of contamination the environmental groups are complaining about are "common to most gas and oil operations," are unlikely to warm the hearts of environmentalists—or even of industry supporters. The newsletter does not deny that pollution of groundwater occurs, but it removes that pollution from any direct connection to the drilling and blames it on above ground spills or mishandling of wastewater. Of course, if it were not for the drilling, above ground spills and mishandling of wastewater would not occur, making this a sort of false dilemma. The industry seems to be arguing that both horizontal drilling and other gas and oil operations are equally hazardous, but they do not consider a third option—no drilling at all.

This is to be expected, given the identity of the author. A gas and oil industry bulletin is unlikely to tolerate a vision that includes no gas and oil drilling.

The bulletin author would have offered a stronger argument had he followed the line of reasoning that he started with his "slaves to Middle Eastern oil" appeal and shown exactly how horizontal drilling for shale gas might give us that kind of freedom from outside markets. As for the pollution argument, which as it stands is extremely weak, had the author presented ways that the industry is combatting mishandling of wastewater or avoiding above ground spills, the argument would have been more convincing.

At present, the newsletter combats "hysteria" with one "truth" that is unsubstantiated and another "truth" that is both weak and alarming. If horizontal drilling is just as bad as other gas and oil operations, and those operations are just as bad as horizontal drilling, is that really a cause for optimism? An argument may exist in favor of horizontal drilling, but this is not it.

499. This essay is clear and credible. The writer uses background knowledge about the topic to counter the argument and points out the need for better support. No errors in English usage or mechanics get in the way of understanding.

Although the congressman's argument is one we have often heard, it contains several straw men and instances of correlation without causation. The congressman is clearly in favor of tax cuts, but his supporting evidence is lacking.

The congressman presents the premise that reducing taxes and regulations leads to saving and investment and thus to accumulation of capital and economic well-being.

He presents it as gospel ("as you know"), not admitting room for argument. Yet many economists would argue that the economy grows from the bottom up, not the top down.

More critically, the congressman states that the plan worked "beautifully" in the 1980s and thus will work well in the future. Many accept that 1980s economic success was due to tax cuts, but it is certainly equally arguable that those tax cuts led to enormous deficits, excessive speculation on dubious projects, and a greater divide between rich and poor. On top of that, our situation in the 2010s is far different from that of 30 years ago. There is no sensible way to compare the two decades and draw the conclusion reached by the Congressman.

The strongest argument against the congressman's premise that "trickle-down economics" has served this country well is this: Are those being trickled down to better off than they were? Certainly, we have a greater percentage of poor people today than we did in the 1980s—and even in the 1980s, there were great disparities of wealth. If there is any trickling down happening today, it is not trickling down very far. The wealthy have benefited hugely from reduced taxes and regulations. The poor have not.

For Congressman Jett's argument to convince me, he would need to include specifics that showed that tax cut A led directly to savings B and trickled down to protect and lift up poor person C, thus improving the overall economy. Barring that, his words seem empty and unsubstantiated despite their widespread appeal.

500. This essay is brief but thorough. For each failure of the argument, the writer presents analysis and a suggestion for improvement. No major errors in English usage or mechanics exist.

The senator's argument is one that we might read quoted in the news. No matter what we think about the terrorist threat, we need spokespeople on our behalf that provide stronger and more principled reasoning than Senator Bellum does.

The senator's use of the childish "two wrongs make a right" argument undermines her entire premise. Because terrorists don't follow the rules of war, she says, we do not need to do so, either. Of course, the guilt of the terrorist does not lessen our guilt if we proceed in a terroristic fashion. Losing our moral center because we are faced with immorality does not strengthen our position. The senator would be more correct and more convincing if she stated, for example, that the Geneva Conventions apply only to declared war, and because the war on terror is not a declared war, the Conventions do not apply.

The senator ends her statement with a non sequitur. We have not experienced a serious foreign terrorist action on our shores in recent years; thus, our tactics are working. Yet she provides no proof that the tactics caused the lack of terrorist action—the causes may vary and are certainly more complex than she leads her readers to believe. Again, she would be more convincing if she could draw direct correlations between periods of detention, wiretapping, and other tactics and specific incidents of terror that were therefore nipped in the bud.

The war on terror is a serious subject, and the tactics used to combat it open serious questions of ethics and legitimacy. While the senator may be sincere in her letter, she is neither logical nor persuasive.